2001 Krause-Minkus

Stamps & Prices

A Mini-Catalog of United States Stamps

Edited by Maurice D. Wozniak

Published by

**krause
publications**

700 E. State Street • Iola, WI 54990-0001
Telephone: 715/445-2214

To place an order or receive our free catalog, call 800-258-0929.
For editorial comment and further information,
use our regular business telephone at (715) 445-2214.

Library of Congress Catalog Number: 00-102618
ISBN: 0-87341-962-6

Printed in the United States of America

Contents

A brief introduction to United States stamps

By Maurice D. Wozniak, Editor

Most collectors trace the history of stamp collecting to 1840, when Great Britain revolutionized postal service by introducing adhesive stamps that signified the sender had paid the fee for delivery. That first stamp featured a portrait of the reigning British monarch, Queen Victoria, and the hobby of stamp collecting commenced almost simultaneously.

The United States followed with its first two postage stamps on July 1, 1847. Issued during the presidency of James K. Polk, the stamps featured two popular figures from the American Revolution – Benjamin Franklin, who had been named the first postmaster general in an age when delivery largely was entrusted to personal couriers or the good will of strangers; and George Washington, the general who became the first president of the republic.

Franklin's picture appeared on the 5¢ stamp, sufficient to carry an ordinary letter up to 300 miles, and Washington's picture was on the 10¢ stamp, used for letters requiring higher postage.

They were the world's first stamps to feature prominent persons of the past, and they set the tone for U.S. stamp-issuing policy. In the first 100 years, especially, portraits of America's heroes were prominent on stamps, which represented the country on mail sent to every country on the globe.

So-called commemorative stamps, issued typically in remembrance of a historical event or to highlight a current event, such as a large stamp exhibition, appeared first in 1893. Those first commemoratives were issued in support of the World's Columbian Exposition in Chicago, Ill., an event designed around the 400th anniversary of the voyage of Christopher Columbus, on which he is credited with the discovery of America.

The 16 stamps in that first commemorative set feature exquisite engravings of paintings of Columbus' voyage. The stamps were enormously popular with the public. In fact, more than 1 billion copies of the dull purple 2¢ stamp, the standard postal value at the time, were printed. That output dwarfs the production of almost all modern U.S. commemorative stamps.

People then could buy a 2¢ stamp as a souvenir of the anniversary and put it away for safekeeping. Many did. Today, you can buy that 2¢ stamp or its companion 1¢ value for less than $20 each. Postally used stamps might cost about 25¢. But the black $5 stamp in the set, which would have placed a strain on the budgets of most Americans at the end of the last century, is now valued at more than $2,500.

While commemoratives helped to sing the praises of America, the workhorse definitives could become dull to most mailers. In fact, for a period of more than 20 years in the early part of the 20th century, familiar portraits of either Washington or Franklin appeared on almost all U.S. stamps. Some collectors today specialize in finding the differences among that array of stamps.

The Presidential Series of definitive stamps, named because it featured profile busts of every deceased president in order of his term in office, extended over 16 years. The Liberty Series, the Prominent Americans Series, Americana Series, and the Great Americans Series, all of which continued to feature famous people and icons of history, followed it.

Then came the Transportation Series, which added an occasional touch of whimsy to the staid postage stamp. (A Tow Truck in a Transportation Series? An Elevator car?)

Today's regular issues are distinguished by variety – flags in various settings, birds and animals, symbols of culture, even berries.

Meanwhile, commemoratives went through a similar evolution in these changing times. Besides recalling famous people and events of history, U.S. stamps became blatantly political and considerably more expansive.

In the 1930s, they extolled the virtue of the Olympics Games, a Roosevelt administration program that was determined to be unconstitutional two years later, Mothers and Baseball.

Today, they have an obvious "topical" bent – art works, trains, professions, extinct animals, living animals, flowers and movie stars. More and more, they are designed to appeal to stamp collectors and entice more people to become stamp collectors. Some of the most difficult stamps to find today are those in the hands (and mounted on the walls) of non-traditional collectors – those for sports stars and Certified Public Accountants.

It may be a reflection of our democratic national character that the most famous U.S. stamp is an airmail error, the "Inverted Jenny" of

1918, on which the center vignette of an airplane was printed upside-down.

Since 1847, the United States has issued approximately 5,000 different postage stamps, not including stamped envelopes and postal cards. In addition, there have been thousands more stamps to raise revenues and signify other business transactions. All of these attract ardent collectors, and the hobby, while changing, remains popular and arguably more interesting than ever. We hope this mini catalog, a more portable version of the Krause-*Minkus Standard Catalog of U.S. Stamps,* will enhance your enjoyment.

How to use this catalog

Stamps issued by the United States government are listed in chronological order according to Minkus catalog number. To the right of the number is a space for you to write in numbers assigned by other catalog makers for that stamp, if you wish. A cross-reference guide to the Scott catalog is available free from Krause Publications, Iola WI 54990-0001.

The date of issue, subject of the stamp image, denomination and color of the stamp are given to help in identification. The prices given for used and unused stamps are based on actual selling prices by dealers or at auction.

Five boxes are provided at the right of each listing for you to customize an inventory of your collection. For example, you might designate the boxes to indicate if you have, in order, a used copy, an unused copy, a mint (never-hinged) copy, a multiple (such as a plate block), and a copy on cover. If you mark the boxes to indicate you have a particular item, you will have a simple, illustrated inventory of your collection that you can carry with you to stamp bourses or stamp club meetings.

	UnFVF	UseFVF

REGULAR POSTAL ISSUES

1 _____   **1847. Benjamin Franklin Issue**

5¢   **red brown**   4,500.00   500.00 ☐☐☐☐☐

SP1 _____   **1875. Benjamin Franklin Special Printing Issue**

5¢   **red brown** (4,779 copies sold)   800.00   ☐☐☐☐☐

2 _____   **1847. George Washington Issue**

10¢ **black**   17,500.00   1,250.00 ☐☐☐☐☐

NOTE: Government imitations of the 5¢ (in blue) and 10¢ (in Venetian red) were printed in 1947 and are listed a CM290 in the commemorative stamp section.

SP2 _____   **1875. George Washington Special Printing Issue**

10¢ **black** (3,883 copies sold)   950.00   ☐☐☐☐☐

3 _____   **1851. Benjamin Franklin Issue**

1¢   **blue** Type I   175,000.00 35,000.00 ☐☐☐☐☐

4 _____   **1857. Benjamin Franklin Type Ia Regular Issue**

1¢   **blue** Type Ia   25,000.00   6,500.00 ☐☐☐☐☐

5 _____   **1851. Benjamin Franklin Type Ib Issue**

1¢   **blue** Type Ib   9,000.00   3,500.00 ☐☐☐☐☐

NOTE: Catalog prices for the above stamp are for nice examples of the type. Stamps with a slightly less complete design at the bottom are worth about one-fourth of the above prices.

6 _____   **1857. Benjamin Franklin Type II Issue**

1¢   **blue** (Plate 1) Type II   500.00   95.00 ☐☐☐☐☐

7 _____   **1851. George Washington Issue**

5¢   **blue** Type III   7,500.00   1,600.00 ☐☐☐☐☐

8 _____   **1851. Benjamin Franklin Type IIIa Issue**

1¢   **blue** (Plate 1E) Type IIIa   2,400.00   550.00 ☐☐☐☐☐

9 _____   **1852. Benjamin Franklin Type IV Issue**

1¢   **blue** Type IV (recut Type IV) (recut once at top & once at bottom)   400.00   85.00 ☐☐☐☐☐

10 _____   **1851. George Washington Issue**

3¢   **orange brown** Type I   1,700.00   50.00 ☐☐☐☐☐

11 _____

3¢   **Venetian red** Type I   120.00   9.00 ☐☐☐☐☐

12 _____   **1856. Thomas Jefferson Issue**

5¢   **red brown** Type I   8,500.00   900.00 ☐☐☐☐☐

13 _____   **1855. George Washington Type I Issue**

10¢ **green** Type I   11,000.00   585.00 ☐☐☐☐☐

14 _____   **1855. George Washington Type II Issue**

10¢ **green** Type II   1,900.00   200.00 ☐☐☐☐☐

15 _____   **1855. George Washington Type III Issue**

10¢ **green** Type III   1,900.00   200.00 ☐☐☐☐☐

16 _____   **1856. George Washington Type IV Issue**

10¢ **green** Type IV (outer line recut at top only)   12,500.00   1,200.00 ☐☐☐☐☐

NOTE: All four types of the 10¢ stamp occur on the same sheet, so that pairs and blocks showing combination of these types exist.

17 _____   **1851. George Washington Type I Issue**

12¢ **black** Type I   2,600.00   225.00 ☐☐☐☐☐

18 _____   **1861. Benjamin Franklin Type I Issue**

1¢   **blue** Type I   725.00   325.00 ☐☐☐☐☐

NOTE: The normal setting of the perforating machine was such that perforations cut the design on almost every stamp Prices quoted are for such copies. Where the perforations do not cut the design No. 18 stamps command very high premiums.

19 _____   **1857. Benjamin Franklin Type Ia Issue**

1¢   **blue** Type Ia   12,000.00   3,250.00 ☐☐☐☐☐

20 _____   **1857. Benjamin Franklin Type II Issue**

1¢   **blue** (Plate 2) Type II   475.00   135.00 ☐☐☐☐☐

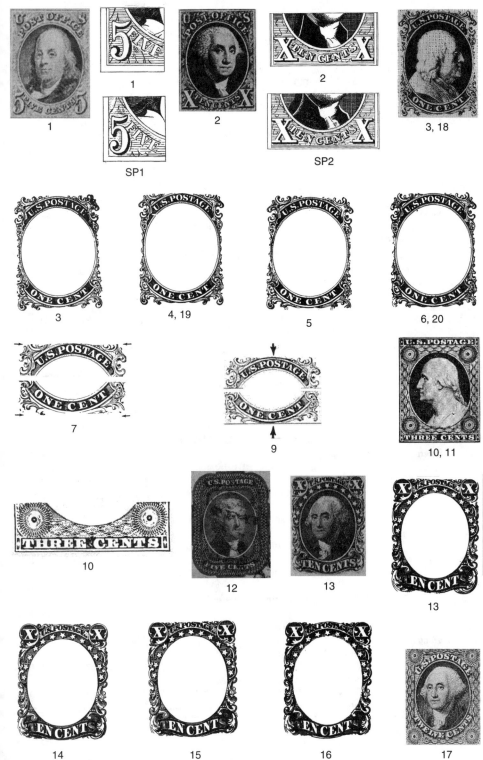

	UnFVF	UseFVF	

21 _____ **1857. Benjamin Franklin Type III Issue**

1¢ **blue** Type III — 5,000.00 — 1,150.00 ☐☐☐☐☐

NOTE: The finest examples of No. 21 are found in position 99R2.

22 _____ **1857. Benjamin Franklin Type IIIa Issue**

1¢ **blue** (Plate 4) Type IIIa — 800.00 — 260.00 ☐☐☐☐☐

23 _____ **1857. Benjamin Franklin Type IV Issue**

1¢ **blue** Type IV recut top and once at bottom — 3,000.00 — 325.00 ☐☐☐☐☐

24 _____ **1857. Benjamin Franklin Type V Issue**

1¢ **blue** Type V — 120.00 — 24.00 ☐☐☐☐☐

25 _____ **1857. George Washington Type I Issue**

3¢ **rose** Type I — 900.00 — 50.00 ☐☐☐☐☐

NOTE: Fakes are known of the horizontal pair, imperforate vertically.

26 _____ **1857. George Washington Type II Issue**

3¢ **Venetian red** Type II — 45.00 — 3.50 ☐☐☐☐☐

27 _____ **1857. George Washington Type III Issue**

3¢ **Venetian red** Type III — 110.00 — 35.00 ☐☐☐☐☐

28 _____ **1857. Thomas Jefferson Type I Issue**

5¢ **red brown** Type I — 3,000.00 — 260.00 ☐☐☐☐☐

28A _____

5¢ **henna brown (Indian red)** — 25,000.00 — 2,500.00 ☐☐☐☐☐

29 _____ **1858. Thomas Jefferson Type I Issue**

5¢ **brick red** Type I — 10,000.00 — 900.00 ☐☐☐☐☐

30 _____ **1859. Thomas Jefferson Type I Issue**

5¢ **brown** Type I — 1,500.00 — 250.00 ☐☐☐☐☐

31 _____ **1860. Thomas Jefferson Type II Issue**

5¢ **brown** Type II — 1,500.00 — 200.00 ☐☐☐☐☐

32 _____ **1861. Thomas Jefferson Type II Issue**

5¢ **orange brown** Type II — 1,100.00 — 800.00 ☐☐☐☐☐

33 _____ **1857. George Washington Type I Issue**

10¢ **green** Type I — 8,250.00 — 500.00 ☐☐☐☐☐

34 _____ **1857. George Washington Type I Issue**

10¢ **green** Type II — 2,500.00 — 200.00 ☐☐☐☐☐

35 _____ **1857. George Washington Type III Issue**

10¢ **green** Type III — 2,600.00 — 200.00 ☐☐☐☐☐

36 _____ **1857. George Washington Type IV Issue**

10¢ **green** Type IV, recut at top — 17,500.00 — 1,500.00 ☐☐☐☐☐

37 _____ **1859. George Washington Type V Issue**

10¢ **green** Type V — 200.00 — 60.00 ☐☐☐☐☐

38 _____ **1857. George Washington Type I Issue**

12¢ **black** Type I — 380.00 — 100.00 ☐☐☐☐☐

39 _____ **1859. George Washington Type II Issue**

12¢ **black** Type II — 360.00 — 115.00 ☐☐☐☐☐

40 _____ **1860. George Washington Issue**

24¢ **gray lilac** — 725.00 — 210.00 ☐☐☐☐☐

41 _____ **1860. Benjamin Franklin Issue**

30¢ **orange** — 850.00 — 300.00 ☐☐☐☐☐

42 _____ **1860. George Washington Issue**

90¢ **deep blue** — 1,300.00 — 5,500.00 ☐☐☐☐☐

NOTE: Many fake cancellations exist on this stamp.

SP3 _____ **1875. Benjamin Franklin Special Printing Issue**

1¢ **brilliant blue** (3,846 copies sold) — 500.00 — ☐☐☐☐☐

SP4 _____ **1875. George Washington Special Printing Issue**

3¢ **bright vermilion** (479 copies) — 2,000.00 — ☐☐☐☐☐

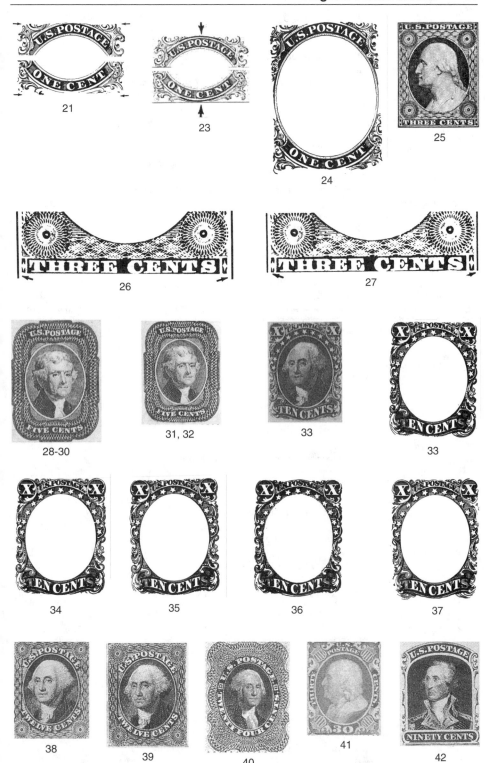

21

23

24

25

26

27

28-30

31, 32

33

33

34

35

36

37

38

39

40

41

42

		UnFVF	UseFVF	

SP5 _____   **1875. Thomas Jefferson Special Printing Issue**
  5¢   **bright orange brown** (878 copies)   950.00   □□□□□
SP6 _____   **1875. George Washington Special Printing Issue**
  10¢ **bluish green** (516 copies)   1,750.00   □□□□□
SP7 _____
  12¢ **greenish black** (489 copies)   2,000.00   □□□□□
SP8 _____
  24¢ **dark violet black** (479 copies)   2,000.00   □□□□□
SP9 _____   **1875. Benjamin Franklin Special Printing Issue**
  30¢ **yellow orange** (480 copies)   2,000.00   □□□□□
SP10 _____   **1875. George Washington Special Printing Issue**
  90¢ **indigo** (454 copies)   3,300.00   □□□□□

NOTE: This set is known imperforated.

43 _____   **1861. Benjamin Franklin Issue**
  1¢   **blue**   150.00   16.00 □□□□□
44 _____   **1863. Andrew Jackson Issue**
  2¢   **black**   175.00   24.00 □□□□□
45 _____   **1861. George Washington Issue**
  3¢   **pink**   4,500.00   450.00 □□□□□

NOTE: It is almost impossible to describe a "pink" in words, but it should be kept in mind that the inking on a "pink" is rather heavy, and the lines of the design do not stand out as sharply as on the other shades. The color, while not as outstanding as a dull pink ribbon, is nevertheless on that order. It is not any of the shades of brown, dull red, rose red, or brown red so often mistaken for the real pink.

46 _____
  3¢   **brown carmine**   625.00   —   □□□□□
47 _____   **1861. Thomas Jefferson Issue**
  5¢   **buff**   9,000.00   425.00 □□□□□
48 _____   **1862. Thomas Jefferson Issue**
  5¢   **red brown**   2,000.00   225.00 □□□□□
49 _____   **1863. Thomas Jefferson Issue**
  5¢   **brown**   —   —   □□□□□
50 _____   **1861. George Washington Type I Issue**
  10¢ **green** Type I   4,500.00   550.00 □□□□□
51 _____   **1861. George Washington Type II Issue**
  10¢ **green** Type II   325.00   30.00 □□□□□
52 _____   **1861. George Washington Issue**
  12¢ **black**   625.00   55.00 □□□□□
53 _____   **1866. Abraham Lincoln Issue**
  15¢ **black**   650.00   72.00 □□□□□
54 _____   **1861. George Washington Issue**
  24¢ **violet**   6,500.00   575.00 □□□□□

NOTE: No. 54 is found only on thin, semi-transparent paper, while Nos. 55 and 56 are on a thicker and more opaque paper.

55 _____
  24¢ **red lilac**   800.00   80.00 □□□□□
56 _____   **1862. George Washington Issue**
  24¢ **lilac**   400.00   55.00 □□□□□
57 _____   **1861. Benjamin Franklin Issue**
  30¢ **orange**   650.00   75.00 □□□□□
58 _____   **1861. George Washington Issue**
  90¢ **blue**   1,500.00   250.00 □□□□□
SP11 _____   **1875. Benjamin Franklin Special Printing Issue**
  1¢   **dark ultramarine** (3,195 copies)   500.00   800.00 □□□□□
SP12 _____   **1875. Andrew Jackson Special Printing Issue**
  2¢   **jet black** (979 copies)   2,300.00 4,000.00 □□□□□

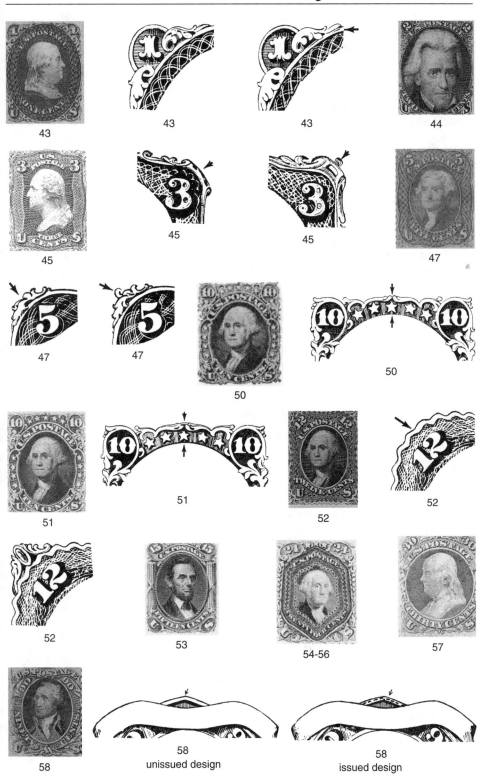

43

43

43

44

45

45

45

47

47

47

50

50

51

52

52

51

52

53

54-56

57

58

58
unissued design

58
issued design

		UnFVF	UseFVF

SP13 _____   **1875. George Washington Special Printing Issue**
    3¢ **brown red** (465 copies)   2,500.00   4,300.00 ☐☐☐☐☐

SP14 _____   **1875. Thomas Jefferson Special Printing Issue**
    5¢ **light yellow brown** (672 copies)   1,850.00   2,300.00 ☐☐☐☐☐

SP15 _____   **1875. George Washington Special Printing Issue**
    10¢ **bluish green** (451 copies)   2,000.00   3,750.00 ☐☐☐☐☐

SP16 _____
    12¢ **deep black** (389 copies)   2,800.00   4,500.00 ☐☐☐☐☐

SP17 _____   **1875. Abraham Lincoln Special Printing Issue**
    15¢ **deep black** (397 copies)   2,250.00   4,800.00 ☐☐☐☐☐

SP18 _____   **1875. George Washington Special Printing Issue**
    24¢ **deep brown violet** (346 copies)   3,250.00   6,000.00 ☐☐☐☐☐

SP19 _____   **1875. Benjamin Franklin Special Printing Issue**
    30¢ **brown orange** (346 copies)   3,500.00   6,000.00 ☐☐☐☐☐

SP20 _____   **1875. George Washington Special Printing Issue**
    90¢ **dark blue** (317 copies)   4,800.00   20,000.00 ☐☐☐☐☐

59 _____   **1867. George Washington w/Grill Issue**
    3¢ **rose** grill A   2,200.00   2,000.00 ☐☐☐☐☐

60 _____   **1867. Thomas Jefferson Grill A Issue**
    5¢ **brown** grill A   42,000.00   — ☐☐☐☐☐

61 _____   **1867. Benjamin Franklin Grill A Issue**
    30¢ **orange** grill A   —   32,500.00 ☐☐☐☐☐

61A _____   **1868. George Washington Grill B Issue**
    3¢ **rose** grill B   —   45,000.00 ☐☐☐☐☐

62 _____   **1867. George Washington Grill C Issue**
    3¢ **rose** grill C   3,000.00   650.00 ☐☐☐☐☐

NOTE: No. 62 shows rows of grill points, not as heavily impressed as the normal grill, forming a grill whose total area is about 18 x 15mm. Caused by a failure to cut deep enough into the grill roller when it was being machined, which left a few areas on the roller only "partially erased."

63 _____   **1868. Andrew Jackson w/Grill D Issue**
    2¢ **black** grill D   9,500.00   1,500.00 ☐☐☐☐☐

64 _____   **1868. George Washington Grill D Issue**
    3¢ **rose** grill D   3,000.00   2,500.00 ☐☐☐☐☐

65 _____   **1868. Benjamin Franklin Grill Z Issue**
    1¢ **blue** grill Z   —   — ☐☐☐☐☐

66 _____   **1868. Andrew Jackson Grill Z Issue**
    2¢ **black** grill Z   3,000.00   400.00 ☐☐☐☐☐

67 _____   **1868. George Washington Grill Z Issue**
    3¢ **rose** grill Z   5,000.00   1,200.00 ☐☐☐☐☐

68 _____
    10¢ **green** grill Z   47,500.00   — ☐☐☐☐☐

69 _____
    12¢ **black** grill Z   4,000.00   600.00 ☐☐☐☐☐

69A _____   **1868. Abraham Lincoln Grill Z Issue**
    15¢ **black** grill Z   100,000.00   — ☐☐☐☐☐

70 _____   **1868. Benjamin Franklin Grill E Issue**
    1¢ **blue** grill E   1,100.00   275.00 ☐☐☐☐☐

71 _____   **1868. Andrew Jackson Grill E Issue**
    2¢ **black** grill E   525.00   75.00 ☐☐☐☐☐

72 _____   **1868. George Washington Grill E Issue**
    3¢ **rose** grill E   375.00   10.00 ☐☐☐☐☐

73 _____
    10¢ **green** grill E   2,000.00   175.00 ☐☐☐☐☐

	UnFVF	UseFVF

74 _____

    12¢ **black** grill E   2,250.00   210.00 ❑❑❑❑❑

75 _____ **1868. Abraham Lincoln Grill E Issue**

    15¢ **black** grill E   4,750.00   460.00 ❑❑❑❑❑

76 _____ **1868. Benjamin Franklin Grill F Issue**

    1¢ **blue** grill F   500.00   100.00 ❑❑❑❑❑

77 _____ **1868. Andrew Jackson Grill F Issue**

    2¢ **black** grill F   200.00   35.00 ❑❑❑❑❑

78 _____ **1868. George Washington Grill F Issue**

    3¢ **rose** grill F   175.00   3.50 ❑❑❑❑❑

79 _____ **1868. Thomas Jefferson Grill F Issue**

    5¢ **brown** grill F   1,500.00   225.00 ❑❑❑❑❑

80 _____ **1868. George Washington Grill F Issue**

    10¢ **yellow green** grill F   1,200.00   120.00 ❑❑❑❑❑

81 _____

    12¢ **black** grill F   1,500.00   125.00 ❑❑❑❑❑

82 _____ **1868. Abraham Lincoln Grill F Issue**

    15¢ **black** grill F   1,500.00   140.00 ❑❑❑❑❑

83 _____ **1869. George Washington Grill F Issue**

    24¢ **gray lilac** grill F   2,100.00   450.00 ❑❑❑❑❑

84 _____ **1868. Benjamin Franklin Grill F Issue**

    30¢ **orange** grill F   2,750.00   400.00 ❑❑❑❑❑

85 _____ **1869. George Washington Grill F Issue**

    90¢ **blue** grill F   5,000.00   850.00 ❑❑❑❑❑

NOTE: Most of the stamps that bear grills can be found with double grills, triple grills, split grills and quadruple split grills. Double grills are two impressions of the grill on the same stamp, triple grills are three impressions of the grill on the same stamp, split grills are those with about half of a normal grill on each end or on each side of the stamp and quadruple split grills are those that show just a small portion of the grill on each corner of the stamp. The split grill varieties were caused by misplacing the stamps under the grill roller so that the grills were not properly placed on the stamps. Fake grills exist.

86 _____ **1869. Benjamin Franklin Issue**

    1¢ **buff**   275.00   65.00 ❑❑❑❑❑

87 _____ **1869. Pony Express Issue**

    2¢ **brown**   225.00   28.00 ❑❑❑❑❑

88 _____ **1869. Early Locomotive Issue**

    3¢ **ultramarine**   175.00   12.00 ❑❑❑❑❑

59

62

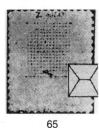

65

86

87

88

		UnFVF	UseFVF	

89 _____ **1869. George Washington Issue**

6¢   ultramarine — 950.00 — 100.00 ☐☐☐☐☐

90 _____ **1869. Shield and Eagle Issue**

10¢ yellow — 1,000.00 — 90.00 ☐☐☐☐☐

91 _____ **1869. Steamship Adriatic Issue**

12¢ green — 975.00 — 100.00 ☐☐☐☐☐

92 _____ **1869. Landing of Columbus Type I Issue**

15¢ brown & blue Type I — 2,500.00 — 350.00 ☐☐☐☐☐

93 _____ **1869. Landing of Columbus Type II Issue**

15¢ brown & blue Type II — 1,200.00 — 160.00 ☐☐☐☐☐

94 _____ **1869. Signing of the Declaration of Independence Issue**

24¢ green & violet — 3,100.00 — 550.00 ☐☐☐☐☐

95 _____ **1869. Shield, Eagle and Flags Issue**

30¢ blue & carmine — 3,100.00 — 350.00 ☐☐☐☐☐

96 _____ **1869. Abraham Lincoln Issue**

90¢ carmine & black — 6,000.00 — 1,800.00 ☐☐☐☐☐

SP21 _____ **1875. Benjamin Franklin Special Printing Pictorial Issue**

1¢   buff (approx. 2,750 copies sold) — 335.00 — 230.00 ☐☐☐☐☐

SP22 _____ **1875. Pony Express Special Printing Pictorial Issue**

2¢   brown (4,755 copies) — 385.00 — 330.00 ☐☐☐☐☐

SP23 _____ **1875. Early Locomotive Special Printing Pictorial Issue**

3¢   ultramarine (1,406 copies) — 3,000.00 — 10,000.00 ☐☐☐☐☐

SP24 _____ **1875. George Washington Special Pictorial Issue**

6¢   ultramarine (2,226 copies) — 900.00 — 600.00 ☐☐☐☐☐

SP25 _____ **1875. Shield and Eagle Special Printing Pictorial Issue**

10¢ yellow (1,947 copies) — 1,400.00 — 1,200.00 ☐☐☐☐☐

SP26 _____ **1875. Steamship Adriatic Special Printing Pictorial Issue**

12¢ bright green (1,584 copies) — 1,500.00 — 1,250.00 ☐☐☐☐☐

SP27 _____ **1875. Landing of Columbus Special Printing Pictorial Issue**

15¢ brown & blue Type III (1,981 copies) — 1,400.00 — 600.00 ☐☐☐☐☐

SP28 _____ **1875. Declaration of Independence Special Printing Pictorial Issue**

24¢ deep green & violet (2,091 copies) — 1,300.00 — 600.00 ☐☐☐☐☐

SP29 _____ **1875. Shield, Eagle and Flags Special Printing Pictorial Issue**

30¢ bright blue & carmine (1,356 copies) — 1,750.00 — 1,000.00 ☐☐☐☐☐

SP30 _____ **1875. Abraham Lincoln Special Printing Pictorial Issue**

90¢ carmine & black (1,356 copies) — 3,800.00 — 4,300.00 ☐☐☐☐☐

SP31 _____ **1880. George Washington Special Printing Pictorial Issue**

1¢   buff without gum (approx. 2,500 copies) — 210.00 — 190.00 ☐☐☐☐☐

97 _____ **1870. Benjamin Franklin Issue**

1¢   ultramarine grill H — 850.00 — 65.00 ☐☐☐☐☐

98 _____ **1870. Andrew Jackson Issue**

2¢   red brown grill H — 480.00 — 38.00 ☐☐☐☐☐

99 _____ **1870. George Washington Issue**

3¢   green grill H — 370.00 — 10.00 ☐☐☐☐☐

100 _____ **1870. Abraham Lincoln Issue**

6¢   carmine grill H — 2,000.00 — 300.00 ☐☐☐☐☐

101 _____ **1871. Edwin Stanton Issue**

7¢   vermillion grill H — 1,325.00 — 275.00 ☐☐☐☐☐

102 _____ **1871. Thomas Jefferson Issue**

10¢ brown — 1,800.00 — 450.00 ☐☐☐☐☐

103 _____ **1872. Henry Clay Issue**

12¢ pale violet — 14,000.00 — 1,750.00 ☐☐☐☐☐

104 _____ **1870. Daniel Webster Portrait Issue**

15¢ orange — 2,600.00 — 750.00 ☐☐☐☐☐

89

90

91

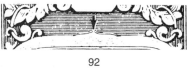

92

92

93 inverted center

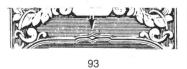

93

94

95

96

97, 108

97, 108

98, 109

98, 109

99, 110

99, 110

100, 111

100, 111

101, 112

101, 112

102, 113

102, 113

103, 114

103, 114

104, 115

104, 115

		UnFVF	UseFVF

		UnFVF	UseFVF	
105 _____	**1870. Gen. Winfield Scott Issue**			
24¢ purple		—	10,000.00	☐☐☐☐☐
106 _____	**1870. Alexander Hamilton Issue**			
30¢ black		3,750.00	550.00	☐☐☐☐☐
107 _____	**1870. Oliver Perry Issue**			
90¢ carmine		4,250.00	550.00	☐☐☐☐☐
108 _____	**1870. Benjamin Franklin Issue**			
1¢ ultramarine		120.00	5.00	☐☐☐☐☐
109 _____	**1870. Andrew Jackson Issue**			
2¢ red brown		90.00	3.50	☐☐☐☐☐
110 _____	**1870. George Washington Issue**			
3¢ green		90.00	.50	☐☐☐☐☐
111 _____	**1870. Abraham Lincoln Issue**			
6¢ carmine		175.00	7.50	☐☐☐☐☐
112 _____	**1871. Edwin Stanton Issue**			
7¢ vermilion		200.00	30.00	☐☐☐☐☐
113 _____	**1870. Thomas Jefferson Issue**			
10¢ brown		185.00	9.00	☐☐☐☐☐
114 _____	**1870. Henry Clay Issue**			
12¢ pale violet		400.00	40.00	☐☐☐☐☐
115 _____	**1870. Daniel Webster Issue**			
15¢ orange		400.00	50.00	☐☐☐☐☐
116 _____	**1870. Gen. Winfield Scott Issue**			
24¢ purple		400.00	50.00	☐☐☐☐☐
117 _____	**1871. Alexander Hamilton Issue**			
30¢ black		950.00	75.00	☐☐☐☐☐
118 _____	**1872. Oliver Perry Issue**			
90¢ carmine		950.00	100.00	☐☐☐☐☐
119 _____	**1873. Benjamin Franklin Issue**			
1¢ ultramarine		70.00	1.25	☐☐☐☐☐
120 _____	**1873. Andrew Jackson Issue**			
2¢ brown		115.00	7.00	☐☐☐☐☐
121 _____	**1875. Andrew Jackson Issue**			
2¢ vermilion		115.00	3.50	☐☐☐☐☐
122 _____	**1873. George Washington Issue**			
3¢ green		40.00	.20	☐☐☐☐☐
123 _____	**1875. Zachary Taylor Issue**			
5¢ Prussian blue		145.00	5.50	☐☐☐☐☐
124 _____	**1873. Abraham Lincoln Issue**			
6¢ dull Venetian red		140.00	7.00	☐☐☐☐☐
125 _____	**1873. Edwin Stanton Issue**			
7¢ vermilion		300.00	30.00	☐☐☐☐☐
126 _____	**1873. Thomas Jefferson Issue**			
10¢ brown		200.00	8.00	☐☐☐☐☐
127 _____	**1874. Henry Clay Issue**			
12¢ blackish violet		500.00	40.00	☐☐☐☐☐
128 _____	**1873. Daniel Webster Issue**			
15¢ yellow orange		475.00	37.50	☐☐☐☐☐
129 _____	**1874. Gen. Winfield Scott Issue**			
24¢ light purple		—	400,000.00	☐☐☐☐☐
130 _____	**1874. Alexander Hamilton Issue**			
30¢ gray black		600.00	37.50	☐☐☐☐☐

NOTE: The 30¢ Continental and 30¢ National are identical except in shade.

105, 116, 129   106, 117   107   119, 132   119

120, 121, 133   120   122, 134   122   123, 136

124, 137   124   125   125   126, 139

126   127   127   128, 140

128   132   133

		UnFVF	UseFVF

131 _____   **1874. Oliver Perry Issue**
90¢   rose carmine   1,100.00   105.00 ☐☐☐☐

NOTE: The 90¢ Continental and the 90¢ National are identical except in shade.

SP32 _____   **1875. Benjamin Franklin Special Printing of the 1873 Pictorial Issue**
1¢   bright ultramarine   7,250.00   ☐☐☐☐

SP33 _____   **1875. Andrew Jackson Special Printing Pictorial Issue**
2¢   blackish brown   3,000.00   ☐☐☐☐

SP34 _____
2¢   carmine vermilion   20,000.00   ☐☐☐☐

SP35 _____   **1875. George Washington Special Pictorial Issue**
3¢   bluish green   9,250.00   ☐☐☐☐

SP36 _____   **1875. Zachary Taylor Special Printing Pictorial Issue**
5¢   bright blue   27,500.00   ☐☐☐☐

SP37 _____   **1875. Abraham Lincoln Special Printing Pictorial Issue**
6¢   pale rose   8,000.00   ☐☐☐☐

SP38 _____   **1875. Edwin Stanton Special Printing Pictorial Issue**
7¢   scarlet vermilion   1,500.00   ☐☐☐☐

SP39 _____   **1875. Thomas Jefferson Special Printing Pictorial Issue**
10¢   yellow brown   8,000.00   ☐☐☐☐

SP40 _____   **1875. Henry Clay Special Printing Pictorial Issue**
12¢   black violet   2,750.00   ☐☐☐☐

SP41 _____   **1875. Daniel Webster Special Printing Pictorial Issue**
15¢   bright orange   8,000.00   ☐☐☐☐

SP42 _____   **1875. Winfield Scott Special Printing Pictorial Issue**
24¢   dull purple   1,750.00   ☐☐☐☐

SP43 _____   **1875. Alexander Hamilton Special Printing Pictorial Issue**
30¢   greenish black   5,750.00   ☐☐☐☐

SP44 _____   **1875. Oliver Perry Special Printing Pictorial Issue**
90¢   violet carmine   7,500.00   ☐☐☐☐

132 _____   **1879. Benjamin Franklin Issue**
1¢   dark ultramarine   75.00   1.00 ☐☐☐☐

133 _____   **1879. Andrew Jackson Issue**
2¢   vermilion   45.00   1.00 ☐☐☐☐

134 _____   **1879. George Washington Issue**
3¢   green   35.00   .25 ☐☐☐☐

135 _____   **1887. George Washington Issue**
3¢   vermilion   45.00   20.00 ☐☐☐☐

136 _____   **1879. Zachary Taylor Issue**
5¢   blue   145.00   6.00 ☐☐☐☐

137 _____   **1879. Abraham Lincoln Issue**
6¢   dull pink   257.00   8.50 ☐☐☐☐

138 _____   **1879. Thomas Jefferson Issue**
10¢   brown like No. 102, but no secret mark   550.00   12.50 ☐☐☐☐

139 _____
10¢   brown like No. 126, with secret mark   425.00   12.50 ☐☐☐☐

140 _____   **1879. Daniel Webster Issue**
15¢   orange   300.00   21.00 ☐☐☐☐

141 _____   **1882. Alexander Hamilton Issue**
30¢   black   300.00   22.50 ☐☐☐☐

142 _____   **1888. Alexander Hamilton Issue**
30¢   orange brown   325.00   40.00 ☐☐☐☐

143 _____   **1880. Oliver Perry Issue**
90¢   carmine   725.00   95.00 ☐☐☐☐

		UnFVF	UseFVF	

144 _____

90¢   dark red violet   750.00   85.00 ☐☐☐☐☐

SP45 _____   **1880. Special Printing of the 1879-88 Issue of 1879.**

1¢   deep ultramarine   4,000.00   ☐☐☐☐☐

145 _____   **1881-82. Re-Engraved Designs of 1873 Issue**

1¢   ultramarine   22.50   .35 ☐☐☐☐☐

146 _____   **1881. Andrew Jackson Issue**

3¢   blue green   27.50   .20 ☐☐☐☐☐

147 _____   **1882. Abraham Lincoln Issue**

6¢   rose   150.00   27.50 ☐☐☐☐☐

148 _____   **1882. Thomas Jefferson Issue**

10¢ brown   50.00   1.50 ☐☐☐☐☐

149 _____   **1887. Benjamin Franklin Issue**

1¢   ultramarine   32.50   .65 ☐☐☐☐☐

150 _____   **1883. George Washington Issue**

2¢   red brown   20.00   .20 ☐☐☐☐☐

151 _____   **1887. George Washington Issue**

2¢   green   15.00   .20 ☐☐☐☐☐

152 _____   **1883. Andrew Jackson Issue**

4¢   deep bluish green   80.00   4.00 ☐☐☐☐☐

SP59 _____   **1883. Special Printing Issue**

2¢   red brown   600.00   ☐☐☐☐☐

SP60 _____

4¢   blue green   14,500.00   ☐☐☐☐☐

153 _____   **1889. Andrew Jackson Issue**

4¢   carmine   75.00   7.50 ☐☐☐☐☐

154 _____   **1882. James Garfield Issue**

5¢   olive brown   80.00   3.00 ☐☐☐☐☐

SP58 _____   **1882. James Garfield Special Printing Issue**

5¢   light brownish gray (2,463 sold)   30,000.00   ☐☐☐☐☐

155 _____   **1888. James Garfield Issue**

5¢   indigo   75.00   4.00 ☐☐☐☐☐

156 _____   **1890. Benjamin Franklin Issue**

1¢   dull blue   17.50   .20 ☐☐☐☐☐

145

146

147

148

149

150

152

154

156

157 _____	**1890. George Washington Issue**			
2¢ lake		125.00	.60	☐☐☐☐☐
158 _____				
2¢ carmine		14.00	.20	☐☐☐☐☐
159 _____	**1890. Andrew Jackson Issue**			
3¢ dark lilac		47.50	5.00	☐☐☐☐☐
160 _____	**1890. Abraham Lincoln Issue**			
4¢ dark brown		47.50	2.00	☐☐☐☐☐
161 _____	**1890. Ulysses S. Grant Issue**			
5¢ chocolate		47.50	2.00	☐☐☐☐☐
162 _____	**1890. James Garfield Issue**			
6¢ brown red		50.00	15.00	☐☐☐☐☐
163 _____	**1890. W. T. Sherman Issue**			
8¢ purple brown		37.50	9.00	☐☐☐☐☐
164 _____	**1890. Daniel Webster Issue**			
10¢ deep bluish green		95.00	2.25	☐☐☐☐☐
165 _____	**1890. Henry Clay Issue**			
15¢ indigo		145.00	16.00	☐☐☐☐☐
166 _____	**1890. Thomas Jefferson Issue**			
30¢ black		225.00	19.00	☐☐☐☐☐
167 _____	**1890. Oliver Hazard Perry Issue**			
90¢ orange		325.00	90.00	☐☐☐☐☐

NOTE: *Stamps of all values of the 1890 issue exist imperforate. They are considered finished proofs.*

168 _____	**1894. Benjamin Franklin Issue**			
1¢ ultramarine		20.00	3.50	☐☐☐☐☐
169 _____				
1¢ blue		47.50	2.00	☐☐☐☐☐
170 _____	**1894. George Washington Issue**			
2¢ **pink** triangle I		15.00	3.00	☐☐☐☐☐
171 _____				
2¢ **carmine lake** triangle I		95.00	2.00	☐☐☐☐☐
172 _____				
2¢ **carmine** triangle I		17.50	.35	☐☐☐☐☐
173 _____				
2¢ **carmine** triangle II		150.00	3.25	☐☐☐☐☐
174 _____				
2¢ **carmine** triangle III		85.00	3.50	☐☐☐☐☐
175 _____	**1894. Andrew Jackson Issue**			
3¢ dark lilac		60.00	6.50	☐☐☐☐☐
176 _____	**1894. Abraham Lincoln Issue**			
4¢ dark brown		75.00	3.50	☐☐☐☐☐
177 _____	**1894. Ulysses S. Grant Issue**			
5¢ chocolate		65.00	4.00	☐☐☐☐☐
178 _____	**1894. James Garfield Issue**			
6¢ red brown		115.00	17.50	☐☐☐☐☐
179 _____	**1894. William T. Sherman Issue**			
8¢ purple brown		95.00	12.50	☐☐☐☐☐
180 _____	**1894. Daniel Webster Issue**			
10¢ blue green		150.00	8.50	☐☐☐☐☐
181 _____	**1894. Henry Clay Issue**			
15¢ indigo		185.00	40.00	☐☐☐☐☐
182 _____	**1894. Thomas Jefferson Issue**			
50¢ orange		275.00	75.00	☐☐☐☐☐
183 _____	**1894. Oliver Hazard Perry Issue**			
$1 **black** Type I		575.00	225.00	☐☐☐☐☐

		UnFVF	UseFVF	

184 _____

   $1   **black** Type II   1,500.00   450.00 ❑❑❑❑❑

185 _____   **1894. James Madison Issue**

   $2   **dark blue**   1,900.00   650.00 ❑❑❑❑❑

186 _____   **1894. John Marshall Issue**

   $5   **dark green**   2,900.00   1,250.00 ❑❑❑❑❑

187 _____   **1895-1898. Bureau of Engraving and Printing Portrait Designs on Watermarked Paper Issue**

   1¢   **deep blue**   5.00   .20 ❑❑❑❑❑

188 _____

   1¢   **deep green**   7.50   .20 ❑❑❑❑❑

189 _____

   2¢   **carmine** Type I   22.50   .90 ❑❑❑❑❑

190 _____

   2¢   **carmine** Type II   20.00   3.00 ❑❑❑❑❑

191 _____

   2¢   **carmine** Type III   4.00   .20 ❑❑❑❑❑

192 _____

   2¢   **red** Type III   7.50   .20 ❑❑❑❑❑

157, 158

159

160

161

162

163

164

165

166

167

168, 169, 187, 188

170-174, 189-192

I

170-72, 189

II

173, 190

III

174, 191-192

175, 193

176, 194, 195

177, 196, 197

178, 198, 199

179, 200

			UnFVF	UseFVF	
193	_____				
	3¢	**dark red violet**	27.50	1.00	☐☐☐☐☐
194	_____				
	4¢	**dark brown**	27.50	1.50	☐☐☐☐☐
195	_____				
	4¢	**chocolate**	22.50	.90	☐☐☐☐☐
196	_____				
	5¢	**dark orange brown**	27.50	1.65	☐☐☐☐☐
197	_____				
	5¢	**dark blue**	25.00	.75	☐☐☐☐☐
198	_____				
	6¢	**red brown**	55.00	4.00	☐☐☐☐☐
199	_____				
	6¢	**lake**	35.00	2.25	☐☐☐☐☐
200	_____				
	8¢	**purple brown**	40.00	1.25	☐☐☐☐☐
201	_____				
	10¢	**dark green** Type I	50.00	1.25	☐☐☐☐☐
202	_____				
	10¢	**brown** Type I	135.00	2.50	☐☐☐☐☐
203	_____				
	10¢	**orange brown** Type II	75.00	2.00	☐☐☐☐☐
204	_____				
	15¢	**indigo**	150.00	9.00	☐☐☐☐☐
205	_____				
	15¢	**olive green**	115.00	7.50	☐☐☐☐☐
206	_____				
	50¢	**orange**	200.00	20.00	☐☐☐☐☐
207	_____				
	$1	**black** Type I	450.00	55.00	☐☐☐☐☐
208	_____				
	$1	**black** Type II	900.00	125.00	☐☐☐☐☐
209	_____				
	$2	**dark blue**	775.00	250.00	☐☐☐☐☐
210	_____				
	$5	**dark green**	1,600.00	375.00	☐☐☐☐☐
211	_____	**1902-03. Regular Issue**			
	1¢	**deep bluish green**	9.00	.20	☐☐☐☐☐
212	_____				
	2¢	**carmine**	12.00	.20	☐☐☐☐☐
213	_____				
	3¢	**dark red violet**	52.50	2.25	☐☐☐☐☐
214	_____				
	4¢	**brown**	57.50	1.00	☐☐☐☐☐
215	_____				
	5¢	**deep blue**	57.50	1.15	☐☐☐☐☐
216	_____				
	6¢	**brown red**	70.00	2.00	☐☐☐☐☐
217	_____				
	8¢	**violet black**	42.50	1.60	☐☐☐☐☐
218	_____				
	10¢	**pale red brown**	60.00	1.15	☐☐☐☐☐
219	_____				
	13¢	**black brown**	42.50	6.50	☐☐☐☐☐

180, 201-203

181, 204, 205

182, 206

183, 194, 207, 208

183, 184, 207

184, 208

185, 209

186, 210

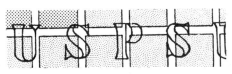

Double-line watermark 187

201, 202

203

211, 225, 228, 230

212

213

214, 226

215, 227, 229

216

217

218

219

			UnFVF	UseFVF	

			UnFVF	UseFVF	
220 _____					
	15¢	**olive green**	150.00	4.50	☐☐☐☐☐
221 _____					
	50¢	**orange**	425.00	20.00	☐☐☐☐☐
222 _____					
	$1	**black**	750.00	45.00	☐☐☐☐☐
223 _____					
	$2	**dark blue**	1,075.00	140.00	☐☐☐☐☐
224 _____					
	$5	**dark green**	2,800.00	525.00	☐☐☐☐☐
225 _____	**1906-08. Regular Issues of 1902-03**				
	1¢	**deep bluish green**	20.00	17.50	☐☐☐☐☐
226 _____					
	4¢	**brown**	22,500.00	15,000.00	☐☐☐☐☐
227 _____					
	5¢	**blue**	375.00	475.00	☐☐☐☐☐

NOTE: *Please exercise caution in buying singles of this stamp, particularly used copies. Certification by respected authorities recommended.*

			UnFVF	UseFVF	
228 _____	**1908. Coil Stamp 1902-03 Series Issue**				
	1¢	**blue green** pair	68,500.00	—	☐☐☐☐☐
229 _____					
	5¢	**blue** pair	9,000.00	—	☐☐☐☐☐

NOTE: *Perforated 12 vertically.*

			UnFVF	UseFVF	
230 _____					
	1¢	**blue green** pair	6,000.00	—	☐☐☐☐☐
231 _____	**1903. Two-Cent Shield Stamp Issue**				
	2¢	**carmine** Type I	4.00	.20	☐☐☐☐☐
232 _____					
	2¢	**lake** Type II	7.50	.50	☐☐☐☐☐
233 _____	**1903. Two-Cent Shield Coil Issue**				
	2¢	**carmine** Type II	20.00	15.00	☐☐☐☐☐
234 _____					
	2¢	**lake** Type II	50.00	40.00	☐☐☐☐☐
235 _____	**1903. Two-Cent Shield Coil Issue**				
	2¢	**carmine** Type I pair	95,000.00	100,000.00	☐☐☐☐☐

NOTE: *Perforated 12 vertically.*

			UnFVF	UseFVF	
236 _____					
	2¢	**scarlet** Type II pair	7,000.00	4,250.00	☐☐☐☐☐
237 _____	**1908-09 Washington & Franklin Issue**				
	1¢	**green**	6.00	.20	☐☐☐☐☐
238 _____					
	2¢	**carmine**	6.00	.20	☐☐☐☐☐
239 _____	**1908. George Washington Type I Issue**				
	3¢	**violet** Type I	27.50	2.50	☐☐☐☐☐
240 _____					
	4¢	**orange brown**	30.00	1.00	☐☐☐☐☐
241 _____					
	5¢	**blue**	40.00	2.00	☐☐☐☐☐
242 _____					
	6¢	**red orange**	47.50	5.00	☐☐☐☐☐
243 _____					
	8¢	**olive green**	37.50	2.50	☐☐☐☐☐
244 _____					
	10¢	**yellow**	55.00	1.50	☐☐☐☐☐

		UnFVF	UseFVF	
245				
13¢	**blue green**	37.50	20.00	❑❑❑❑❑
246				
15¢	**gray blue**	50.00	6.00	❑❑❑❑❑
247				
50¢	**gray lilac**	250.00	17.50	❑❑❑❑❑
248				
$1	**violet brown**	375.00	75.00	❑❑❑❑❑

1908. Washington & Franklin Type I Issue

		UnFVF	UseFVF	
249				
1¢	**green**	6.00	4.00	❑❑❑❑❑
250				
2¢	**carmine**	7.50	3.00	❑❑❑❑❑
251				
3¢	**violet** Type I	17.50	20.00	❑❑❑❑❑
252				
4¢	**brown**	27.50	22.50	❑❑❑❑❑
253				
5¢	**blue**	42.50	30.00	❑❑❑❑❑

1908-10. Washington & Franklin Coil Issue

		UnFVF	UseFVF	
254				
1¢	**green**	22.50	12.50	❑❑❑❑❑
255				
2¢	**carmine**	37.50	8.00	❑❑❑❑❑
256				
4¢	**brown**	85.00	70.00	❑❑❑❑❑
257				
5¢	**blue**	100.00	85.00	❑❑❑❑❑
258				
1¢	**green**	50.00	30.00	❑❑❑❑❑
259				
2¢	**carmine**	47.50	7.50	❑❑❑❑❑
260				
4¢	**brown**	115.00	55.00	❑❑❑❑❑

220

221

222

223, 365

224, 366

226

231-236

237

239

239

239 *George Washington. Type I: All stamps of this design and perforated 12 are Type I. Top line of toga from front of neck to top of button is very weak, as are upper parts of five lines of shading that join top line; line between the lips is thin.*

			UnFVF	UseFVF	

261 _____

    5¢ **blue**   125.00   75.00 ☐☐☐☐☐

262 _____

    10¢ yellow   1,750.00   850.00 ☐☐☐☐☐

263 _____ **1909. Washington & Franklin Issue**

    1¢ green   85.00   85.00 ☐☐☐☐☐

264 _____

    2¢ carmine   75.00   70.00 ☐☐☐☐☐

265 _____

    3¢ **deep violet** Type I   1,600.00 1,600.00 ☐☐☐☐☐

266 _____

    4¢ **orange brown**   15,000.00   — ☐☐☐☐☐

267 _____

    5¢ **blue**   3,500.00 3,750.00 ☐☐☐☐☐

268 _____

    6¢ **red orange**   1,150.00 1,000.00 ☐☐☐☐☐

269 _____

    8¢ **olive green**   16,000.00   — ☐☐☐☐☐

270 _____

    10¢ yellow   1,400.00 1,150.00 ☐☐☐☐☐

271 _____

    13¢ **blue green**   2,350.00 1,450.00 ☐☐☐☐☐

272 _____

    15¢ **pale ultramarine**   1,150.00 1,000.00 ☐☐☐☐☐

273 _____ **1910-14. Washington & Franklin Issue**

    1¢ green   6.00   .20 ☐☐☐☐☐

274 _____

    2¢ carmine   5.75   .20 ☐☐☐☐☐

275 _____ **1911. George Washington Issue**

    3¢ violet Type I   15.00   1.50 ☐☐☐☐☐

276 _____

    4¢ **brown**   22.50   .75 ☐☐☐☐☐

277 _____

    5¢ **blue**   22.50   .75 ☐☐☐☐☐

278 _____

    6¢ **red orange**   30.00   .85 ☐☐☐☐☐

279 _____

    7¢ **black**   70.00   8.50 ☐☐☐☐☐

280 _____

    8¢ **light olive green**   95.00   12.50 ☐☐☐☐☐

281 _____

    10¢ yellow   85.00   4.00 ☐☐☐☐☐

282 _____

    15¢ **pale ultramarine**   225.00   15.00 ☐☐☐☐☐

283 _____ **1910. George Washington Issue**

    1¢ green   3.00   2.75 ☐☐☐☐☐

284 _____

    2¢ carmine   5.50   3.00 ☐☐☐☐☐

285 _____ **1910. Washington & Franklin Coil Issue**

    1¢ green   22.50   12.50 ☐☐☐☐☐

286 _____

    2¢ carmine   37.50   17.50 ☐☐☐☐☐

287 _____

    1¢ green   85.00   37.50 ☐☐☐☐☐

			UnFVF	UseFVF	

288 _____
| | 2¢ | carmine | | 575.00 | 250.00 ☐☐☐☐☐ |

289 _____ **1910. George Washington Orangeburg Coil Issue**
| | 3¢ | deep violet Type I | | 28,500.00 | 7,000.00 ☐☐☐☐☐ |

290 _____ **1910. Washington & Franklin Coil Issue**
| | 1¢ | green | | 4.50 | 5.00 ☐☐☐☐☐ |

291 _____
| | 2¢ | carmine | | 30.00 | 12.50 ☐☐☐☐☐ |

292 _____
| | 1¢ | green | | 20.00 | 20.00 ☐☐☐☐☐ |

293 _____
| | 2¢ | carmine | | 40.00 | 10.00 ☐☐☐☐☐ |

294 _____
| | 3¢ | violet Type I | | 50.00 | 50.00 ☐☐☐☐☐ |

295 _____
| | 4¢ | brown | | 50.00 | 50.00 ☐☐☐☐☐ |

296 _____
| | 5¢ | blue | | 50.00 | 50.00 ☐☐☐☐☐ |

297 _____ **1912. Modified George Washington Issue**
| | 1¢ | green | | 5.00 | .20 ☐☐☐☐☐ |

298 _____
| | 2¢ | carmine Type I | | 4.50 | .20 ☐☐☐☐☐ |

299 _____
| | 1¢ | green | | 1.25 | .60 ☐☐☐☐☐ |

300 _____
| | 2¢ | carmine Type I | | 1.30 | .60 ☐☐☐☐☐ |

301 _____ **1912. George Washington Modified Design Coil Issue**
| | 1¢ | green | | 5.50 | 4.50 ☐☐☐☐☐ |

302 _____
| | 2¢ | carmine Type I | | 7.50 | 4.50 ☐☐☐☐☐ |

303 _____
| | 1¢ | green | | 22.50 | 6.25 ☐☐☐☐☐ |

273   275-262   276   297

298

298 *George Washington, Type I. The following detailed description is provided, although any 2¢ that fits Point 1 is a Type I.* 1. The line from the front of the neck to and over the top of the button is very weak. The shading lines that run into this line (top of toga) are thin in the area above the cross hatching lines. 2. One shading line in the first (upper) curve of the ribbon above the left numeral and one line in the second (middle) curve above the right numeral. 3. There is a white dash below the ear. 4. The shading lines of the face terminate in front of the ear and are not joined with each other. 5. The lock of hair behind the ear is formed at the bottom by two lines of shading, the lower one being considerably shorter than the other. 6. The hair lines above the ear and slightly to the right form an arrowhead. 7. The shading lines just to the left of the ear form a fairly solid color.

			UnFVF	UseFVF	

304	_____				
	2¢	carmine Type I	35.00	1.25	☐☐☐☐☐
305	_____	**1912-14. Benjamin Franklin Redesigned Issue**			
	8¢	pale olive green	30.00	1.25	☐☐☐☐☐
306	_____				
	9¢	salmon pink	45.00	12.50	☐☐☐☐☐
307	_____				
	10¢	orange yellow	32.50	.50	☐☐☐☐☐
308	_____				
	12¢	chocolate	40.00	4.25	☐☐☐☐☐
309	_____				
	15¢	gray black	65.00	4.00	☐☐☐☐☐
310	_____				
	20¢	gray blue	150.00	17.50	☐☐☐☐☐
311	_____				
	30¢	orange red	115.00	17.50	☐☐☐☐☐
312	_____				
	50¢	violet	350.00	20.00	☐☐☐☐☐
313	_____				
	50¢	violet	225.00	20.00	☐☐☐☐☐
314	_____				
	$1	violet brown	425.00	65.00	☐☐☐☐☐
315	_____	**1914-15. Washington & Franklin Issue**			
	1¢	green	2.75	.20	☐☐☐☐☐
316	_____				
	2¢	rose red Type I	2.25	.20	☐☐☐☐☐
317	_____				
	3¢	violet Type I	12.50	2.00	☐☐☐☐☐
318	_____				
	4¢	brown	30.00	.75	☐☐☐☐☐
319	_____				
	5¢	blue	27.50	.70	☐☐☐☐☐
320	_____				
	6¢	red orange	45.00	2.00	☐☐☐☐☐
321	_____				
	7¢	black	75.00	5.00	☐☐☐☐☐
322	_____				
	8¢	yellow olive	30.00	1.25	☐☐☐☐☐
323	_____				
	9¢	salmon	35.00	2.00	☐☐☐☐☐
324	_____				
	10¢	orange yellow	40.00	.40	☐☐☐☐☐
325	_____				
	11¢	deep bluish green	20.00	9.00	☐☐☐☐☐
326	_____				
	12¢	maroon	23.00	4.25	☐☐☐☐☐

NOTE: So-called vertical pair, imperforate between, really have at least one perforation hole between the stamps.

327	_____				
	15¢	gray black	110.00	8.50	☐☐☐☐☐
328	_____				
	20¢	pale ultramarine	175.00	4.50	☐☐☐☐☐
329	_____				
	30¢	orange red	225.00	20.00	☐☐☐☐☐
330	_____				
	50¢	violet	525.00	22.50	☐☐☐☐☐

			UnFVF	UseFVF	

331 _____ **1914-15. Benjamin Franklin Issue**

    $1   **violet black**   725.00   85.00 ☐☐☐☐☐

332 _____ **1915. George Washington Issue**

    2¢   **rose red** Type I   100.00   225.00 ☐☐☐☐☐

333 _____ **1914. George Washington Coil Issue**

    1¢   **green**   1.25   1.25 ☐☐☐☐☐

334 _____

    2¢   **carmine** Type I   8.50   8.00 ☐☐☐☐☐

335 _____

    1¢   **green**   22.50   7.50 ☐☐☐☐☐

336 _____

    2¢   **carmine** Type I   32.50   1.75 ☐☐☐☐☐

337 _____

    3¢   **violet** Type I   225.00   125.00 ☐☐☐☐☐

338 _____

    4¢   **brown**   120.00   47.50 ☐☐☐☐☐

339 _____

    5¢   **blue**   47.50   32.50 ☐☐☐☐☐

340 _____ **1914-16. Washington & Franklin Rotary Press Coil Issue**

    1¢   **green**   6.50   4.25 ☐☐☐☐☐

341 _____

    2¢   **carmine** Type III   10.00   4.25 ☐☐☐☐☐

342 _____ **1914. Washington Rotary Press Sidewise Coil Issue**

    2¢   **carmine** Type I   375.00   750.00 ☐☐☐☐☐

343 _____ **1914-16. Washington Issue**

    1¢   **green**   10.00   2.50 ☐☐☐☐☐

344 _____

    2¢   **carmine** Type III   10.00   1.15 ☐☐☐☐☐

345 _____

    3¢   **violet** Type I   225.00   115.00 ☐☐☐☐☐

346 _____

    4¢   **yellow brown**   27.50   20.00 ☐☐☐☐☐

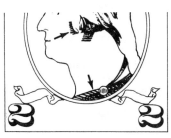

305-314   315-321   322-331   333 and 340

341 *Type III. Same as Type II except two lines of shading in the curves of the ribbons.*

344

344 *Type II. Shading lines in ribbons same as Type I. The top line of toga rope is heavy and the rope is heavily shaded. The shading lines on the face, in front of the ear, are joined by a heavy vertical curved line.*

			UnFVF	UseFVF	

347 _____

5¢	blue		32.50	17.50	☐☐☐☐☐

348 _____   **1916-17. Washington & Franklin Issue**

1¢	green		6.00	.50	☐☐☐☐☐

349 _____

2¢	carmine Type I		4.00	.35	☐☐☐☐☐

350 _____

3¢	violet Type I		65.00	15.00	☐☐☐☐☐

351 _____

4¢	yellow brown		42.50	2.25	☐☐☐☐☐

352 _____

5¢	blue		65.00	2.25	☐☐☐☐☐

353 _____

5¢	carmine		550.00	700.00	☐☐☐☐☐

NOTE: 353 The "Five Cent Red Error" was caused by mistakenly using a 5¢ transfer roll in reentering three positions on plate 7942, a plate of the 2¢ stamps. Of the 400 positions on the plate, 397 copies were 2¢ and three copies were 5¢. The error was not discovered until a considerable number of sheets were in the post offices, and many of them were picked up by collectors. The errors exist perforated 10 (No. 353), perforated 11 (No. 385), and imperforate (No. 370). The shade actually is carmine, but the stamp commonly is called the "Red Error."

354 _____

6¢	red orange		80.00	7.50	☐☐☐☐☐

355 _____

7¢	black		100.00	12.50	☐☐☐☐☐

356 _____

8¢	yellow olive		55.00	6.50	☐☐☐☐☐

357 _____

9¢	salmon		50.00	15.00	☐☐☐☐☐

358 _____

10¢	orange yellow		95.00	1.25	☐☐☐☐☐

359 _____

11¢	deep bluish green		35.00	22.50	☐☐☐☐☐

360 _____

12¢	chocolate		45.00	5.50	☐☐☐☐☐

361 _____

15¢	gray black		165.00	12.50	☐☐☐☐☐

362 _____

20¢	pale blue		225.00	12.50	☐☐☐☐☐

362A _____

30¢	orange red		4,500.00	—	☐☐☐☐☐

NOTE: 362A Two sheets of 100 stamps of the 30¢ denomination were discovered without any trace of watermark, as authenticated by The Philatelic Foundation's expert committee.

363 _____

50¢	light violet		950.00	65.00	☐☐☐☐☐

364 _____

$1	violet black		625.00	20.00	☐☐☐☐☐

365 _____   **1917. James Madison Issue**

$2	dark blue		325.00	45.00	☐☐☐☐☐

366 _____   **1917. John Marshall Issue**

$5	light green		250.00	50.00	☐☐☐☐☐

367 _____   **1916-1917. George Washington Issue**

1¢	green		1.15	1.00	☐☐☐☐☐

368 _____

2¢	carmine Type I		1.40	1.30	☐☐☐☐☐

369 _____

3¢	violet Type I		15.00	8.50	☐☐☐☐☐

		UnFVF	UseFVF	

370 _____

5¢   **carmine**   12,500.00   ☐☐☐☐☐

NOTE: This stamp commonly is called the "Red Error," but really is carmine. See note with No. 353.

371 _____   **1916-22. Washington Rotary Press Coil Issue**

1¢   **green**   .75   .20 ☐☐☐☐☐

372 _____

2¢   **carmine** Type III   3.00   1.75 ☐☐☐☐☐

373 _____

3¢   **violet** Type I   4.50   1.50 ☐☐☐☐☐

374 _____   **1916-22. Washington Issue**

1¢   **green**   .60   .20 ☐☐☐☐☐

375 _____

2¢   **carmine** Type III   8.50   .20 ☐☐☐☐☐

376 _____

3¢   **violet** Type II   11.50   1.25 ☐☐☐☐☐

377 _____

4¢   **yellow brown**   10.50   4.00 ☐☐☐☐☐

378 _____

5¢   **blue**   3.50   1.25 ☐☐☐☐☐

379 _____

10¢   **orange yellow**   19.00   12.50 ☐☐☐☐☐

380 _____   **1917-19 Washington & Franklin Issue**

1¢   **green**   .55   .20 ☐☐☐☐☐

381 _____

2¢   **rose red** Type I   .50   .20 ☐☐☐☐☐

NOTE: Type Ia is similar to Type I, but lines of the design are stronger. This is particularly noticeable on the toga button, toga rope and rope shading lines, which are heavy. Lines in the ribbons are similar to Type I.

382 _____

3¢   **violet** Type I   12.50   .20 ☐☐☐☐☐

382A _____

3¢   **violet** Type II   15.00   .40 ☐☐☐☐☐

383 _____

4¢   **yellow brown**   11.50   .30 ☐☐☐☐☐

384 _____

5¢   **blue**   8.50   .25 ☐☐☐☐☐

385 _____

5¢   **carmine**   400.00   500.00 ☐☐☐☐☐

NOTE: This stamp commonly is called the "Red Error" but really is carmine. See note with No. 353.

386 _____

6¢   **red orange**   12.50   .40 ☐☐☐☐☐

387 _____

7¢   **black**   25.00   1.25 ☐☐☐☐☐

388 _____

8¢   **yellow olive**   12.50   1.00 ☐☐☐☐☐

365

366

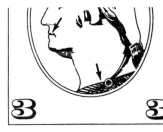

369

369 3¢. On Type II the top line of the toga rope is heavy, and the rope shading lines are also heavy and complete. The line between the lips is heavy.

			UnFVF	UseFVF

			UnFVF	UseFVF	
389					
	9¢	salmon	14.00	2.50	☐☐☐☐☐
390					
	10¢	orange yellow	17.50	.25	☐☐☐☐☐
391					
	11¢	deep bluish green	9.00	3.00	☐☐☐☐☐
392					
	12¢	brown purple	9.00	.65	☐☐☐☐☐
393					
	13¢	apple green	10.50	6.50	☐☐☐☐☐
394					
	15¢	gray black	37.50	1.25	☐☐☐☐☐
395					
	20¢	pale blue	47.50	.50	☐☐☐☐☐
396					
	30¢	orange red	37.50	1.25	☐☐☐☐☐
397					
	50¢	reddish violet	65.00	.90	☐☐☐☐☐
398					
	$1	black purple	55.00	1.75	☐☐☐☐☐
399		**1917. George Washington Issue**			
	2¢	carmine	275.00	450.00	☐☐☐☐☐
400		**1918-20. Benjamin Franklin Issue**			
	$2	orange & black	650.00	225.00	☐☐☐☐☐
401					
	$2	carmine & black	190.00	40.00	☐☐☐☐☐
402					
	$5	deep green & black	225.00	35.00	☐☐☐☐☐
403		**1918-20. George Washington Issue**			
	1¢	dull green	2.00	.75	☐☐☐☐☐
404					
	2¢	rose red Type VII	17.50	.35	☐☐☐☐☐
404A					
	2¢	rose red Type V	15.00	1.00	☐☐☐☐☐
404B					
	2¢	rose red Type Va	8.00	.35	☐☐☐☐☐
404C					
	2¢	rose red Type VI	45.00	1.50	☐☐☐☐☐
404D					
	2¢	rose red Type IV	25.00	4.25	☐☐☐☐☐
405		**1918. George Washington Issue**			
	3¢	purple Type III	3.00	.40	☐☐☐☐☐
405A					
	3¢	purple Type IV	1.25	.20	☐☐☐☐☐
406		**1919-20. George Washington Issue**			
	1¢	dull green	10.00	8.50	☐☐☐☐☐
407					
	2¢	rose red Type IV	35.00	30.00	☐☐☐☐☐
407A					
	2¢	rose red Type V	190.00	85.00	☐☐☐☐☐
407B					
	2¢	rose red Type Va	12.50	8.50	☐☐☐☐☐
407C					
	2¢	rose red Type VI	35.00	22.50	☐☐☐☐☐

400, 401   402   403

Type IV: *Top line of toga rope is broken. Lines inside toga button read "D (reversed) ID." The line of color in the left "2" is very thin and is usually broken.*

Type V: *Top line of the toga is complete. Five vertical shading lines in toga button. Line of color in left "2" is very thin and usually broken. Shading dots on nose form a triangle with six dots in third row from bottom.*

Type Va: *Same as Type V except on the shading dots on the nose, in which the third row from the bottom has only four dots instead of six.*

Type VI: *Same as Type V but there is a heavy line of color in the left "2."*

Type VII: *The line of color in the left "2" is clear and unbroken, heavier than on Type V or Va but not as heavy as on Type VI. An extra vertical row of dots has been added on the lip, making four rows of three dots instead of two dots. Additional dots have been added to the hair on top of the head.*

404-404D

405

Type III: *Top line of toga is strong but the fifth shading line is missing. The center shading line of the toga button consists of two vertical dashes with a dot between them. The "P" and "O" of "POSTAGE" have a line of color between them.*

Type IV: *The "P" and "O" of "POSTAGE" are joined with no line of color between them. The center shading line runs right through the dot in the toga button.*

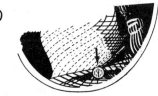

		UnFVF	UseFVF

407D _____

2¢ **rose red** Type VII   1,500.00   575.00 ☐☐☐☐☐

408 _____

3¢ **violet** Type IV   8.75   6.00 ☐☐☐☐☐

409 _____   **1919. George Washington Issue**

1¢ **dull green**   14.00   16.50 ☐☐☐☐☐

410 _____

1¢ **green**   8.00   8.00 ☐☐☐☐☐

411 _____

2¢ **carmine red** Type II   2,500.00   3,200.00 ☐☐☐☐☐

411A _____

2¢ **carmine red** Type III   10.00   9.00 ☐☐☐☐☐

412 _____

3¢ **gray lilac** Type II   32.50   35.00 ☐☐☐☐☐

413 _____   **1920. George Washington Issue**

1¢ **green**   10.00   1.00 ☐☐☐☐☐

414 _____   **1921. George Washington Issue**

1¢ **green**   .55   .20 ☐☐☐☐☐

415 _____   **1922. George Washington Issue**

1¢ **green**   12,000.00   2,400.00 ☐☐☐☐☐

416 _____   **1921. George Washington Issue**

1¢ **green**   120.00   130.00 ☐☐☐☐☐

417 _____

2¢ **carmine** Type III   85.00   115.00 ☐☐☐☐☐

418 _____   **1925. Nathan Hale Issue**

1/2¢ **olive brown**   .25   .20 ☐☐☐☐☐

419 _____   **1923. Benjamin Franklin Issue**

1¢ **green**   1.45   .20 ☐☐☐☐☐

420 _____   **1925. Warren Harding Issue**

1-1/2¢ **yellow brown**   2.75   .25 ☐☐☐☐☐

NOTE: See also CM60-63, a 2¢ black Harding of the same design as 420. Some include it with the 1922-34 Regular Issue Series.

421 _____   **1923. George Washington Type I Issue**

2¢ **carmine** Type I   1.75   .20 ☐☐☐☐☐

422 _____   **1923. Abraham Lincoln Issue**

3¢ **reddish violet**   17.50   1.25 ☐☐☐☐☐

423 _____   **1923. Martha Washington Issue**

4¢ **yellow brown**   17.50   .20 ☐☐☐☐☐

424 _____   **1922. Theodore Roosevelt Issue**

5¢ **Prussian blue**   17.50   .20 ☐☐☐☐☐

425 _____   **1922. James Garfield Issue**

6¢ **red orange**   32.50   .85 ☐☐☐☐☐

426 _____   **1923. William McKinley Issue**

7¢ **black**   8.00   .75 ☐☐☐☐☐

427 _____   **1923. Ulysses S. Grant Issue**

8¢ **yellow olive**   42.50   .85 ☐☐☐☐☐

428 _____   **1923. Thomas Jefferson Issue**

9¢ **carmine rose**   16.50   1.25 ☐☐☐☐☐

429 _____   **1923. James Monroe Issue**

10¢ **orange yellow**   22.50   .25 ☐☐☐☐☐

430 _____   **1922. Rutherford B. Hayes Issue**

11¢ **turquoise blue**   1.50   .50 ☐☐☐☐☐

NOTE: No. 430 is known in a wide range of color shades between yellow green and light blue.

431 _____   **1923. Grover Cleveland Issue**

12¢ **maroon**   7.50   .25 ☐☐☐☐☐

410	411	412	416	417

418, 473	419, 443, 446, 448, 449A 450, 461, 469, 474, 495, 506	420, 444, 451, 462, 470, 472, 475, 496, 507	421, 445, 447, 449, 452, 463, 471, 476, 476A, 497, 508	422, 453, 464, 477, 498, 509

423, 454, 465, 478, 499, 510	424, 455, 466, 479, 500, 511	425, 456, 467, 480, 501, 512	426, 457, 481, 502, 513	427, 458, 482, 503, 514

428, 459, 483, 504, 515	429, 460, 468, 484, 505, 516	430, 485	431, 486	432, 487

433, 488	434, 489	435, 490	436, 491

437, 492	438, 493	439, 494	440

		UnFVF	UseFVF

432 _____ **1926. Benjamin Harrison Issue**

13¢ green   14.00   .65 ☐☐☐☐☐

433 _____ **1923. American Indian Issue**

14¢ blue   4.75   .80 ☐☐☐☐☐

434 _____ **1922. Statue of Liberty Issue**

15¢ gray black   22.50   .20 ☐☐☐☐☐

435 _____ **1925. Woodrow Wilson Issue**

17¢ black   17.50   .35 ☐☐☐☐☐

436 _____ **1923. Golden Gate Issue**

20¢ carmine red   22.50   .20 ☐☐☐☐☐

437 _____ **1922. Niagara Falls Issue**

25¢ green   17.50   .75 ☐☐☐☐☐

438 _____ **1923. Bison Issue**

30¢ olive brown   32.50   .50 ☐☐☐☐☐

439 _____ **1922. Arlington Issue**

50¢ gray lilac   55.00   .20 ☐☐☐☐☐

440 _____ **1923. Lincoln Memorial Issue**

$1 purple brown   45.00   .50 ☐☐☐☐☐

441 _____ **1923. U. S. Capitol Issue**

$2 blue   100.00   10.00 ☐☐☐☐☐

442 _____ **1923. Head of Freedom Issue**

$5 carmine & blue   200.00   13.50 ☐☐☐☐☐

443 _____ **1923. Issue**

1¢ green   7.50   4.50 ☐☐☐☐☐

444 _____

1-1/2¢ yellow brown   1.50   1.45 ☐☐☐☐☐

NOTE: No. 444 exists in a rotary press printing, No. 472.

445 _____

2¢ carmine   1.50   1.45 ☐☐☐☐☐

446 _____ **1923-24. Rotary Press Printings**

1¢ green   70.00   110.00 ☐☐☐☐☐

447 _____

2¢ carmine   55.00   100.00 ☐☐☐☐☐

448 _____

1¢ green   15,000.00 4,000.00 ☐☐☐☐☐

449 _____

2¢ carmine   185.00   235.00 ☐☐☐☐☐

NOTE: Nos. 448 and 449 were made from coil waste. Design 18 1/2 to 19mm wide by 22 1/2mm high.

449A _____

1¢ green   —   42,500.00 ☐☐☐☐☐

450 _____ **1923-26. Rotary Press Printing Issue**

1¢ green   7.50   1.00 ☐☐☐☐☐

451 _____

1-1/2¢ yellow brown   3.75   1.00 ☐☐☐☐☐

452 _____

2¢ carmine   2.00   .35 ☐☐☐☐☐

453 _____

3¢ reddish violet   20.00   2.50 ☐☐☐☐☐

454 _____

4¢ yellow brown   14.00   .80 ☐☐☐☐☐

455 _____

5¢ blue   14.00   .80 ☐☐☐☐☐

456 _____

6¢ orange   6.25   .75 ☐☐☐☐☐

		UnFVF	UseFVF	

457 _____
    7¢ **black**   9.00   6.50 ☐☐☐☐☐

458 _____
    8¢ **yellow olive**   20.00   4.00 ☐☐☐☐☐

459 _____
    9¢ **red**   4.25   2.50 ☐☐☐☐☐

460 _____
    10¢ **orange yellow**   50.00   .45 ☐☐☐☐☐

461 _____ **1923-26. Rotary Press Coil Issue**
    1¢ **yellow green**   .35   .20 ☐☐☐☐☐

462 _____
    1-1/2¢ **yellow brown**   .75   .20 ☐☐☐☐☐

463 _____
    2¢ **carmine** Type I   .45   .20 ☐☐☐☐☐

464 _____
    3¢ **reddish violet**   5.50   .30 ☐☐☐☐☐

465 _____
    4¢ **yellow brown**   3.75   .50 ☐☐☐☐☐

466 _____
    5¢ **blue**   1.75   .20 ☐☐☐☐☐

467 _____
    6¢ **orange**   9.50   .35 ☐☐☐☐☐

468 _____
    10¢ **orange yellow**   3.50   .20 ☐☐☐☐☐

469 _____ **1924. Rotary Press Coil Issue**
    1¢ **yellow green**   .35   .20 ☐☐☐☐☐

470 _____
    1-1/2¢ **yellow brown**   .35   .20 ☐☐☐☐☐

471 _____
    2¢ **carmine**   .35   .20 ☐☐☐☐☐

472 _____ **1926. Rotary Press Issue**
    1-1/2¢ **yellow brown**   2.25   2.00 ☐☐☐☐☐

473 _____ **1926-34. Rotary Press Issue**
    1/2¢ **olive brown**   .25   .20 ☐☐☐☐☐

474 _____
    1¢ **green**   .25   .20 ☐☐☐☐☐

475 _____
    1-1/2¢ **yellow brown**   2.00   .20 ☐☐☐☐☐

476 _____
    2¢ **carmine red** Type I   .25   .20 ☐☐☐☐☐

476A _____
    2¢ **carmine red** Type II   220.00   15.00 ☐☐☐☐☐

477 _____
    3¢ **reddish violet**   .55   .20 ☐☐☐☐☐

441

442

463 Type 1 (left); Type II (right)

463 Type II

		UnFVF	UseFVF	

478 _____
    4¢   **yellow brown** — 2.75 — .20 ☐☐☐☐☐

479 _____
    5¢   **blue** — 2.25 — .20 ☐☐☐☐☐

480 _____
    6¢   **orange** — 2.25 — .20 ☐☐☐☐☐

481 _____
    7¢   **black** — 2.25 — .20 ☐☐☐☐☐

482 _____
    8¢   **yellow olive** — 2.25 — .20 ☐☐☐☐☐

483 _____
    9¢   **red** — 2.00 — .20 ☐☐☐☐☐

484 _____
    10¢   **orange yellow** — 4.00 — .20 ☐☐☐☐☐

485 _____
    11¢   **turquoise green** — 2.75 — .20 ☐☐☐☐☐

486 _____
    12¢   **brown purple** — 6.00 — .20 ☐☐☐☐☐

487 _____
    13¢   **yellow green** — 2.25 — .20 ☐☐☐☐☐

488 _____
    14¢   **blue** — 4.00 — .50 ☐☐☐☐☐

489 _____
    15¢   **gray black** — 8.00 — .20 ☐☐☐☐☐

490 _____   **1931. Rotary Press Issue**
    17¢   **black** — 5.50 — .20 ☐☐☐☐☐

491 _____
    20¢   **carmine rose** — 9.50 — .20 ☐☐☐☐☐

492 _____
    25¢   **green** — 11.00 — .20 ☐☐☐☐☐

493 _____
    30¢   **olive brown** — 17.50 — .20 ☐☐☐☐☐

494 _____
    50¢   **lilac** — 42.50 — .20 ☐☐☐☐☐

495 _____   **1929. Kansas and Nebraska Overprints Issue**
    1¢   **green** — 2.00 — 1.50 ☐☐☐☐☐

496 _____
    1-1/2¢ **yellow brown** — 3.00 — 2.25 ☐☐☐☐☐

497 _____
    2¢   **carmine red** — 3.00 — 1.00 ☐☐☐☐☐

498 _____
    3¢   **reddish violet** — 15.00 — 11.00 ☐☐☐☐☐

499 _____
    4¢   **yellow brown** — 15.00 — 8.50 ☐☐☐☐☐

500 _____
    5¢   **blue** — 12.50 — 9.00 ☐☐☐☐☐

501 _____
    6¢   **orange** — 25.00 — 15.00 ☐☐☐☐☐

502 _____
    7¢   **black** — 25.00 — 20.00 ☐☐☐☐☐

503 _____
    8¢   **yellow olive** — 70.00 — 60.00 ☐☐☐☐☐

504 _____
    9¢   **salmon** — 12.50 — 10.00 ☐☐☐☐☐

	UnFVF	UseFVF	

505 _____
  10¢ orange yellow — 20.00 — 12.50 ☐☐☐☐☐

506 _____
  1¢ green — 2.25 — 2.00 ☐☐☐☐☐

507 _____
  1-1/2¢ yellow brown — 2.25 — 2.00 ☐☐☐☐☐

508 _____
  2¢ carmine red — 2.25 — 1.00 ☐☐☐☐☐

509 _____
  3¢ reddish violet — 11.00 — 8.00 ☐☐☐☐☐

510 _____
  4¢ yellow brown — 15.00 — 10.00 ☐☐☐☐☐

511 _____
  5¢ blue — 12.50 — 11.50 ☐☐☐☐☐

512 _____
  6¢ orange — 35.00 — 17.50 ☐☐☐☐☐

513 _____
  7¢ black — 18.50 — 12.50 ☐☐☐☐☐

514 _____
  8¢ yellow olive — 25.00 — 17.50 ☐☐☐☐☐

515 _____
  9¢ salmon — 30.00 — 22.50 ☐☐☐☐☐

516 _____
  10¢ orange yellow — 85.00 — 17.50 ☐☐☐☐☐

517 _____
1930-32. Warren G. Harding New Design Issue
  1-1/2¢ yellow brown — .25 — .20 ☐☐☐☐☐

518 _____
1930-32. George Washington Issue
  3¢ reddish violet — .25 — .20 ☐☐☐☐☐

519 _____
1930-32 William H. Taft Issue
  4¢ yellow brown — .90 — .20 ☐☐☐☐☐

520 _____
1930-32. Warren G. Harding New Design Coil Issue
  1-1/2¢ yellow brown — 1.50 — .20 ☐☐☐☐☐

521 _____
1930-32. George Washington Coil Issue
  3¢ reddish violet — 1.75 — .20 ☐☐☐☐☐

522 _____
1930-32. William H. Taft Coil Issue
  4¢ yellow brown — 2.75 — .75 ☐☐☐☐☐

Kans.

Kans.

Nebr.

495-505   503   506-516

516   517, 520   518, 521, 523   519, 522   520 Line Pair

		UnFVF	UseFVF	

523 _____ **1930-32. George Washington Coil Issue**
3¢   reddish violet   1.00   .75 ☐☐☐☐☐
524 _____ **1938. Benjamin Franklin Issue**
1/2¢ red orange   .25   .20 ☐☐☐☐☐
525 _____ **1938. George Washington Issue**
1¢   green   .25   .20 ☐☐☐☐☐
526 _____ **1938. Martha Washington Issue**
1-1/2¢ yellow brown   .25   .20 ☐☐☐☐☐
527 _____ **1938. John Adams Issue**
2¢   rose   .25   .20 ☐☐☐☐☐
528 _____ **1938. Thomas Jefferson Issue**
3¢   violet   .25   .20 ☐☐☐☐☐
529 _____ **1938. James Madison Issue**
4¢   bright purple   1.15   .20 ☐☐☐☐☐
530 _____ **1938. White House Issue**
4-1/2¢ gray   .25   .20 ☐☐☐☐☐
531 _____ **1938. James Monroe Issue**
5¢   light blue   .25   .20 ☐☐☐☐☐
532 _____ **1938. John Quincy Adams Issue**
6¢   orange   .35   .20 ☐☐☐☐☐
533 _____ **1938. Andrew Jackson Issue**
7¢   sepia   .45   .20 ☐☐☐☐☐
534 _____ **1938. Martin Van Buren Issue**
8¢   olive green   .45   .20 ☐☐☐☐☐
535 _____ **1938. William Henry Harrison Issue**
9¢   rose pink   .50   .20 ☐☐☐☐☐
536 _____ **1938. John Tyler Issue**
10¢ Venetian red   .45   .20 ☐☐☐☐☐
537 _____ **1938. James Knox Polk Issue**
11¢ cobalt   .75   .15 ☐☐☐☐☐
538 _____ **1938. Zachary Taylor Issue**
12¢ light reddish violet   1.40   .20 ☐☐☐☐☐
539 _____ **1938. Millard Fillmore Issue**
13¢ blue green   2.25   .20 ☐☐☐☐☐
540 _____ **1938. Franklin Pierce Issue**
14¢ blue   1.15   .20 ☐☐☐☐☐
541 _____ **1938. James Buchanan Issue**
15¢ slate   .65   .20 ☐☐☐☐☐
542 _____ **1938. Abraham Lincoln Issue**
16¢ black   1.25   .60 ☐☐☐☐☐
543 _____ **1938. Andrew Johnson Issue**
17¢ rose red   1.25   .20 ☐☐☐☐☐
544 _____ **1938. Ulysses S. Grant Issue**
18¢ brown carmine   2.25   .25 ☐☐☐☐☐
545 _____ **1938. Rutherford B. Hayes Issue**
19¢ light reddish violet   2.00   .60 ☐☐☐☐☐
546 _____ **1938. James A. Garfield Issue**
20¢ blue green   1.25   .20 ☐☐☐☐☐
547 _____ **1938. Chester A. Arthur Issue**
21¢ slate blue   2.25   .20 ☐☐☐☐☐
548 _____ **1938. Grover Cleveland Issue**
22¢ vermilion   1.50   .75 ☐☐☐☐☐
549 _____ **1938. Benjamin Harrison Issue**
24¢ gray green   4.25   .35 ☐☐☐☐☐

524

525, 556, 565

526, 557, 566

527, 558, 567

528, 559, 568

529, 560

530, 561

531, 562

532, 563

533

534

535

536, 564

537

538

539

540

541

542

543

544

545

546

547

548

549

550

551

552

553

		UnFVF	UseFVF	

550 _____ **1938. William McKinley Issue**
25¢ claret — 1.20 / .20 ☐☐☐☐☐

551 _____ **1938. Theodore Roosevelt Issue**
30¢ deep ultramarine — 5.00 / .20 ☐☐☐☐☐

552 _____ **1938. William Howard Taft Issue**
50¢ light red violet — 8.50 / .20 ☐☐☐☐☐

NOTE: Flat plate printing, perforated 11.

553 _____ **1938. Woodrow Wilson Issue**
$1 dark purple and black — 10.00 / .20 ☐☐☐☐☐

NOTE: 553a is printed on pre-gummed, whiter and thicker paper. It was printed on "dry" print; No. 553 was printed on pre-dampened paper.

554 _____ **1938. Warren G. Harding Issue**
$2 green and black — 27.50 / 4.75 ☐☐☐☐☐

555 _____ **1938. Calvin Coolidge Issue**
$5 carmine and black — 115.00 / 4.50 ☐☐☐☐☐

556 _____ **1939. Presidential Coil Issue**
1¢ green — .25 / .20 ☐☐☐☐☐

557 _____
1-1/2¢ yellow brown — .25 / .20 ☐☐☐☐☐

558 _____
2¢ rose — .25 / .20 ☐☐☐☐☐

559 _____
3¢ violet — .25 / .20 ☐☐☐☐☐

560 _____
4¢ bright purple — 7.50 / .75 ☐☐☐☐☐

561 _____
4-1/2¢ gray — .75 / .50 ☐☐☐☐☐

562 _____
5¢ bright blue — 6.00 / .50 ☐☐☐☐☐

563 _____
6¢ orange — 1.25 / .50 ☐☐☐☐☐

564 _____
10¢ Venetian red — 12.50 / 1.25 ☐☐☐☐☐

565 _____ **1939. Presidential Coil Issue**
1¢ green — .75 / .25 ☐☐☐☐☐

566 _____
1-1/2¢ yellow brown — 1.50 / .75 ☐☐☐☐☐

567 _____
2¢ rose — 2.50 / .75 ☐☐☐☐☐

568 _____
3¢ violet — 2.25 / .75 ☐☐☐☐☐

		MNHVF	UseVF	

569 _____ **1955. Benjamin Franklin Issue**
1/2¢ vermilion wet print — .25 / .20 ☐☐☐☐☐

570 _____ **1954. George Washington Issue**
1¢ dull green wet print — .25 / .20 ☐☐☐☐☐

571 _____ **1956. Mount Vernon Issue**
1-1/2¢ brown carmine dry print — .25 / .20 ☐☐☐☐☐

572 _____ **1954. Thomas Jefferson Issue**
2¢ rose dry print — .25 / .20 ☐☐☐☐☐

NOTE: Silkote paper was used for only 50,000 stamps. Silkote varieties need expertization.

	MNHVF	UseVF

573 _____   **1954. Statue of Liberty Issue**

3¢   **violet** wet print   .25   .20

NOTE: Type I tagging: mat tagging. The four separate mats used did not cover the entire sheet of 400 stamps and certain untagged areas help to identify this variety.

NOTE: Type II tagging: roll tagging. Continuously surfaced rolls replaced the previously used tagging mats. Only the plate number selvage margin is partially tagged, and the plate number blocks have one untagged margin.

NOTE: Type III tagging: curved metal plate tagging. Sheet margins are almost fully tagged but a "hot line" of intense phosphor-tagging or untagged narrow gap, 1mm or less in width, can appear on stamps from any position in the pane.

574 _____   **1954. Abraham Lincoln Issue**

4¢   **magenta** wet print   .25   .20 ⬜⬜⬜⬜⬜

575 _____   **1954. James Monroe Issue**

5¢   **blue** dry print   .25   .20 ⬜⬜⬜⬜⬜

576 _____   **1955. Theodore Roosevelt Issue**

6¢   **rose red** wet print   .25   .20 ⬜⬜⬜⬜⬜

577 _____   **1956. Woodrow Wilson Issue**

7¢   **carmine red** dry print   .25   .20 ⬜⬜⬜⬜⬜

578 _____   **1954. Statue of Liberty Issue**

8¢   **deep blue & carmine**   .25   .20 ⬜⬜⬜⬜⬜

NOTE: This stamp was produced on both flat-bed and rotary presses. See also 591 for Type II.

579 _____   **1956. The Alamo Issue**

9¢   **rose lilac** dry print   .25   .20 ⬜⬜⬜⬜⬜

580 _____   **1956. Independence Hall Issue**

10¢ **brown purple** dry print   .25   .20 ⬜⬜⬜⬜⬜

581 _____   **1956. Monticello Issue**

20¢ **bright blue** dry print   .50   .20 ⬜⬜⬜⬜⬜

582 _____   **1955. Robert E. Lee Issue**

30¢ **black** wet print   1.50   .25 ⬜⬜⬜⬜⬜

554	555	569	570, 587	571
572, 588	573, 589	574, 590	575	576
577	578	579	580	581

	MNHVF	UseVF

583 _____ **1955. John Marshall Issue**

40¢ **brown carmine** wet print | 2.75 | .25 □□□□□

584 _____ **1955. Susan B. Anthony Issue**

50¢ **red violet** wet print | 2.00 | .20 □□□□□

585 _____ **1955. Patrick Henry Issue**

$1 **dark lilac** wet print | 7.00 | .20 □□□□□

586 _____ **1956. Alexander Hamilton Issue**

$5 **black** dry print | 70.00 | 6.50 □□□□□

587 _____ **1954. George Washington Issue**

1¢ **dull green** wet print | .45 | .25 □□□□□

588 _____ **1954. Thomas Jefferson Issue**

2¢ **rose** wet print | .25 | .20 □□□□□

589 _____ **1954. Statue of Liberty Issue**

3¢ **purple** wet print, large holes | .25 | .20 □□□□□

NOTE: No. 589psz1, the so-called "Look Coil," was prepared for Look magazine in coil rolls of 3,000 subjects. All but 99,000 of this issue were affixed to outgoing mail and return addressed envelopes on an automatic labeling machine at Des Moines, Iowa. The earliest known use was Dec. 29, 1966. The common usage was in combination with a 2¢ Jefferson coil (No. 588). The paper on which the stamps were printed is plain, without fluorescent content, and tagging is uniform and brilliant. A special printing was issued, in coils of 500 subjects, to satisfy collector demands (No. 589psz1). The original printing had a sharper, more well-defined design, and a more intense shade of purple ink. The philatelic examples were on slightly fluorescent paper, the tagging was less intense and on some coils across-the-web tagging marks known as "hot lines" repeat every 24th stamp.

590 _____ **1958. Abraham Lincoln Issue**

4¢ **bright purple** wet print (Bureau precancel only) | 25.00 | 1.00 □□□□□

591 _____ **1958. Statue of Liberty Issue**

8¢ **deep blue & carmine** | .25 | .20 □□□□□

592 _____ **1958. John Jay Issue**

15¢ **brown purple** dry print | .75 | .20 □□□□□

593 _____ **1958. Paul Revere Issue**

25¢ **deep blue green** | 1.50 | .20 □□□□□

594 _____ **1959. Bunker Hill Monument Issue**

2-1/2¢ **slate blue** dry print | .25 | .20 □□□□□

595 _____ **1959. Hermitage Issue**

4-1/2¢ **blue green** dry print | .25 | .20 □□□□□

596 _____ **1959. Benjamin Harrison Issue**

12¢ **carmine red** dry print | .30 | .20 □□□□□

NOTE: Type IIa tagging: wide roll tagging. All margins are fully tagged.

597 _____ **1959. Hermitage Coil Issue**

4-1/2¢ **blue green** large holes | 2.00 | 1.25 □□□□□

598 _____ **1959. Bunker Hill Monument Coil Issue**

2-1/2¢ **slate blue** large holes. | 25 | .20 □□□□□

599 _____ **1960. Palace of the Governors**

1-1/4¢ **turquoise blue.** | 25 | .20 □□□□□

600 _____ **1960. Palace of the Governors Coil Issue**

1-1/4¢ **turquoise blue** large holes | 15.00 | .25 □□□□□

601 _____ **1961. Statue of Liberty Issue**

11¢ **carmine red & blue** | .30 | .20 □□□□□

NOTE: Type OP tagging: Used on multicolor stamps previously designated to be printed on Giori presses.

602 _____ **1961. John J. Pershing Issue**

8¢ **brown** | .25 | .20 □□□□□

NOTE: There is disagreement concerning whether No. 602 is actually part of the Liberty Series. Although printed within the same period, it does not match the design characteristics of other stamps in the series.

603 _____ **1962. Evergreen Wreath and Burning Candles Issue**

4¢ **green & red** | .25 | .20 □□□□□

604 _____ **1962. George Washington Issue**

5¢ **gray blue** | .25 | .20 □□□□□

		MNHVF	UseVF	

		MNHVF	UseVF	
605 _____	**1962. George Washington Coil Issue**			
5¢ gray blue		.25	.20 ☐☐☐☐☐
606 _____	**1963. U.S. Flag and White House Issue**			
5¢ blue & red		.25	.20 ☐☐☐☐☐
607 _____	**1963. Andrew Jackson Issue**			
1¢ green		.25	.20 ☐☐☐☐☐
608 _____	**1963. Andrew Jackson Coil Issue**			
1¢ green		.25	.20 ☐☐☐☐☐
609 _____	**1963. Christmas Tree and White House**			
5¢ dark blue, indigo & red		.25	.20 ☐☐☐☐☐
610 _____	**1964. Holiday Evergreens Issue**			
5¢ Holly		.25	.20 ☐☐☐☐☐
611 _____				
5¢ Mistletoe		.25	.20 ☐☐☐☐☐
612 _____				
5¢ Poinsettia		.25	.20 ☐☐☐☐☐

582

583

584

585

586

591

592

593, 614

594, 598

595, 597

596

599, 600

601

602

603

604, 605

606

607, 608

609

	MNHVF	UseVF

613 _____

5¢   **Conifer sprig**   .25   .20 ☐☐☐☐☐

614 _____   **1965. Paul Revere Coil Issue**

25¢ **deep blue green** small holes   .45   .25 ☐☐☐☐☐

615 _____   **1965. Angel Gabriel Issue**

5¢   **red, green & yellow**   .25   .20 ☐☐☐☐☐

616 _____   **1968. Thomas Jefferson Issue**

1¢   **green** tagged Type II or III   .25   .20 ☐☐☐☐☐

617 _____   **1967. Albert Gallatin Issue**

1-1/4¢ **light green**   .25   .20 ☐☐☐☐☐

618 _____   **1966. Frank Lloyd Wright Issue**

2¢   **blue** tagged Type II or III   .25   .20 ☐☐☐☐☐

619 _____   **1967. Francis Parkman Issue**

3¢   **purple** tagged Type II   .25   .20 ☐☐☐☐☐

620 _____   **1965. Abraham Lincoln Issue**

4¢   **black**   .25   .20 ☐☐☐☐☐

621 _____   **1965. George Washington Issue**

5¢   **deep blue**   .25   .20 ☐☐☐☐☐

622 _____   **1966. Franklin D. Roosevelt Issue**

6¢   **black brown**   .25   .20 ☐☐☐☐☐

623 _____   **1966. Albert Einstein Issue**

8¢   **violet**   .25   .20 ☐☐☐☐☐

624 _____   **1967. Andrew Jackson Issue**

10¢ **lavender** tagged Type II or III   .25   .20 ☐☐☐☐☐

624A _____   **1968. Henry Ford Issue**

12¢ **black** tagged Type II   .25   .20 ☐☐☐☐☐

625 _____   **1967. John F. Kennedy Issue**

13¢ **brown** tagged Type II or III   .25   .20 ☐☐☐☐☐

626 _____   **1968. Oliver Wendell Holmes Issue**

15¢ **maroon** design Type I, tagged Type III   .25   .20 ☐☐☐☐☐

NOTE: Type I: crosshatching on tie complete and strong; bottom of necktie just touches coat. Type II: crosshatching on tie (lines running upper left to lower right) very faint; necktie does not touch coat. Type III (only known on booklet pane) overall design smaller and "15¢" closer to head.

626A _____

15¢ **maroon** design Type II, tagged   .50   .20 ☐☐☐☐☐

626B _____

15¢ **maroon** design Type III   .25   .20 ☐☐☐☐☐

627 _____   **1967. George C. Marshall Issue**

20¢ **olive brown**   .35   .20 ☐☐☐☐☐

628 _____   **1967. Frederick Douglass Issue**

25¢ **maroon**   .50   .20 ☐☐☐☐☐

629 _____   **1968. John Dewey Issue**

30¢ **purple**   .55   .25 ☐☐☐☐☐

630 _____   **1968. Thomas Paine Issue**

40¢ **dark blue**   .75   .25 ☐☐☐☐☐

631 _____   **1968. Lucy Stone Issue**

50¢ **maroon**   1.00   .25 ☐☐☐☐☐

632 _____   **1967. Eugene O'Neill Issue**

$1   **dark purple**   2.25   .50 ☐☐☐☐☐

633 _____   **1966. John Bassett Moore Issue**

$5   **dark gray**   10.00   3.00 ☐☐☐☐☐

634 _____   **1968. Thomas Jefferson Coil Issue**

1¢   **green** tagged   .25   .20 ☐☐☐☐☐

635 _____   **1966. Abraham Lincoln Coil Issue**

4¢   **black** tagged Type II   .25   .20 ☐☐☐☐☐

610-613

615

616, 634

617

618

619, 693

620, 635

621, 636

622

623

624

624A

625

626, 721, 721A

627

628

629

630

631

632, 672

633

644

(637), 638

645

646, 747A

647, 650, 654

	MNHVF	UseVF	

636 _____   **1966. George Washington Coil Issue**

5¢ **deep blue** tagged Type II   .25   .20 ☐☐☐☐☐

637 _____   **1968. Franklin D. Roosevelt Coil Issue**

6¢ **black brown** tagged   .25   .20 ☐☐☐☐☐

638 _____   **1967. Franklin D. Roosevelt Coil Issue**

6¢ **black brown** tagged   .25   .20 ☐☐☐☐☐

NOTE: Nos. 639-643 are not assigned.

644 _____   **1966. Traditional Christmas Issue**

5¢ **multicolored**   .25   .20 ☐☐☐☐☐

645 _____   **1967. Traditional Christmas Issue**

5¢ **multicolored**   .25   .20 ☐☐☐☐☐

646 _____   **1967. George Washington Issue**

5¢ **deep blue** tagged, shiny gum   .25   .20 ☐☐☐☐☐

647 _____   **1968. Flag Over White House Issue**

6¢ **dark blue, green & red** tagged Type OP   .25   .20 ☐☐☐☐☐

648 _____   **1968. Serviceman's Airlift Issue**

$1 **multicolored**   3.00   2.00 ☐☐☐☐☐

649 _____   **1968. Traditional Christmas Issue**

6¢ **multicolored** tagged Type B   .25   .20 ☐☐☐☐☐

NOTE: Type B tagging: Billet or bar-like shapes designed to register within the limits of a single stamp. Untagged areas surround the design and were intended to register with the perforations.

650 _____   **1969. Flag Over White House Coil Stamp Issue**

6¢ **dark blue, green & red** tagged   .25   .20 ☐☐☐☐☐

651 _____   **1969. Contemporary Christmas Issue**

6¢ **multicolored** tagged   .25   .20 ☐☐☐☐☐

NOTE: Experimental precanceled stamps were sold for use by the public, imprinted, "ATLANTA, GA," "BALTIMORE, MD," "MEMPHIS, TN," and "NEW HAVEN, CT."

652 _____   **1970. Dwight D. Eisenhower Issue**

6¢ **blue** tagged Type II   .25   .20 ☐☐☐☐☐

653 _____   **1970. Dwight D. Eisenhower Coil Issue**

6¢ **blue** tagged   .25   .20 ☐☐☐☐☐

654 _____   **1970. Flag Over White House Issue**

6¢ **dark blue, green & red** tagged Type B   .25   .20 ☐☐☐☐☐

655 _____   **1970. Contemporary Christmas Issue**

6¢ **multicolored** tagged   .25   .20 ☐☐☐☐☐

656 _____

6¢ **multicolored** tagged   .25   .20 ☐☐☐☐☐

657 _____

6¢ **multicolored** tagged   .25   .20 ☐☐☐☐☐

658 _____

6¢ **multicolored** tagged   .25   .20 ☐☐☐☐☐

659 _____   **1970. Traditional Christmas Issue**

6¢ **multicolored** tagged design Type I   .25   .20 ☐☐☐☐☐

NOTE: Type I has a slightly blurry impression and no gum breaker ridges. Type II has a shiny surfaced paper, sharper impression, and both horizontal and vertical gum breaker ridges. Type I precancel is gray black; Type II precancel is intense black.

660 _____   **1971. Ernie Pyle Issue**

16¢ **brown** tagged   .30   .20 ☐☐☐☐☐

661 _____   **1971. Flag Over White House Issue**

8¢ **dark blue, red & slate green** tagged Type B   .25   .20 ☐☐☐☐☐

662 _____   **1971. Flag Over White House Coil Issue**

8¢ **dark blue, red & slate green** tagged Type B   .20   .20 ☐☐☐☐☐

663 _____   **1971. Dwight D. Eisenhower Issue**

8¢ **black, blue gray & red** tagged Type OP   .25   .20 ☐☐☐☐☐

	MNHVF	UseVF

663A _____ **1971. Dwight D. Eisenhower Booklet Issue**

8¢ **reddish brown** tagged Type II, in booklet form only or III, in booklet form only..25 .20 ☐☐☐☐☐

NOTE: All these booklet stamps have 1 or 2 straight edges.

664 _____ **1971. Dwight D. Eisenhower Coil Issue**

8¢ **reddish brown** tagged .25 .20 ☐☐☐☐☐

665 _____ **1971. U.S. Postal Service Issue**

8¢ **multicolored** tagged .25 .20 ☐☐☐☐☐

666 _____ **1971. Contemporary Christmas Issue**

8¢ **multicolored** tagged .25 .20 ☐☐☐☐☐

667 _____ **1971. Traditional Christmas Issue**

8¢ **multicolored** tagged .25 .20 ☐☐☐☐☐

668 _____ **1972. Fiorello H. LaGuardia Issue**

14¢ **dark brown** tagged .25 .20 ☐☐☐☐☐

669 _____ **1972. Benjamin Franklin Issue**

7¢ **light blue** shiny gum, tagged .25 .20 ☐☐☐☐☐

CHRISTMAS 6c

UNITED STATES

649

648

651

EISENHOWER·USA

652, 653

Ernie Pyle

660

661, 662

659

655-658

663

663A, 664

665

666

667

668

669

	MNHVF	UseVF

670 _____ **1972. Contemporary Christmas Issue**
8¢ **multicolored** tagged — .25 — .20 ☐☐☐☐☐

671 _____ **1972. Traditional Christmas Issue**
8¢ **multicolored** tagged — .25 — .20 ☐☐☐☐☐

672 _____ **1973. Eugene O'Neill Coil Issue**
$1 **dark purple** tagged — 2.00 — .75 ☐☐☐☐☐

673 _____ **1973. Amadeo P. Giannini Issue**
21¢ **banknote green** tagged — .40 — .25 ☐☐☐☐☐

674 _____ **1973. Traditional Christmas Issue**
8¢ **multicolored** tagged — .25 — .20 ☐☐☐☐☐

675 _____ **1973. Contemporary Christmas Issue**
8¢ **multicolored** tagged — .25 — .20 ☐☐☐☐☐

676 _____ **1973. Crossed Flags Issue**
10¢ **red & blue** tagged — .25 — .20 ☐☐☐☐☐

677 _____ **1973. Crossed Flags Coil Issue**
10¢ **red & blue** tagged — .40 — .25 ☐☐☐☐☐

NOTE: The lines on this issue, which can occur every 4 stamps, are usually incomplete. Full, complete lines sell for a premium.

678 _____ **1973. Jefferson Memorial Issue**
10¢ **blue** tagged, Type II or III — .25 — .20 ☐☐☐☐☐

679 _____ **1973. Jefferson Memorial Coil Issue**
10¢ **blue** tagged — .25 — .20 ☐☐☐☐☐

680 _____ **1974. ZIP Code Issue**
10¢ **multicolored** tagged with small rectangle in center of stamp — .25 — .20 ☐☐☐☐☐

681 _____ **1974. Elizabeth Blackwell Issue**
18¢ **purple** tagged — .30 — .25 ☐☐☐☐☐

682 _____ **1974. Swinging Bell Coil Issue**
6.3¢ **brick red** tagged — .25 — .20 ☐☐☐☐☐

683 _____ **1974. Contemporary Christmas Issue**
10¢ **multicolored** tagged — .25 — .20 ☐☐☐☐☐

684 _____ **1974. Dove of Peace Issue**
10¢ **multicolored** self-adhesive — .25 — .20 ☐☐☐☐☐

NOTE: Two types of rouletting were used on backing paper.

685 _____ **1974. Traditional Christmas Issue**
10¢ **multicolored** tagged — .25 — .20 ☐☐☐☐☐

686 _____ **1975. Contemporary Christmas Issue**
10¢ **multicolored** tagged — .30 — .20 ☐☐☐☐☐

686A _____
10¢ **multicolored** tagged — .30 — .20 ☐☐☐☐☐

686B _____
10¢ **multicolored** tagged — .60 — .20 ☐☐☐☐☐

687 _____ **1975. Traditional Christmas Issue**
10¢ **multicolored** tagged — .30 — .20 ☐☐☐☐☐

688 _____ **1975. Capitol Dome Issue**
9¢ **green** on gray paper, tagged — .25 — .20 ☐☐☐☐☐

689 _____ **1975. Colonial Printing Press Issue**
11¢ **orange** on gray paper, tagged — .25 — .20 ☐☐☐☐☐

690 _____ **1975. Flag over Independence Hall Issue**
13¢ **dark blue & red** tagged — .25 — .20 ☐☐☐☐☐

691 _____ **1975. Eagle and Shield Issue**
13¢ **multicolored** tagged with eagle-shape untagged area — .25 — .20 ☐☐☐☐☐

691A _____
13¢ **multicolored** perforated 11 (L-perforation) — 40.00 — 15.00 ☐☐☐☐☐

670

671

673

674

675

676, 677

678, 679

680

681

682

683

684

685

686

687

688, 697, 702, 702A

689

690, 694, 782

691

692

693

694

695, 696

697

		MNHVF	UseVF

692 _____ 1975. Old North Church Issue

24¢ **red** on blue paper, tagged ... .50 ... .25 ☐☐☐☐☐

693 _____ 1975. Francis Parkman Coil Issue

3¢ **purple** tagged ... .25 ... .20 ☐☐☐☐☐

694 _____ 1975. Flag over Independence Hall Coil Issue

13¢ **dark blue & red** tagged ... .25 ... .20 ☐☐☐☐☐

695 _____ 1975. Liberty Bell Issue

13¢ **brown** from booklet panes only, tagged ... .25 ... .20 ☐☐☐☐☐

696 _____ 1975. Liberty Bell Coil Issue

13¢ **brown** shiny gum, tagged ... .25 ... .20 ☐☐☐☐☐

697 _____ 1976. Capitol Dome Coil Issue

9¢ **green** on gray paper, shiny gum, tagged ... .25 ... .20 ☐☐☐☐☐

698 _____ 1976. American Eagle and Drum Coil Issue

7.9¢ **red** on canary paper, shiny gum, tagged ... .25 ... .20 ☐☐☐☐☐

699 _____ 1976. Contemporary Christmas Issue

13¢ **multicolored** overall tagged ... .40 ... .25 ☐☐☐☐☐

699A _____

13¢ **multicolored** block tagged ... .40 ... .25 ☐☐☐☐☐

700 _____ 1976. Traditional Christmas Issue

13¢ **multicolored** tagged ... .40 ... .25 ☐☐☐☐☐

701 _____ 1976. Saxhorns Issue

7.7¢ **brown** on canary paper, tagged ... .25 ... .20 ☐☐☐☐☐

702 _____ 1977. Capitol Dome Booklet Issue

9¢ **green** tagged, perforated 11 x 10 1/2 ... 1.00 ... .20 ☐☐☐☐☐

702A _____

9¢ **green** tagged ... 35.00 ... 22.50 ☐☐☐☐☐

703 _____ 1977. Flag over Capitol Booklet Issue

13¢ **red & blue** tagged ... .25 ... .20 ☐☐☐☐☐

703A _____ 1977. Flag over Capitol Issue

13¢ **red & blue** tagged ... .75 ... .50 ☐☐☐☐☐

704 _____ 1977. Rural Mail Box Issue

13¢ **multicolored** tagged ... .40 ... .20 ☐☐☐☐☐

705 _____ 1977. Washington Kneeling At Prayer Issue

13¢ **multicolored** tagged ... .40 ... .20 ☐☐☐☐☐

NOTE: The multicolor Combination Press issue (No. 705) has "floating" plate numbers, a set of five numbers sandwiched between two or three blanks, so that on a plate strip of 20 there are five numbers and five blanks, six numbers and four blanks, seven numbers and three blanks or eight numbers and two blanks. There are no ZIP or Mail Early slogans.

NOTE: Nos. 706-707 are not assigned.

708 _____ 1977. Contemplation of Justice Issue

10¢ **purple** on gray paper, shiny gum, tagged ... .25 ... .20 ☐☐☐☐☐

709 _____ 1977. Contemplation of Justice Coil Issue

10¢ **purple** on gray paper, tagged ... .25 ... .20 ☐☐☐☐☐

710 _____ 1977. Quill Pen and Inkwell Issue

1¢ **blue** on green paper, tagged ... .25 ... .20 ☐☐☐☐☐

711 _____ 1977. Symbols of Speech Issue

2¢ **brown** on green paper, shiny gum, tagged ... .25 ... .20 ☐☐☐☐☐

711A _____ 1981. Symbols of Speech Issue

2¢ **brown** on cream paper, matte gum, tagged ... .25 ... .20 ☐☐☐☐☐

712 _____ 1977. Ballot Box Issue

3¢ **olive** on green paper, shiny gum, tagged ... .25 ... .20 ☐☐☐☐☐

713 _____ 1977. Reading and Learning Issue

4¢ **maroon** on cream paper, tagged ... .25 ... .20 ☐☐☐☐☐

714 _____ 1978. Indian Head Penny Issue

13¢ **brown & blue** on tan paper ... .25 ... .20 ☐☐☐☐☐

698

699, 699A

700

701

702, 702A, 703, 703A

704

705

708, 709

710, 742

711, 711A

712

713

714

715, 716

716

717

718-720

722, 722A, 723

724

725

726

727

728

729

	MNHVF	UseVF

715 _____   1978. Statue of Liberty Issue
16¢ **blue** tagged   .30   .20 ◻◻◻◻◻
716 _____   1978. Statue of Liberty Coil Issue
16¢ **blue** overall tagged   .35   .20 ◻◻◻◻◻
716A _____
16¢ **multicolored** block tagged, B Press (design slightly narrower than 716,   ◻◻◻◻◻
no joint line)   —   ◻◻◻◻◻
717 _____   1978. Sandy Hook Lighthouse Issue
29¢ **blue** on blue paper, shiny gum, tagged   .50   .65 ◻◻◻◻◻
718 _____   1978. "A" Stamp Issue
15¢ **orange** perforated 11, tagged   .30   .25 ◻◻◻◻◻
718A _____   1978. "A" Stamp Issue
15¢ **orange** perforated 11 1/4, tagged   .30   .25 ◻◻◻◻◻
719 _____   1978. "A" Booklet Stamp Issue
15¢ **orange** tagged   .25   .20 ◻◻◻◻◻
720 _____   1978. "A" Stamp Coil Issue
15¢ **orange** tagged   .25   .15 ◻◻◻◻◻
721 _____   1978. Oliver Wendell Holmes Issue
15¢ **maroon** Type I, tagged   .25   .20 ◻◻◻◻◻
721A _____   1978. Oliver Wendell Holmes Issue
15¢ **maroon** Type II matte gum, tagged   .25   .20 ◻◻◻◻◻
NOTE: For booklet pane issued the same date see No. 626.
722 _____   1978. American Flag Issue
15¢ **red, blue & gray** perforated 11, tagged   .30   .20 ◻◻◻◻◻
722A _____   1978. American Flag Booklet Issue
15¢ **red, blue & gray** booklet stamp, perforated 11 x 10 1/2, tagged   .35   .20 ◻◻◻◻◻
723 _____   1978. American Flag Coil Issue
15¢ **red, blue & gray**   .40   .20 ◻◻◻◻◻
724 _____   1978. American Roses Booklet Issue
15¢ **orange, red & green** tagged   .25   .20 ◻◻◻◻◻
725 _____   1978. Steinway Grand Piano Coil Issue
8.4¢ **blue** on canary paper, shiny gum, tagged   .25   .20 ◻◻◻◻◻
726 _____   1978. Blockhouse Issue
28¢ **brown** on blue paper, tagged, shiny gum   .50   .20 ◻◻◻◻◻
727 _____   1978. Contemporary Christmas Issue
15¢ **multicolored** tagged   .40   .20 ◻◻◻◻◻
728 _____   1978. Madonna and Child with Cherubim Issue
15¢ **multicolored** tagged   .40   .20 ◻◻◻◻◻
729 _____   1978. Kerosene Table Lamp Issue
$2 **multicolored** tagged   3.50   1.00 ◻◻◻◻◻
730 _____   1979. Rush Lamp and Candle Holder Issue
$1 **multicolored** tagged   2.00   .25 ◻◻◻◻◻
731 _____   1979. Railroad Conductor's Lantern Issue
$5 **multicolored** tagged   8.50   2.25 ◻◻◻◻◻
732 _____   1979. Country Schoolhouse Issue
30¢ **green** on blue paper, tagged   1.00   .30 ◻◻◻◻◻
733 _____   1979. Iron "Betty" Lamp Issue
50¢ **black, orange & tan** tagged   1.00   .20 ◻◻◻◻◻
734 _____   1979. Santa Claus Christmas Tree Ornament Issue
15¢ **multicolored** tagged   .40   .20 ◻◻◻◻◻
735 _____   1979. Traditional Christmas Issue
15¢ **multicolored** tagged   .40   .20 ◻◻◻◻◻
736 _____   1979. Standard Six-string Guitar Coil Issue
3.1¢ **brown** on canary paper, tagged   .25   .20 ◻◻◻◻◻

	MNHVF	UseVF

737 _____   **1980. Historic Windmills Issue**
15¢ **Virginia, brown** on yellow paper, tagged   .30   .20 ☐☐☐☐☐
738 _____
15¢ **Rhode Island, brown** on yellow paper, tagged   .30   .20 ☐☐☐☐☐
739 _____
15¢ **Massachusetts, brown,** on yellow paper, tagged   .30   .20 ☐☐☐☐☐
740 _____
15¢ **Illinois, brown** on yellow paper, tagged   .30   .20 ☐☐☐☐☐
741 _____
15¢ **Texas, brown** on yellow paper, tagged   .30   .20 ☐☐☐☐☐
742 _____   **1980. Quill Pen and Inkwell Coil Issue**
1¢   **blue** on green paper, shiny gum, tagged   .25   .20 ☐☐☐☐☐
743 _____   **1980. Dolley Madison Issue**
15¢ **red brown & sepia** tagged   .40   .20 ☐☐☐☐☐
744 _____   **1980. Weaver Manufactured Violins Coil Issue**
3.5¢ **purple** on yellow paper, tagged   .25   .20 ☐☐☐☐☐
745 _____   **1980. Contemporary Christmas Issue**
15¢ **multicolored** tagged   .50   .20 ☐☐☐☐☐
746 _____   **1980. Traditional Christmas Issue**
15¢ **multicolored** tagged   .50   .20 ☐☐☐☐☐
747 _____   **1980. Sequoyah Issue**
19¢ **brown** overall tagged   .30   .20 ☐☐☐☐☐
747A _____   **1980. Washington Coil Issue**
5¢   **deep blue** tagged   .25   .20 ☐☐☐☐☐
748 _____   **1981. Non-Denominated "B" Stamp Issue**
18¢ **purple** tagged   .30   .20 ☐☐☐☐☐

730

731

732

733

734

735

736

737-741

743

744

745

746

747

		MNHVF	UseVF

749 _____ **1981. Non-Denominated "B" Booklet Issue**

18¢ **purple** tagged   .30   .20 ☐☐☐☐☐

750 _____ **1981. Non-Denominated "B" Coil Issue**

18¢ **purple** tagged   .40   .20 ☐☐☐☐☐

751 _____ **1981. Freedom Of Conscience Issue**

12¢ **brown** on beige paper, tagged   .25   .20 ☐☐☐☐☐

NOTE: **U.S. Postal Service Plate-Numbering Change** *In response to collector complaints that its plate-numbering system resulted in many inconvenient and costly blocks of 10, 12 and 20 stamps, the USPS in January 1981 instituted a new plate number arrangement. Under the new system, most sheets were to contain a single plate number consisting of one (for monocolor stamps) to six digits, each digit representing a given printing plate and color. Thus, under this system, most plate blocks returned to blocks of four.*

NOTE: *Booklet panes hereafter also contain a plate number in the selvage.*

NOTE: *In coils, a plate number was incorporated into some stamps in the roll, at various intervals between stamps, depending on press used.*

752 _____ **1981. Freedom of Conscience Coil Issue**

12¢ **red brown** on beige paper, tagged   .25   .20 ☐☐☐☐☐

753 _____ **1981. America The Beautiful Issue**

18¢ **multicolored** tagged   .30   .20 ☐☐☐☐☐

754 _____ **1981. America The Beautiful Issue**

18¢ **multicolored** tagged   .30   .20 ☐☐☐☐☐

755 _____ **1981. America The Beautiful Combination Booklet**

6¢ **blue** tagged   .55   .25 ☐☐☐☐☐

756 _____

18¢ **multicolored** tagged   .30   .20 ☐☐☐☐☐

757 _____ **1981. George Mason Issue**

18¢ **blue** overall tagged   .30   .20 ☐☐☐☐☐

758 _____ **1981. Wildlife Booklet Issue**

18¢ **Bighorn sheep, brown,** tagged   .50   .20 ☐☐☐☐☐

759 _____

18¢ **Puma, brown,** tagged   .50   .20 ☐☐☐☐☐

760 _____

18¢ **Harbor seal, brown,** tagged   .50   .20 ☐☐☐☐☐

761 _____

18¢ **Bison, brown,** tagged   .50   .20 ☐☐☐☐☐

762 _____

18¢ **Brown bear, brown,** tagged   .50   .20 ☐☐☐☐☐

763 _____

18¢ **Polar bear, brown,** tagged   .50   .20 ☐☐☐☐☐

764 _____

18¢ **Elk (Wapiti), brown,** tagged   .50   .20 ☐☐☐☐☐

765 _____

18¢ **Moose, brown,** tagged   .50   .20 ☐☐☐☐☐

766 _____

18¢ **White-tailed deer, brown,** tagged   .50   .20 ☐☐☐☐☐

767 _____

18¢ **Pronghorn antelope, brown,** tagged   .50   .20 ☐☐☐☐☐

768 _____ **1981. Surrey Issue**

18¢ **brown** tagged   .35   .20 ☐☐☐☐☐

769 _____ **1981. Rachel Carson Issue**

17¢ **green** overall tagged   .30   .20 ☐☐☐☐☐

770 _____ **1981. Charles R. Drew Issue**

35¢ **gray** overall tagged   .50   .25 ☐☐☐☐☐

NOTE: *Note: Plate blocks from plates 3 & 4 carry a premium.*

771 _____ **1981. Electric Auto Issue**

17¢ **blue** tagged   .35   .20 ☐☐☐☐☐

		MNHVF	UseVF

		MNHVF	UseVF
772 _____	**1981. Non-Denominated "C" Issue**		
	20¢ **brown** tagged	.35	.20 ☐☐☐☐☐
773 _____	**1981. Non-Denominated "C" Booklet Pane Issue**		
	20¢ **brown** tagged	.50	.20 ☐☐☐☐☐
774 _____	**1981. Non-Denominated "C" Coil Issue**		
	20¢ **brown** tagged	.60	.20 ☐☐☐☐☐
775 _____	**1981. Christmas Issue**		
	20¢ **multicolored** tagged	.50	.20 ☐☐☐☐☐
776 _____			
	20¢ **multicolored** tagged	.50	.20 ☐☐☐☐☐
777 _____	**1981. Fire Pumper Issue**		
	20¢ **red** tagged	.40	.20 ☐☐☐☐☐
778 _____	**1981. Mail Wagon Issue**		
	9.3¢ **dark red** tagged	.25	.20 ☐☐☐☐☐
779 _____	**1981. Flag Over Supreme Court Issue**		
	20¢ **black, dark blue & red** perforated 11, tagged	.35	.20 ☐☐☐☐☐

748-750

751, 752

753

754

755, 756

757

758-767

768

769

770

771

772-774

775

	MNHVF	UseVF

779A _____
20¢ **black, dark blue & red** perforated 11 1/4, tagged .35 .20 ☐☐☐☐☐
780 _____ **1981. Flag Over Supreme Court Coil Issue**
20¢ **black, dark blue & red** tagged .35 .20 ☐☐☐☐☐
781 _____ **1981. Flag Over Supreme Court Issue**
20¢ **black, dark red & blue** tagged .35 .20 ☐☐☐☐☐
782 _____ **1981. Flag Over Independence Hall Issue**
13¢ **dark blue & red** block tagged .60 .25 ☐☐☐☐☐
783 _____ **1982. Bighorn Sheep Issue**
20¢ **blue** Type I, overall tagged .45 .20 ☐☐☐☐☐
783A _____
20¢ **blue** Type II, block tagged .45 .20 ☐☐☐☐☐
NOTE: Type I: is 18 3/4mm wide, Type II: is 18 1/2mm wide.
784 _____ **1982. Ralph Bunche Issue**
20¢ **maroon** overall tagged .35 .20 ☐☐☐☐☐
785 _____ **1982. Crazy Horse Issue**
13¢ **light maroon** overall tagged .35 .20 ☐☐☐☐☐
786 _____ **1982. Robert Millikan Issue**
37¢ **blue** overall tagged .60 .20 ☐☐☐☐☐
787 _____ **1982. High Wheeler Bicycle Issue**
5.9¢ **blue** tagged .25 .20 ☐☐☐☐☐
788 _____ **1982. Hansom Cab Issue**
10.9¢ **purple** tagged .25 .20 ☐☐☐☐☐
789 _____ **1982. Consumer Education Issue**
20¢ **blue** tagged .50 .20 ☐☐☐☐☐
790 _____ **1982. Locomotive Issue**
2¢ **black** tagged .25 .20 ☐☐☐☐☐
NOTE: (For similar design with "2 USA" see No. 873.)
791 _____ **1982. Stagecoach Issue**
4¢ **brown** tagged .25 .20 ☐☐☐☐☐
NOTE: For similar design with "Stagecoach 1890s" measuring 17mm long. see No. 868.
792 _____ **1982. Christmas Issue**
20¢ **Sledding, multicolored,** tagged .35 .20 ☐☐☐☐☐
793 _____
20¢ **Building snowman, multicolored,** tagged .35 .20 ☐☐☐☐☐
794 _____
20¢ **Skating, multicolored,** tagged .35 .20 ☐☐☐☐☐
795 _____
20¢ **Decorating tree, multicolored,** tagged .35 .20 ☐☐☐☐☐
796 _____ **1982. Traditional Christmas Issue**
20¢ **multicolored** tagged .35 .20 ☐☐☐☐☐
797 _____ **1982. Kitten and Puppy Issue**
13¢ **multicolored** tagged .35 .20 ☐☐☐☐☐
798 _____ **1982. Igor Stravinsky Issue**
2¢ **brown** overall tagged .25 .20 ☐☐☐☐☐
799 _____ **1983. Sleigh Issue**
5.2¢ **red** tagged .25 .20 ☐☐☐☐☐
800 _____ **1983. Handcar Issue**
3¢ **green** tagged .25 .20 ☐☐☐☐☐
801 _____ **1983. Carl Schurz Issue**
4¢ **purple** overall tagged .25 .20 ☐☐☐☐☐
802 _____ **1983. Thomas H. Gallaudet Issue**
20¢ **green** overall tagged .35 .20 ☐☐☐☐☐
803 _____ **1983. Pearl Buck Issue**
5¢ **red brown** overall tagged .25 .20 ☐☐☐☐☐

776

777

778

779-781

782

783, 783A

784

785

786

787

788

789

790

791

792-795

796

797

798

799

800

801

802

803

804

805

	MNHVF	UseVF	

804 _____ **1983. Henry Clay Issue**
3¢ **olive** overall tagged — .25 — .20 ☐☐☐☐☐

805 _____ **1983. Express Mail Issue**
$9.35 **multicolored** tagged — 25.00 — 20.00 ☐☐☐☐☐

806 _____ **1983. Omnibus Issue**
1¢ **purple** tagged — .25 — .20 ☐☐☐☐☐

NOTE: For similar design with "1 USA" see No. 867.

807 _____ **1983. Dorothea Dix Issue**
1¢ **black** tagged (small block) perforated 11 1/4 — .25 — .20 ☐☐☐☐☐

807A _____
1¢ **black** tagged (small block) perforated 10 3/4 — .25 — .20 ☐☐☐☐☐

808 _____ **1983. Motorcycle Issue**
5¢ **dark green** tagged — .25 — .20 ☐☐☐☐☐

809 _____ **1983. Christmas Issue**
20¢ **multicolored** tagged — .35 — .20 ☐☐☐☐☐

810 _____
20¢ **multicolored** tagged — .35 — .20 ☐☐☐☐☐

811 _____ **1984. Harry S. Truman Issue**
20¢ **black** tagged (small block) — .35 — .20 ☐☐☐☐☐

NOTE: (See also No. 904.)

812 _____ **1984. Railroad Caboose Issue**
11¢ **red** tagged — .25 — .20 ☐☐☐☐☐

813 _____ **1984. Lillian Gilbreth Issue**
40¢ **green,** tagged (small block) perforated 11 — .60 — .20 ☐☐☐☐☐

813A _____
40¢ **green** tagged (large block) perforated 11 1/4 (1987) — .60 — .20 ☐☐☐☐☐

814 _____ **1984. Baby Buggy Issue**
7.4¢ **brown** tagged — .25 — .20 ☐☐☐☐☐

815 _____ **1984. Richard Russell Issue**
10¢ **blue** tagged (small block) — .25 — .20 ☐☐☐☐☐

NOTE: Imperforate printer's waste is known to exist, and in one case was used as postage.

816 _____ **1984. Frank C. Laubach Issue**
30¢ **green** tagged (small block) perforated 11 — .75 — .20 ☐☐☐☐☐

816A _____
30¢ **green** tagged (large block) perforated 11 1/4 — .75 — .20 ☐☐☐☐☐

817 _____ **1984. Christmas Issue**
20¢ **multicolored** tagged — .25 — .20 ☐☐☐☐☐

818 _____
20¢ **multicolored** tagged — .25 — .20 ☐☐☐☐☐

819 _____ **1985. Abraham Baldwin Issue**
7¢ **red** tagged (small block) — .25 — .20 ☐☐☐☐☐

820 _____ **1985. Non-Denominated "D" Issue**
22¢ **green** tagged — .45 — .20 ☐☐☐☐☐

821 _____ **1985. Non-Denominated "D" Coil Issue**
22¢ **green** tagged perforated 11 — .80 — .20 ☐☐☐☐☐

822 _____ **1985. Non-Denominated "D" Rate Booklet Issue**
22¢ **green** tagged — .40 — .20 ☐☐☐☐☐

823 _____ **1985. Alden Partridge Issue**
11¢ **blue** overall tagged — .25 — .20 ☐☐☐☐☐

824 _____ **1985. Chester W. Nimitz Issue**
50¢ **brown** overall tagged, perforated 11, shiny gum — .90 — .20 ☐☐☐☐☐

824A _____
50¢ **brown** tagged (large block) perforated 11 1/4, matte gum — .90 — .20 ☐☐☐☐☐

	MNHVF	UseVF

825 _____ **1985. Grenville Clark Issue**
   39¢ **purple** tagged (small block) perforated 11   .75   .20 ☐☐☐☐☐
825A _____
   39¢ **purple** tagged (large block), perforated 11 1/4   .75   .20 ☐☐☐☐☐
826 _____ **1985. Sinclair Lewis Issue**
   14¢ **gray** tagged (small block)   .25   .20 ☐☐☐☐☐
827 _____ **1985. Iceboat Issue**
   14¢ **blue** Type I, overall tagged   .25   .20 ☐☐☐☐☐
827A _____
   14¢ **blue** Type II, block tagged   .25   .20 ☐☐☐☐☐
NOTE: Type I is 17 1/2 mm wide with overall tagging. Type II is 17 1/4 mm wide with block tagging.
828 _____ **1985. Flag over the Capitol Issue**
   22¢ **black, blue, & red** tagged   .35   .20 ☐☐☐☐☐
829 _____ **1985. Flag Over the U.S. Capitol Coil Issue**
   22¢ **black, blue, & red** tagged   .40   .20 ☐☐☐☐☐
NOTE: For similar design with "T" at bottom, see No. 876.

806

807

808

809

810

811

812

813

814

815

816, 816A

817

818

819

820-822

823

824, 824A

825, 825A

826

827, 827A

	MNHVF	UseVF

830 _____ 1985. Flag Over the Capitol Booklet Issue

22¢ **black, blue, & red** tagged .... .40 .20 ☐☐☐☐☐

NOTE: Issued for use in vending machines, and was available with one or two panes.

831 _____ 1985. Stanley Steamer Issue

12¢ **blue** Type I, tagged .... .25 .20 ☐☐☐☐☐

831A _____

12¢ **blue** Type II, untagged (Bureau precancel: "PRESORTED FIRST-CLASS") .25 .20 ☐☐☐☐☐

NOTE: Type I: "Stanley Steamer 1909" is 18mm long;

NOTE: Type II: "Stanley Steamer 1909" is 17 1/2 mm long.

832 _____ 1985. Seashell Booklet Issue

22¢ **Frilled dogwinkle, black & brown** tagged .... .35 .20 ☐☐☐☐☐

833 _____

22¢ **Reticulated helmet, black & multicolored** tagged .... .35 .20 ☐☐☐☐☐

834 _____

22¢ **New England neptune, black & brown,** tagged .... .35 .20 ☐☐☐☐☐

835 _____

22¢ **Calico scallop, black & purple** tagged .... .35 .20 ☐☐☐☐☐

836 _____

22¢ **Lightning whelk, multicolored,** tagged .... .35 .20 ☐☐☐☐☐

NOTE: Mis-registered tagging is common on this issue.

837 _____ 1985. Oil Wagon Issue

10.1¢ **blue** tagged .... .25 .20 ☐☐☐☐☐

838 _____ 1985. Pushcart Issue

12.5¢ **olive** tagged .... .25 .20 ☐☐☐☐☐

839 _____ 1985. John J. Audubon Issue

22¢ **blue** tagged (small block) perforated 11 .... .40 .20 ☐☐☐☐☐

839A _____

22¢ **blue** tagged (large block) perforated 11 1/4 .... .40 .20 ☐☐☐☐☐

840 _____ 1985. Express Mail Issue

$10.75 **multicolored** Type I, tagged .... 15.00 9.00 ☐☐☐☐☐

NOTE: Type I: overall dull appearance, "$10.75" appears grainy. Type II: more intense colors, "$10.75" smoother, much less grainy.

841 _____ 1985. Tricycle Issue

6¢ **brown** tagged .... .25 .20 ☐☐☐☐☐

842 _____ 1985. Sylvanus Thayer Issue

9¢ **green** tagged (small block) .... .25 .20 ☐☐☐☐☐

843 _____ 1985. School Bus Issue

3.4¢ **green** tagged .... .25 .20 ☐☐☐☐☐

844 _____ 1985. Stutz Bearcat Issue

11¢ **green** tagged .... .25 .20 ☐☐☐☐☐

845 _____ 1985. Ambulance Issue

8.3¢ **green** Type I, tagged .... .25 .20 ☐☐☐☐☐

845A _____

8.3¢ **green** Type II, untagged (Bureau precancel: "Blk. Rt./CAR-RT/SORT") .25 .20 ☐☐☐☐☐

NOTE: Type I: "Ambulance 1860s" is 18 1/2mm long. Type II: "Ambulance 1860s" is 18mm long.

846 _____ 1985. Buckboard Issue

4.9¢ **brown** tagged .... .25 .20 ☐☐☐☐☐

847 _____ 1985. Henry Knox Issue

8¢ **olive** overall tagged .... .25 .20 ☐☐☐☐☐

848 _____ 1985. Walter Lippmann Issue

6¢ **orange** tagged (large block) .... .25 .20 ☐☐☐☐☐

849 _____ 1985. Envelope Stamp Issue

21.1¢ **multicolored** tagged .... .35 .20 ☐☐☐☐☐

NOTE: Some precanceled stamps are known with light tagging.

828, 829, 876

830

831, 831A

Frilled Dogwinkle

837

838

USA $10.75

840

Reticulated Helmet

New England Neptune

Calico Scallop

839, 839A

Tricycle 1880s

841

842

School Bus 1920s

843

Stutz Bearcat 1933

844

Ambulance 1860s

845, 845A

Lightning Whelk

832-836

Buckboard 1880s

846

Henry Knox

847

Walter Lippmann

848

ZIP+4

849

Season's Greetings USA 22

850

CHRISTMAS

USA 22
Luca della Robbia. Detroit Institute of Arts

851

852

Jack London

853, 888, 889

	MNHVF	UseVF

850 _____ **1985. Contemporary Christmas Issue**
22¢ **multicolored** tagged ... .35 ... .20 ☐☐☐☐☐

851 _____ **1985. Traditional Christmas Issue**
22¢ **multicolored** tagged ... .35 ... .20 ☐☐☐☐☐

852 _____ **1985. George Washington & Monument Issue**
18¢ **multicolored** tagged ... .35 ... .20 ☐☐☐☐☐

NOTE: Some precanceled stamps are known with light tagging.

853 _____ **1986. Jack London Issue**
25¢ **blue** tagged (large block) perforated 11 ... .45 ... .20 ☐☐☐☐☐

NOTE: For booklet panes of 10 and 6, see Nos. 888-889.

854 _____ **1986. Hugo L. Black Issue**
5¢ **deep olive green** tagged (large block) ... .25 ... .20 ☐☐☐☐☐

855 _____ **1986. William Jennings Bryan Issue**
$2 **purple** tagged (large block) ... 3.25 ... .75 ☐☐☐☐☐

856 _____ **1986. Belva Ann Lockwood Issue**
17¢ **blue green** tagged (large block) ... .35 ... .20 ☐☐☐☐☐

857 _____ **1986. Margaret Mitchell Issue**
1¢ **brown** tagged (large block) ... .25 ... .20 ☐☐☐☐☐

858 _____ **1986. Father Flanagan Issue**
4¢ **purple** tagged (large block) ... .25 ... .20 ☐☐☐☐☐

859 _____ **1986. Dog Sled Issue**
17¢ **blue** tagged ... .30 ... .20 ☐☐☐☐☐

860 _____ **1986. John Harvard Issue**
56¢ **crimson** tagged (large block) ... 1.10 ... .20 ☐☐☐☐☐

861 _____ **1986. Paul Dudley White Issue**
3¢ **blue** tagged (large block), matte gum ... .25 ... .20 ☐☐☐☐☐

862 _____ **1986. Bernard Revel Issue**
$1 **blue** tagged (large block) ... 2.00 ... .25 ☐☐☐☐☐

863 _____ **1986. Christmas Issue**
22¢ **multicolored** tagged ... .50 ... .20 ☐☐☐☐☐

864 _____
22¢ **multicolored** tagged ... .50 ... .20 ☐☐☐☐☐

865 _____ **1986. Star Route Truck Issue**
5.5¢ **maroon** tagged ... .25 ... .20 ☐☐☐☐☐

866 _____ **1986. Bread Wagon Issue**
25¢ **orange brown** tagged, plates 2, 3, 4 ... .40 ... .20 ☐☐☐☐☐

867 _____ **1986. Omnibus Issue**
1¢ **violet** tagged ... .25 ... .20 ☐☐☐☐☐

NOTE: (For similar design with "USA 1¢" see No. 806)

868 _____ **1986. Stagecoach Issue**
4¢ **red brown** block tagged ... .25 ... .20 ☐☐☐☐☐

869 _____ **1987. Tow Truck Issue**
8.5¢ **dark gray** tagged ... .50 ... .20 ☐☐☐☐☐

870 _____ **1987. Tractor Issue**
7.1¢ **dark red** tagged ... .25 ... .20 ☐☐☐☐☐

871 _____ **1987. Julia Ward Howe Issue**
14¢ **red** tagged (large block) ... .25 ... .20 ☐☐☐☐☐

872 _____ **1987. Mary Lyon Issue**
2¢ **blue** tagged (large block) ... .25 ... .20 ☐☐☐☐☐

873 _____ **1987. Locomotive Issue**
2¢ **black** tagged ... .25 ... .20 ☐☐☐☐☐

NOTE: (For similar design with "USA 2¢" see No. 790.)

874 _____ **1987. Canal Boat Issue**
10¢ **sky blue** block tagged matte gum ... .25 ... .20 ☐☐☐☐☐

	MNHVF	UseVF	

875 _____ **1987. Flag With Fireworks Issue**

22¢ **multicolored** tagged — .35 — .20

876 _____ **1987. Flag Over Capitol Coil Issue**

22¢ **black, blue, & red** with "T" at bottom — .40 — .20

877 _____ **1987. Red Cloud Issue**

10¢ **carmine red** tagged (large block) — .25 — .20

878 _____ **1987. Bret Harte Issue**

$5 **Venetian red** tagged (large block) — 8.00 — 2.00

879 _____ **1987. Milk Wagon Issue**

5¢ **charcoal** tagged — .25 — .20

854

855

856

857

858

859

860

861

862

863

864

865

866

867

868

869

870

871

872

873

874

875

877

878

879

	MNHVF	UseVF	

880 _____ **1987. Racing Car Issue**
  17.5¢ **blue violet** tagged .30 .20 ☐☐☐☐☐
881 _____ **1987. Christmas Issue**
  22¢ **multicolored** tagged .50 .20 ☐☐☐☐☐
882 _____
  22¢ **multicolored** tagged .50 .20 ☐☐☐☐☐
883 _____ **1988. Conestoga Wagon Coil Issue**
  3¢ **dark lilac purple** tagged .25 .20 ☐☐☐☐☐
884 _____ **1988. Non-Denominated "E" Issue**
  28¢ **multicolored** tagged .50 .20 ☐☐☐☐☐
885 _____ **1988. Non-Denominated "E" Coil Issue**
  25¢ **multicolored** tagged .50 .20 ☐☐☐☐☐
886 _____ **1988. Non-Denominated "E" Booklet Issue**
  25¢ **multicolored** tagged .50 .20 ☐☐☐☐☐
887 _____ **1988. Pheasant Booklet Issue**
  25¢ **multicolored** tagged .50 .20 ☐☐☐☐☐
NOTE: Fully imperforate panes were cut from printer's waste.
888 _____ **1988. Jack London Booklet Issue**
  25¢ **blue** tagged (large block) perforated 11 .45 .20 ☐☐☐☐☐
889 _____
  25¢ **blue** tagged, perforated 10 .50 .20 ☐☐☐☐☐
890 _____ **1988. Flags With Clouds Issue**
  25¢ **multicolored** tagged .35 .20 ☐☐☐☐☐
890A _____ **1988. Flags With Clouds Booklet Issue**
  25¢ **multicolored** tagged .50 .20 ☐☐☐☐☐
891 _____ **1988. Flag Over Yosemite Issue**
  25¢ **multicolored** tagged .40 .20 ☐☐☐☐☐
892 _____ **1988. Owl and Grosbeak Issue**
  25¢ **multicolored** tagged .40 .20 ☐☐☐☐☐
893 _____
  25¢ **multicolored** tagged .40 .20 ☐☐☐☐☐
894 _____ **1988. Buffalo Bill Cody Issue**
  15¢ **maroon** tagged (large block) .30 .20 ☐☐☐☐☐
895 _____ **1988. Harvey Cushing Issue**
  45¢ **blue** tagged (large block) 1.00 .20 ☐☐☐☐☐
NOTE: Nos. 896 and 897 are not assigned.
898 _____ **1988. Popcorn Wagon Issue**
  16.7¢ **dark rose** (Bureau-printed service indicator "Bulk Rate") .20 .35 ☐☐☐☐☐
899 _____ **1988. Tugboat Issue**
  15¢ **purple** block tagged .30 .20 ☐☐☐☐☐
900 _____ **1988. Coal Car Issue**
  13.2¢ **dark green** (Bureau-printed red service indicator "Bulk Rate") .30 .20 ☐☐☐☐☐
901 _____ **1988. Wheel Chair Issue**
  8.4¢ **dark violet** (Bureau-printed red service indicator: "Non-profit") .30 .20 ☐☐☐☐☐
902 _____ **1988. Railroad Mail Car Issue**
  21¢ **green** (Bureau-printed red service indicator "Presorted 1st Class") .35 .20 ☐☐☐☐☐
903 _____ **1988. Carreta Issue**
  7.6¢ **brown** Bureau-printed red service indicator: "Nonprofit" .25 .20 ☐☐☐☐☐
904 _____ **1988. Harry S. Truman Issue**
  20¢ **black** tagged (large block), matte gum .35 .20 ☐☐☐☐☐
NOTE: (See also No. 811)
905 _____ **1988. Honeybee Issue**
  25¢ **multicolored** tagged .40 .20 ☐☐☐☐☐
906 _____ **1988. Elevator Issue**
  5.3¢ **black** (Bureau-printed red service indicator: "Nonprofit/Carrier Route Sort") .25 .20 ☐☐☐☐☐

	MNHVF	UseVF

907 _____ **1988. Fire Engine Issue**

20.5¢ **red** (Bureau-printed black service indicator: "ZIP+4 Presort")   .35   .20 ☐☐☐☐☐

908 _____ **1988. Eagle and Moon Issue**

$8.75 **multicolored** tagged   25.00   8.00 ☐☐☐☐☐

909 _____ **1988. Christmas Issue**

25¢ **multicolored,** tagged   .40   .20 ☐☐☐☐☐

910 _____ **1988. Madonna And Child by Botticelli Issue**

25¢ **multicolored** tagged   .40   .20 ☐☐☐☐☐

911 _____ **1988. Chester Carlson Issue**

21¢ **blue violet** tagged (large block)   .35   .20 ☐☐☐☐☐

880

881

882

883

884-886

887

890, 890A

891

892

893

894

895

898

899

900

901

902

903

905

906

907

908

909

910

	MNHVF	UseVF

912 _____ **1988. Tandem Bicycle Issue**

24.1¢ **deep blue violet** (Bureau-printed red service indicator: "ZIP+4")   .40   .20 ☐☐☐☐☐

913 _____ **1988. Cable Car Issue**

20¢ **dark violet,** block tagged   .35   .20 ☐☐☐☐☐

914 _____ **1988. Police Patrol Wagon Issue**

13¢ **black** (Bureau-printed red service indicator: "Presorted First Class")   .30   .20 ☐☐☐☐☐

915 _____ **1988. Mary Cassatt Issue**

23¢ **purple** tagged (large block)   .45   .20 ☐☐☐☐☐

916 _____ **1988. H.H. "Hap" Arnold Issue**

65¢ **dark blue** tagged (large block)   1.25   .20 ☐☐☐☐☐

NOTE: No. 917 not assigned.

918 _____ **1989. Johns Hopkins Issue**

$1 **blackish blue** tagged (large block) matte gum   2.00   .30 ☐☐☐☐☐

919 _____ **1989. Sitting Bull Issue**

28¢ **green** tagged (large block)   .50   .20 ☐☐☐☐☐

920 _____ **1989. Sleigh with Gifts Issue**

25¢ **multicolored** tagged   .40   .20 ☐☐☐☐☐

921 _____ **1989. Sleigh with Gifts Booklet Issue**

25¢ **multicolored** booklet stamp, tagged   .40   .20 ☐☐☐☐☐

922 _____ **1989. The Dream of St. Alexandria Issue**

25¢ **multicolored** tagged   .40   .20 ☐☐☐☐☐

NOTE: No. 923 is not assigned.

924 _____ **1989. Eagle and Shield Self-Adhesive Issue**

25¢ **multicolored** tagged   .40   .20 ☐☐☐☐☐

NOTE: No. 925 is not assigned.

926 _____ **1990. Beach Umbrella Issue**

15¢ **multicolored** booklet stamp, tagged   .30   .20 ☐☐☐☐☐

927 _____ **1990. Luis Muñoz Marin Issue**

5¢ **dark rose,** overall tagged   .25   .20 ☐☐☐☐☐

928 _____ **1990. Seaplane Issue**

$1 **dark blue & red** tagged   2.00   .50 ☐☐☐☐☐

929 _____ **1990. Flag Issue for Automatic Teller Machines**

25¢ **red & dark blue** tagged   .50   .50 ☐☐☐☐☐

930 _____ **1990. Bobcat Issue**

$2 **multicolored** tagged   4.00   1.25 ☐☐☐☐☐

931 _____ **1990. Circus Wagon Issue**

5¢ **carmine red** tagged   .25   .20 ☐☐☐☐☐

NOTE: For stamps of this design inscribed "USA 5¢" see No. 1007 (gravure) or No. 1077 (intaglio).

932 _____ **1990. Claire Lee Chennault Issue**

40¢ **dark blue** overall tagged, matte gum   .75   .20 ☐☐☐☐☐

933 _____ **1990. Contemporary Christmas Issue**

25¢ **multicolored** tagged   .40   .20 ☐☐☐☐☐

934 _____

25¢ **multicolored** booklet stamp, tagged   .40   .20 ☐☐☐☐☐

935 _____ **1990. Madonna and Child Booklet Issue**

25¢ **multicolored** tagged   .40   .20 ☐☐☐☐☐

936 _____

25¢ **multicolored** booklet stamp, tagged   .40   .20 ☐☐☐☐☐

NOTE: The booklet version has a much heavier shading in the Madonna's veil where it meets the right frame line.

937 _____ **1991. "F" (Flower) Non-Denominated Issue**

29¢ **multicolored** tagged   .50   .20 ☐☐☐☐☐

938 _____ **1991. "F" (Flower) Non-Denominated Booklet Issue**

29¢ **multicolored** booklet stamp, tagged   .50   .20 ☐☐☐☐☐

939 _____

29¢ **multicolored** booklet stamp, printed by KCS Industries, tagged   .50   .20 ☐☐☐☐☐

	MNHVF	UseVF
940 _____ 1991. "F" (Flower) Non-Denominated Coil Issue		
29¢ **multicolored** tagged	.60	.20 ▢▢▢▢▢
941 _____ 1991. Non-Denominated 4¢ Make Up Issue		
4¢ **bister & carmine**	.25	.20 ▢▢▢▢▢
942 _____ 1991. "F" Non-Denominated ATM Flag Issue		
29¢ **black, dark blue & red** tagged	.50	.20 ▢▢▢▢▢
943 _____ 1991. Steam Carriage Issue		
4¢ **maroon** tagged	.25	.20 ▢▢▢▢▢
944 _____ 1991. Fawn Issue		
19¢ **multicolored** tagged	.40	.20 ▢▢▢▢▢

911

912

913

914

915

916

918

919

920, 921

922

924

926

927

928

929

930

931

932

933, 934

935, 936

937-940

941

942

943

944

		MNHVF	UseVF

945 _____   **1991. Flag Over Mount Rushmore**
29¢ **red, blue, & maroon** tagged   .50   .20 ⬜⬜⬜⬜⬜

945A _____
29¢ **red, blue & brown** color change (error), tagged   .50   .20 ⬜⬜⬜⬜⬜

NOTE: For gravure version of this design, see No. 963.

946 _____   **1991. Dennis Chavez Issue**
35¢ **black** phosphored paper mottled tagging   .75   .20 ⬜⬜⬜⬜⬜

947 _____   **1991. Flower Issue**
29¢ **multicolored** tagged, perforated 11   .45   .20 ⬜⬜⬜⬜⬜

947A _____
29¢ **multicolored** tagged, perforated 12 1/2 x 13   .45   .20 ⬜⬜⬜⬜⬜

948 _____   **1991. Flower Booklet Issue**
29¢ **multicolored** booklet stamp, tagged, perforated 11   .45   .20 ⬜⬜⬜⬜⬜

NOTE: For coil version of the Flower Issue, see Nos. 966 and 982.

949 _____   **1991. Lunch Wagon Issue**
23¢ **blue** tagged, matte gum   .50   .20 ⬜⬜⬜⬜⬜

950 _____   **1991. Wood Duck Issue**
29¢ **multicolored** booklet stamp, black inscription (B.E.P.), tagged   .75   .20 ⬜⬜⬜⬜⬜

951 _____
29¢ **multicolored** booklet stamp, red inscription (KCS Industries), tagged   1.00   .20 ⬜⬜⬜⬜⬜

952 _____   **1991. U.S. Flag with Olympic Rings Issue**
29¢ **multicolored** booklet stamp, tagged   .75   .20 ⬜⬜⬜⬜⬜

953 _____   **1991. Hot Air Balloon Issue**
19¢ **multicolored** booklet stamp, tagged   .30   .20 ⬜⬜⬜⬜⬜

954 _____   **1991. Tractor Trailer Issue**
10¢ **green** (Bureau-printed gray service indicator: "Additional Presort Postage Paid").25   .20 ⬜⬜⬜⬜⬜

NOTE: For version with service indicator in black, see No. 1042.

955 _____   **1991. Canoe Issue**
5¢ **brown** (printed gray service indicator: "Additional Nonprofit Postage Paid")   .25   .20 ⬜⬜⬜⬜⬜

NOTE: For gravure version of No. 955 in red, see No. 979.

956 _____   **1991. Flags on Parade Issue**
29¢ **multicolored** tagged   .50   .20 ⬜⬜⬜⬜⬜

957 _____   **1991. Hubert H. Humphrey Issue**
52¢ **purple** phosphored paper (solid)   1.50   .20 ⬜⬜⬜⬜⬜

958 _____   **1991. Eagle and Olympic Rings Issue**
$9.95 **multicolored** tagged   15.00   7.50 ⬜⬜⬜⬜⬜

959 _____   **1991. American Kestrel Issue**
1¢ **multicolored**   .25   .20 ⬜⬜⬜⬜⬜

NOTE: For versions inscribed "USA 1¢", see No. 1079 (sheet) and No. 1115 (Coil).

960 _____   **1991. Bluebird Issue**
3¢ **Eastern bluebird**   .25   .20 ⬜⬜⬜⬜⬜

961 _____   **1991. Cardinal Issue**
30¢ **multicolored** on phosphored paper   .45   .20 ⬜⬜⬜⬜⬜

962 _____   **1991. Statue of Liberty Torch Issue**
29¢ **black, gold & green** tagged, die cut   .60   .30 ⬜⬜⬜⬜⬜

963 _____   **1991. Flag Over Mount Rushmore Coil Issue**
29¢ **blue, red & brown** tagged   .50   .25 ⬜⬜⬜⬜⬜

NOTE: For intaglio version of the same design, see No. 945.

964 _____   **1991. Eagle and Olympic Rings Issue**
$2.90 **multicolored** tagged   5.00   2.75 ⬜⬜⬜⬜⬜

965 _____   **1991. Fishing Boat Coil Issue**
19¢ **multicolored** Type I, tagged   .40   .20 ⬜⬜⬜⬜⬜

NOTE: Imperforates in this design came from printer's waste. For version with one loop of rope tying boat to piling, see No. 1044.

966 _____   **1991. Flower Coil Issue**
29¢ **multicolored** tagged   .75   .20 ⬜⬜⬜⬜⬜

945, 945A   946   947, 947A, 948, 962   949   950, 951

952   953   954   955   956

957   959   960

958

961   962   963

964

965   966   967

969   971, 972, 972A   973   970

		MNHVF	UseVF	

967 _____ **1991. Eagle Over Coastline, Olympic Rings Issue**

$14 **multicolored** tagged   30.00   17.50 ☐☐☐☐☐

NOTE: No. 968 is not assigned.

969 _____ **1991. U.S. Flag Issue**

23¢ **red & blue** printed service indicator: "Presorted First Class"   .65   .20 ☐☐☐☐☐

970 _____ **1991. USPS Olympic Sponsor Issue**

$1 **multicolored** tagged   2.75   .75 ☐☐☐☐☐

971 _____ **1991. Santa Descending a Chimney Issue**

29¢ **multicolored** tagged   .45   .20 ☐☐☐☐☐

972 _____ **1991. Santa Booklet Issue**

29¢ **multicolored** booklet stamp, Type I, tagged   .45   .20 ☐☐☐☐☐

972A _____

29¢ **multicolored** booklet stamp, Type II, tagged   .45   .20 ☐☐☐☐☐

NOTE: Type I has an extra vertical line of brick in the top row of bricks at left; Type II is missing that vertical line of brick.

973 _____

29¢ **multicolored** booklet stamp, tagged   .45   .20 ☐☐☐☐☐

974 _____

29¢ **multicolored** booklet stamp, tagged   .45   .20 ☐☐☐☐☐

975 _____

29¢ **multicolored** booklet stamp, tagged   .45   .20 ☐☐☐☐☐

976 _____

29¢ **multicolored** booklet stamp, tagged   .45   .20 ☐☐☐☐☐

977 _____ **1991. Traditional Christmas Issue**

29¢ **multicolored** tagged   .45   .20 ☐☐☐☐☐

NOTE: No. 978 is not assigned.

979 _____ **1991. Canoe Issue**

5¢ **red** (printed service indicator: "Additional Nonprofit Postage Paid")   .25   .20 ☐☐☐☐☐

NOTE: For intaglio version in brown, see No. 955.

980 _____ **1991. Eagle and Shield Non-Denominated Issue**

10¢ **multicolored** (printed service indicator: "Bulk Rate")   .25   .20 ☐☐☐☐☐

NOTE: See Nos. 1011 and 1012 for similar stamps printed by the Bureau of Engraving and Printing and Stamp Venturers.

981 _____ **1992. Wendell L. Willkie Issue**

75¢ **maroon** phosphored paper (taggant on surface), matte gum   1.25   .50 ☐☐☐☐☐

982 _____ **1992. Flower Perforated Coil Issue**

29¢ **multicolored** tagged   .75   .20 ☐☐☐☐☐

983 _____ **1992. Earl Warren Issue**

29¢ **blue** tagged, phosphored paper   .50   .20 ☐☐☐☐☐

984 _____ **1992. Flag Over White House Issue**

29¢ **blue & red** tagged, phosphored paper   .50   .20 ☐☐☐☐☐

985 _____ **1992. USA Issue**

23¢ **multicolored** (printed service indicator: "Presorted First-Class")   .50   .20 ☐☐☐☐☐

NOTE: See Nos. 994 and 1010 for similar stamps printed by the Bureau of Engraving and Printing and by Stamp Venturers.

986 _____ **1992. ECA GARD Variable Denominated Issue**

29¢ **red & blue** tagged (solid), denomination (.01 to 9.99) printed in black,
matte gum   1.50   .50 ☐☐☐☐☐

NOTE: For narrow, tall format, see No. 1040.

987 _____ **1992. Pledge of Allegiance Issue**

29¢ **multicolored** black inscription, booklet stamp, tagged   .75   .20 ☐☐☐☐☐

NOTE: For version with red inscription see No. 1008.

988 _____ **1992. Eagle and Shield Self-Adhesive Issue**

29¢ **multicolored** red inscription, tagged   .45   .30 ☐☐☐☐☐

NOTE: No. 989 is not assigned.

990 _____

29¢ **multicolored** green inscription, tagged   .45   .30 ☐☐☐☐☐

NOTE: No. 991 is not assigned.

	MNHVF	UseVF

992 _____

  29¢ **multicolored** brown inscription, tagged   .45   .30 ☐☐☐☐☐

NOTE: No. 993 is not assigned.

994 _____   **1992. "USA" Issue**

  23¢ **multicolored** printed service indicator: "Presorted First-Class," shiny gum   .50   .20 ☐☐☐☐☐

NOTE: In this version, "23" is 7mm long. See Nos. 985 and 1010 for versions printed by the American Bank Note Co. or by Stamp Venturers.

995 _____   **1992. Contemporary Christmas Issue**

  29¢ **Locomotive multicolored,** tagged   .45   .20 ☐☐☐☐☐

996 _____

  29¢ **Pony & rider multicolored,** tagged   .45   .20 ☐☐☐☐☐

997 _____

  29¢ **Fire engine multicolored,** tagged   .45   .20 ☐☐☐☐☐

998 _____

  29¢ **Steamship multicolored,** tagged   .45   .20 ☐☐☐☐☐

999 _____   **1992. Contemporary Booklet Issue**

  29¢ **Locomotive multicolored,** booklet single   .45   .20 ☐☐☐☐☐

1000 _____

  29¢ **Pony & rider multicolored,** booklet single   .45   .20 ☐☐☐☐☐

974   975   976   977   979

980   981   982   983   984

985   986   987, 1008   988, 990, 992   994

995, 999, 1005 (upper left)
996, 1000 (upper right)
997, 1001 (lower left)
998, 1002 (lower right)

1003   1005

	MNHVF	UseVF

1001 _____
29¢ **Fire engine multicolored,** booklet single ... .45 ... .20 ☐☐☐☐☐
1002 _____
29¢ **Steamship multicolored,** booklet single ... .45 ... .20 ☐☐☐☐☐
1003 _____ **1992. Traditional Christmas Issue**
29¢ **multicolored** tagged ... .45 ... .20 ☐☐☐☐☐
NOTE: No. 1004 is not assigned.
1005 _____ **1992. Contemporary Christmas Self-Adhesive ATM Issue**
29¢ **multicolored** tagged ... .75 ... .20 ☐☐☐☐☐
1006 _____ **1992. Pumpkinseed Sunfish Issue**
45¢ **multicolored** tagged ... 1.00 ... .20 ☐☐☐☐☐
1007 _____ **1992. Circus Wagon Issue**
5¢ **red** untagged ... .25 ... .20 ☐☐☐☐☐
NOTE: For intaglio stamps of this design see No. 931 ("05 USA") and No. 1077 ("USA 5¢").
1008 _____ **1993. Pledge of Allegiance Issue**
29¢ **multicolored** red inscription, tagged ... .75 ... .20 ☐☐☐☐☐
NOTE: For similar stamp with black inscription see No. 987.
1009 _____ **1993. Thomas Jefferson Issue**
29¢ **indigo** phosphored paper ... .50 ... .30 ☐☐☐☐☐
1010 _____ **1993. USA Issue**
23¢ **multicolored** printed service indicator: "Presorted First-Class" ... .75 ... .20 ☐☐☐☐☐
NOTE: In this version, "23" is 8 1/2mm long. See No. 985 and No. 994 for versions printed by the American Bank Note Co. and by the Bureau of Engraving and Printing.
1011 _____ **1993. Eagle and Shield Non-Denominated Issue**
10¢ **multicolored** (B.E.P.) ... .30 ... .20 ☐☐☐☐☐
1012 _____
10¢ **multicolored** (Stamp Venturers) ... .30 ... .20 ☐☐☐☐☐
NOTE: See No. 980 for similar design printed by the American Bank Note Co.
1013 _____ **1993. Futuristic Space Shuttle Issue**
$2.90 **multicolored** ... 6.50 ... 2.50 ☐☐☐☐☐
1014 _____ **1993. Red Squirrel Issue**
29¢ **multicolored** from booklet, tagged ... .50 ... .20 ☐☐☐☐☐
NOTE: No. 1015 is not assigned.
1016 _____ **1993. Rose Issue**
29¢ **multicolored** from booklet, tagged ... .50 ... .20 ☐☐☐☐☐
NOTE: No. 1017 is not assigned.
1018 _____ **1993. African Violet Booklet Issue**
29¢ **multicolored** from booklet, tagged ... .75 ... .20 ☐☐☐☐☐
1019 _____ **1993. Contemporary Christmas Issue**
29¢ **Jack-in-the-box,** tagged ... .50 ... .20 ☐☐☐☐☐
1020 _____
29¢ **Reindeer,** tagged ... .50 ... .20 ☐☐☐☐☐
1021 _____
29¢ **Snowman,** tagged ... .50 ... .20 ☐☐☐☐☐
1022 _____
29¢ **Toy soldier,** tagged ... .50 ... .20 ☐☐☐☐☐
1023 _____
29¢ **Jack-in-the-box,** tagged (single) ... .50 ... .20 ☐☐☐☐☐
1024 _____
29¢ **Reindeer,** tagged (single) ... .50 ... .20 ☐☐☐☐☐
1025 _____
29¢ **Snowman,** tagged (single) ... .50 ... .20 ☐☐☐☐☐
1026 _____
29¢ **Toy soldier,** tagged ... .50 ... .20 ☐☐☐☐☐
1027 _____ **1993. Traditional Christmas Issue**
29¢ **multicolored** tagged ... .50 ... .20 ☐☐☐☐☐

	MNHVF	UseVF

1028 _____
    29¢ **multicolored** booklet single, tagged   .50   .20
1029 _____ **1993. Contemporary Christmas Self-adhesive Issue**
    29¢ **Jack-in-the-box,** tagged (single)   .50   .20
1030 _____
    29¢ **Reindeer,** tagged (single)   .50   .20
1031 _____
    29¢ **Snowman,** tagged (single)   .50   .20
1032 _____
    29¢ **Toy soldier,** tagged (single)   .50   .20
NOTE: Nos. 1033-1036 are not assigned.
1037 _____ **1993. Snowman ATM Pane Issue**
    29¢ **Snowman,** tagged (single)   .75   .25
NOTE: Although the placement is different, the Snowmen depicted on Nos. 1021 and 1031 have three buttons and seven snowflakes beneath the nose. No. 1025 has two buttons and five snowflakes beneath the nose.
1038 _____ **1993. Pine Cone Issue**
    29¢ **multicolored** from booklet, tagged   .50   .20
1039 _____ **1994. Eagle Issue**
    29¢ **red, cream & blue** tagged (single)   .50   .20

1006

1009

1011, 1012

USA $2.90
1013

1014

1016

1019, 1023, 1029
(upper left)
1020, 1024, 1030
(upper right)
1021, 1025, 1031
(lower left)
1022, 1026, 1032
(lower right)

1018

1027, 1028

1037

1038

1039

1040

1041

1042

	MNHVF	UseVF	

1040 _____ 1994. Postage and Mail Center (PMC) Issue

32¢ **(variable rate) red and blue,** denomination 20¢-$99.99 printed in black, phosphored paper — 1.50 — .50 ☐☐☐☐☐

1041 _____ 1994. Surrender of Burgoyne at Saratoga Issue

$1 **dark blue** tagged — 2.00 — .75 ☐☐☐☐☐

1042 _____ 1994. Tractor Trailer Issue

10¢ **green** Bureau-printed service indicator (in gray): "Additional Presort Postage Paid" — .25 — .20 ☐☐☐☐☐

1043 _____ 1994. Statue of Liberty Issue

29¢ **multicolored** tagged (single) — .50 — .20 ☐☐☐☐☐

1044 _____ 1994. Fishing Boat Issue

19¢ **multicolored** tagged — .50 — .20 ☐☐☐☐☐

1045 _____ 1994. Moon Landing Issue

$9.95 **multicolored** tagged — 25.00 — 10.00 ☐☐☐☐☐

1046 _____ 1994. Washington and Jackson Issue

$5 **dark green** tagged — 10.00 — 3.75 ☐☐☐☐☐

1047 _____ 1994. Contemporary Christmas Issue

29¢ **multicolored** tagged — .50 — .20 ☐☐☐☐☐

1048 _____ 1994. Traditional Christmas Issue

29¢ **multicolored** tagged — .50 — .20 ☐☐☐☐☐

1049 _____

29¢ **multicolored** tagged (single) self-adhesive — .50 — .20 ☐☐☐☐☐

1050 _____ 1994. Contemporary Santa Claus Booklet Issue

29¢ **multicolored** tagged — .50 — .20 ☐☐☐☐☐

1051 _____ 1994. Cardinal in Snow ATM Issue

29¢ **multicolored** tagged — .50 — .20 ☐☐☐☐☐

1052 _____ 1994. Virginia Apgar Issue

29¢ **brown** tagged, phosphored — .50 — .20 ☐☐☐☐☐

1053 _____ 1994. Postage and Mail Center (PMC) Issue

32¢ **(variable rate) red & blue,** embedded taggant, denomination printed in black, shiny gum — .75 — .50 ☐☐☐☐☐

1054 _____ 1994. Black "G" Sheet Issue

32¢ **red, blue, gray & black** tagged — .50 — .20 ☐☐☐☐☐

1055 _____ 1994. Red "G" Sheet Booklet Issue

32¢ **red, blue, gray & black** tagged — .50 — .20 ☐☐☐☐☐

1056 _____ 1994. Black "G" Booklet Issue

32¢ **red, blue, gray & black** tagged — .50 — .20 ☐☐☐☐☐

1057 _____ 1994. Blue "G" Booklet Issue

32¢ **red, blue, gray & black** tagged — .50 — .20 ☐☐☐☐☐

1058 _____ 1994. Red "G" Booklet Issue

32¢ **red, blue, gray & black** tagged — .50 — .20 ☐☐☐☐☐

1059 _____ 1994. Black "G" Coil Issue

32¢ **red, blue, gray & black** tagged — .50 — .20 ☐☐☐☐☐

1060 _____ 1994. Blue "G" Coil Issue

32¢ **red, blue, gray & black** tagged — .50 — .20 ☐☐☐☐☐

1061 _____ 1994. Red "G" Coil Issue

32¢ **red, blue, gray & black** tagged — .50 — .20 ☐☐☐☐☐

1061A _____

32¢ **red, blue, gray & black** tagged — .50 — .20 ☐☐☐☐☐

1062 _____ 1994. "G" Self Adhesive Issue

32¢ **red, dark blue, light blue, gray & black,** tagged — 1.00 — .35 ☐☐☐☐☐

1063 _____ 1994. "G" Self Adhesive ATM Issue

32¢ **red, blue & black** tagged — 1.00 — .35 ☐☐☐☐☐

1064 _____ 1994. "G" First-Class Presort Rate Issue

25¢ **red, dark blue, gray, black & light blue** — .75 — .20 ☐☐☐☐☐

		MNHVF	UseVF	
1065 _____	**1994. Black "G" Postcard Rate Issue**			
	20¢ **red, blue, gray, yellow & black** tagged	.50	.20	☐☐☐☐☐
1066 _____	**1994. Red "G" Postcard Rate Issue**			
	20¢ **red, blue, gray, yellow & black,** tagged	.50	.20	☐☐☐☐☐
1067 _____	**1994. Non-Denominated "Make-Up " Rate Issue**			
	3¢ **red, bright blue & tan**	.25	.20	☐☐☐☐☐
1068 _____				
	3¢ **red, dark blue & tan**	.25	.20	☐☐☐☐☐
1069 _____	**1995. "G" Nonprofit Presort Coil Issue**			
	5¢ **green & multicolored** untagged	.25	.20	☐☐☐☐☐

NOTE: *First-day covers received a Dec. 13, 1994 cancellation although these stamps were not yet available on that date.*

		MNHVF	UseVF	
1070 _____	**1995. Butte and "Nonprofit Organization" Issue**			
	5¢ **yellow, blue & red** untagged	.25	.20	☐☐☐☐☐
1071 _____	**1995. Car Hood and "Bulk Rate" Issue**			
	10¢ **black, brown & red brown** untagged	.30	.20	☐☐☐☐☐
1072 _____	**1995. Tail Fin Presorted First-Class Coil Issue**			
	15¢ **yellow orange & multicolored** untagged	.40	.30	☐☐☐☐☐

1043

1044

25th Anniversary First Moon Landing, 1969

1045

1046

Greetings

1047

Elisabetta Sirani, 1663
National Museum of Women in the Arts

1048, 1049

Greetings

1050

Old Glory
USA G
For U.S. addresses only

1054-1063

Greetings

1051

Virginia Apgar   Physician
1909 1974

1052

USA

1053

Old Glory
USA G
First-Class Presort

1064

Old Glory
USA G
Postcard Rate

1065, 1066

USA
The 'G' Rate make-up stamp

1067, 1068

Old Glory
USA G
Nonprofit Presort

1069

USA
NONPROFIT ORG.

1070

	MNHVF	UseVF	

1073 _____

15¢ **buff & multicolored** untagged .40 .30 ☐☐☐☐☐

1074 _____   **1995. Juke Box Presorted First-Class Coil Issue**

25¢ **dark red, yellow green & multicolored,** untagged .65 .40 ☐☐☐☐☐

1075 _____

25¢ **orange red, bright yellow green & multicolored** untagged .65 .40 ☐☐☐☐☐

1076 _____   **1995. Flag Over Field ATM Issue**

32¢ **multicolored** tagged 1.00 .30 ☐☐☐☐☐

1077 _____   **1995. Circus Wagon Issue**

5¢ **red** untagged .25 .20 ☐☐☐☐☐

NOTE: For intaglio & gravure versions of this design inscribed "05 USA" see Nos. 931 & 1007.

1078 _____   **1995. Flag Over Porch Self Adhesive Booklet Issue**

32¢ **multicolored** phosphored paper, large "1995" 1.00 .30 ☐☐☐☐☐

1078a _____

☐☐☐☐☐

1079 _____   **1995. American Kestrel Issue**

1¢ **multicolored** tagged .25 .20 ☐☐☐☐☐

NOTE: For version inscribed "USA 01" see No. 959. For coil see No. 1115.

1080 _____   **1995. Flag Over Porch Issue**

32¢ **multicolored** tagged .70 .20 ☐☐☐☐☐

1081 _____   **1995. Flag Over Porch Booklet Issue**

32¢ **multicolored** tagged .80 .20 ☐☐☐☐☐

1082 _____   **1995. Flag Over Porch Coil Issue**

32¢ **multicolored** tagged, red "1995" .50 .20 ☐☐☐☐☐

1083 _____

32¢ **multicolored** tagged, blue "1995" .75 .20 ☐☐☐☐☐

1084 _____   **1995. Pink Rose Issue**

32¢ **pink, green & black** phosphored .80 .30 ☐☐☐☐☐

1085 _____   **1995. Ferryboat Issue**

32¢ **deep blue** phosphored paper .75 .20 ☐☐☐☐☐

1086 _____   **1995. Cog Railway Issue**

20¢ **green** phosphored paper .40 .20 ☐☐☐☐☐

1087 _____   **1995. Blue Jay Issue**

20¢ **multicolored** phosphored paper .45 .20 ☐☐☐☐☐

1088 _____   **1995. Space Shuttle Challenger Issue**

$3 **multicolored** phosphored paper 6.00 3.00 ☐☐☐☐☐

1089 _____   **1995. Peaches and Pear Issue**

32¢ **multicolored** phosphored paper .75 .20 ☐☐☐☐☐

1090 _____

32¢ **multicolored** phosphored paper .75 .20 ☐☐☐☐☐

1091 _____   **1995. Peaches and Pear Self-Adhesive Issue**

32¢ **multicolored** phosphored paper .85 .30 ☐☐☐☐☐

1091A _____   **1995. Peaches and Pear Self-Adhesive Coil Issue**

32¢ **multicolored** .85 .30 ☐☐☐☐☐

1092 _____   **1995. Peaches and Pear Self-Adhesive Issue**

32¢ **multicolored** phosphored paper .85 .30 ☐☐☐☐☐

1092A _____   **1995. Peaches and Pear Self-Adhesive Coil Issue**

32¢ **multicolored** .85 .30 ☐☐☐☐☐

1093 _____   **1995. Alice Hamilton Issue**

55¢ **green** phosphored paper, grainy tagging 1.10 .20 ☐☐☐☐☐

1094 _____   **1995. Space Shuttle Endeavor Issue**

10.75¢ **multicolored** phosphored paper 21.00 8.00 ☐☐☐☐☐

1095 _____   **1995. Alice Paul Issue**

78¢ **purple** phosphored paper 1.75 .25 ☐☐☐☐☐

	MNHVF	UseVF

1096 _____ **1995. Milton S. Hershey Issue**
32¢ **chocolate brown** phosphored paper — .65 — .20 ☐☐☐☐☐

1097 _____ **1995. Eddie Rickenbacker Issue**
60¢ **multicolored** phosphored paper — .75 — .20 ☐☐☐☐☐

1098 _____ **1995. Contemporary Christmas Issue**
32¢ **Santa on rooftop,** phosphored paper — .60 — .20 ☐☐☐☐☐

1099 _____
32¢ **Child and jumping jack,** phosphored paper — .60 — .20 ☐☐☐☐☐

1100 _____
32¢ **Child and tree,** phosphored paper — .60 — .20 ☐☐☐☐☐

1071

1072 First-Class Card

1073, 1133 First-Class Card

1074-75, 1134, 1153 Presorted First-Class

1076

1077

1078, 1080-83

1079

1084

1085

1086

1087, 1135-36

1088

1089, 1091, 1091A (left)
1090, 1092, 1092A (right)

1093

1094

1095

1096

1097, 1250

1098, 1102, 1106 (upper left)
1099, 1103, 1107 (upper right)
1100, 1104, 1108 (lower left)
1101, 1105, 1109 (lower right)

		MNHVF	UseVF	

1101 _____
| 32¢ **Santa in workshop,** phosphored paper | .60 | .20 ☐☐☐☐☐ |

1102 _____ **1995. Contemporary Christmas Coil Issue**
| 32¢ **Santa on rooftop,** phosphored paper | .60 | .20 ☐☐☐☐☐ |

1103 _____
| 32¢ **Child and Jumping Jack,** phosphored paper | .60 | .20 ☐☐☐☐☐ |

1104 _____
| 32¢ **Child and tree,** phosphored paper | .60 | .20 ☐☐☐☐☐ |

1105 _____
| 32¢ **Santa in workshop,** phosphored paper | .60 | .20 ☐☐☐☐☐ |

1106 _____ **1995. Contemporary Christmas Booklet ATM Issue**
| 32¢ **multicolored** phosphored paper | .60 | .20 ☐☐☐☐☐ |

1107 _____
| 32¢ **multicolored** phosphored paper | .60 | .20 ☐☐☐☐☐ |

1108 _____
| 32¢ **multicolored** phosphored paper | .60 | .20 ☐☐☐☐☐ |

1109 _____
| 32¢ **multicolored** phosphored paper | .60 | .20 ☐☐☐☐☐ |

1110 _____ **1995. Midnight Angel Christmas Booklet Issue**
| 32¢ **multicolored** phosphored paper | 1.75 | .45 ☐☐☐☐☐ |

1110A _____ **1995. Midnight Angel Christmas Coil Issue**
| 32¢ **multicolored** phosphored paper | .75 | .45 ☐☐☐☐☐ |

1111 _____ **1995. Contemporary Christmas Booklet ATM Issue**
| 32¢ **multicolored** phosphored lacquer on surface of stamps | .75 | .45 ☐☐☐☐☐ |

1112 _____ **1995. Traditional Christmas Issue**
| 32¢ **multicolored** phosphored paper, perforated 11 1/4 | .75 | .20 ☐☐☐☐☐ |

1113 _____
| 32¢ **multicolored** phosphored paper, perforated 9 3/4 x 11 | .75 | .20 ☐☐☐☐☐ |

1114 _____ **1995. Ruth Benedict Issue**
| 45¢ **carmine** phosphored paper | 1.00 | .25 ☐☐☐☐☐ |

1115 _____ **1996. American Kestrel Issue**
| 1¢ **multicolored** untagged | .25 | .20 ☐☐☐☐☐ |

NOTE: For sheet version see No. 1079. For version inscribed "USA 01" see No. 959.

1116 _____ **1996. Flag Over Porch Issue**
| 32¢ **multicolored** phosphored paper | .75 | .30 ☐☐☐☐☐ |

1117 _____ **1996. Unisys Variable Denomination Issue**
| 32¢ **red & blue** denomination (.20 to $20.00) printed in black, tagged | .95 | .50 ☐☐☐☐☐ |

1118 _____ **1996. Red-headed Woodpecker Issue**
| 2¢ **multicolored** untagged | .25 | .20 ☐☐☐☐☐ |

1119 _____ **1996. Space Shuttle Challenger Issue**
| $3 **multicolored** phosphored paper | 6.00 | 3.00 ☐☐☐☐☐ |

1120 _____ **1996. Jacqueline Cochran Issue**
| 50¢ **multicolored** phosphored paper | 1.20 | .40 ☐☐☐☐☐ |

1121 _____ **1996. Mountain Coil Issue**
| 5¢ **purple & multicolored** untagged | .25 | .20 ☐☐☐☐☐ |

1122 _____
| 5¢ **blue & multicolored** untagged | .25 | .20 ☐☐☐☐☐ |

1123 _____ **1996. Eastern Bluebird Issue**
| 3¢ **multicolored** untagged | .25 | .20 ☐☐☐☐☐ |

1124 _____ **1996. Cal Farley Issue**
| 32¢ **green** phosphored paper | .65 | .20 ☐☐☐☐☐ |

1125 _____ **1996. Flag Over Porch Booklet Stamp Issue**
| 32¢ **multicolored** phosphored paper | .75 | .30 ☐☐☐☐☐ |

1126 _____ **1996. Flag Over Porch Coil Stamp Issue**
| 32¢ **multicolored** phosphored paper | 1.00 | .30 ☐☐☐☐☐ |

	MNHVF	UseVF

1127 _____
  32¢ **multicolored** phosphored paper — 1.50 — .50 ☐☐☐☐☐
1128 _____
  32¢ **multicolored** phosphored paper — .70 — .20 ☐☐☐☐☐
NOTE: On this issue, stamps are spaced apart on the 10,000 stamp coil roll.
1129 _____ **1996. Eagle and Shield Non-Denominated Self-Adhesive Coil Issue**
  10¢ **multicolored** untagged — .25 — .20 ☐☐☐☐☐
1130 _____ **1996. Butte Coil Issue**
  5¢ **yellow, blue & red** untagged — .25 — .20 ☐☐☐☐☐
1131 _____ **1996. Mountains Coil Issue**
  5¢ **purple & multicolored** untagged — .25 — .20 ☐☐☐☐☐
1132 _____ **1996. Automobile Coil Issue**
  10¢ **black, brown & red brown** untagged — .25 — .20 ☐☐☐☐☐
1133 _____ **1996. Auto Tail Fin Coil Issue**
  15¢ **buff & multicolored** untagged — .35 — .30 ☐☐☐☐☐
1134 _____ **1996. Juke Box Coil Issue**
  25¢ **orange red, bright yellow green & multicolored** untagged — .60 — .30 ☐☐☐☐☐
1135 _____ **1996. Blue Jay Booklet Issue**
  20¢ **multicolored** phosphored paper — .45 — .25 ☐☐☐☐☐

1110, 1110A   1111   1112, 1113   1114   1115

1116   1117   1118   1119   1120

1121, 1122   1123   1124   1125-1128   1129   1130

1131

1132

1133

1134

1135, 1136

		MNHVF	UseVF

1136 _____   **1996. Blue Jay Coil Issue**

20¢ **multicolored** phosphored paper   .40   .20 ☐☐☐☐☐

1137 _____   **1996. Contemporary Christmas Issue**

32¢ **Family at yule hearth,** phosphored paper   .60   .20 ☐☐☐☐☐

1138 _____

32¢ **Family trimming tree,** phosphored paper   .60   .20 ☐☐☐☐☐

1139 _____

32¢ **Dreaming of Santa,** phosphored paper   .60   .20 ☐☐☐☐☐

1140 _____

32¢ **Holiday shopping,** phosphored paper   .60   .20 ☐☐☐☐☐

1141 _____   **1996. Contemporary Self Adhesive Booklet Issue**

32¢ **Family at yule hearth,** phosphored paper   .60   .20 ☐☐☐☐☐

1142 _____

32¢ **Family trimming tree,** phosphored paper   .60   .20 ☐☐☐☐☐

1143 _____

32¢ **Dreaming of Santa,** phosphored paper   .60   .20 ☐☐☐☐☐

1144 _____

32¢ **Holiday shopping,** phosphored paper   .60   .20 ☐☐☐☐☐

1145 _____   **1996. Holiday Skaters Booklet ATM Issue**

32¢ **multicolored,** phosphored lacquer on surface of stamps   .75   .30 ☐☐☐☐☐

1146 _____   **1996. Traditional Christmas Issue**

32¢ **multicolored** phosphored paper, perforated 11 1/4   .70   .20 ☐☐☐☐☐

1147 _____

32¢ **multicolored** tagged, serpentine die cut   .95   .30 ☐☐☐☐☐

1149 _____   **1996. Yellow Rose Issue**

32¢ **yellow & multicolored** phosphored paper   .75   .25 ☐☐☐☐☐

1150 _____   **1997. Flag Over Porch Booklet Issue**

32¢ **multicolored** phosphored paper   .75   .30 ☐☐☐☐☐

1151 _____   **1997. Flag Over Porch Coil Issue**

32¢ **multicolored** phosphored paper   .75   .30 ☐☐☐☐☐

1152 _____   **1997. Mountain Coil Issue**

5¢ **purple & multicolored** untagged   .25   .20 ☐☐☐☐☐

1153 _____   **1997. Juke Box Coil Issue**

25¢ **multicolored** untagged   .60   .20 ☐☐☐☐☐

1154 _____   **1997. Statue of Liberty Issue**

32¢ **multicolored** phosphored paper   .75   .20 ☐☐☐☐☐

1155 _____   **1997. Citron and Insect Issue**

32¢ **multicolored** tagged   .75   .20 ☐☐☐☐☐

1156 _____   **1997. Flowering Pineapple Issue**

32¢ **multicolored** tagged   .75   .20 ☐☐☐☐☐

1157 _____   **1997. Citron and Insect Booklet Issue**

32¢ **multicolored** tagged   .75   .20 ☐☐☐☐☐

1158 _____   **1997. Flowering Pineapple Booklet Issue**

32¢ **multicolored** tagged   .75   .20 ☐☐☐☐☐

1159 _____   **1997. Citron and Insect Booklet Issue**

32¢ **multicolored** tagged   1.25   .50 ☐☐☐☐☐

1160 _____   **1997. Flowering Pineapple Booklet Issue**

32¢ **multicolored** tagged   1.25   .50 ☐☐☐☐☐

NOTE: Nos. 1159-60, which are die cut on all four sides, have a single irregular large serration near the middle of the right side created by die cutting.

1161 _____   **1997. Juke Box Issue**

25¢ **multicolored** untagged   .60   .20 ☐☐☐☐☐

1162 _____   **1997. Flag Over Porch Issue**

32¢ **multicolored** tagged   .60   .20 ☐☐☐☐☐

1137, 1141
(upper left)
1138, 1142
(upper right)
1139, 1143
(lower left)
1140, 1144
(lower right)

1145

1146, 1147

1149, 1163

1150-1151

1152

1153

1154

1155

1156

1157, 1159

1158, 1160

1161

1162

1163

1164

American Holly 32 USA

1165

1166, 1167

MARS PATHFINDER
JULY 4, 1997

Mars Rover Sojourner

$3.00 usa

1168

1169

1170, 1177

1171

1172, 1173, 1248

	MNHVF	UseVF

1163 _____ **1997. Rose Issue**
32¢ yellow & multicolored tagged .65 .20 ⬜⬜⬜⬜⬜
1164 _____ **1997. Christmas Issue**
32¢ multicolored tagged (single) .50 .20 ⬜⬜⬜⬜⬜
1165 _____
32¢ multicolored tagged (single) .50 .20 ⬜⬜⬜⬜⬜
1166 _____ **1997. Mars Pathfinder Issue**
$3 multicolored tagged *(15,000,000 printed)* 4.50 2.50 ⬜⬜⬜⬜⬜
1167 _____ **1998. Mars Pathfinder Press Sheet Issue**
$3 multicolored tagged (single) 15.00 — ⬜⬜⬜⬜⬜
1168 _____ **1998. Henry R. Luce Issue**
32¢ lake tagged .50 .20 ⬜⬜⬜⬜⬜
1169 _____ **1998. Swamp Coil Issue**
5¢ multicolored .25 .20 ⬜⬜⬜⬜⬜
1169A _____ **1998. Swamp Self-adhesive Coil Issue**
5¢ multicolored .20 .20 ⬜⬜⬜⬜⬜
1170 _____ **1998. Diner Non-Denominated Coil Issue**
25¢ multicolored tagged .40 .20 ⬜⬜⬜⬜⬜
1171 _____ **1998. Lila and De Witt Wallace Issue**
32¢ blue tagged (solid) .50 .20 ⬜⬜⬜⬜⬜
1172 _____ **1998. Ring-necked Pheasant Coil Issue**
20¢ multicolored tagged .40 .20 ⬜⬜⬜⬜⬜
1173 _____ **1998. Ring-necked Pheasant Booklet Issue**
20¢ multicolored tagged (single) .40 .20 ⬜⬜⬜⬜⬜
1174 _____ **1998. Red Fox Issue**
$1 multicolored tagged 1.50 .75 ⬜⬜⬜⬜⬜
1175 _____ **1998. Bicycle Coil Issue**
10¢ multicolored untagged .30 .20 ⬜⬜⬜⬜⬜
1176 _____ **1998. Bicycle Self Adhesive Coil Issue**
10¢ multicolored untagged .30 .20 ⬜⬜⬜⬜⬜
1177 _____ **1998. Diner Coil Issue**
25¢ multicolored untagged .30 .20 ⬜⬜⬜⬜⬜
1178 _____ **1998. Traditional Christmas Issue**
32¢ multicolored .50 .20 ⬜⬜⬜⬜⬜
1179 _____ **1998. Contemporary Christmas Issue**
32¢ Traditional wreath, tagged .50 .20 ⬜⬜⬜⬜⬜
1180 _____
32¢ Colonial wreath, tagged .50 .20 ⬜⬜⬜⬜⬜
1181 _____
32¢ Chili wreath, tagged .50 .20 ⬜⬜⬜⬜⬜
1182 _____
32¢ Tropical wreath, tagged .50 .20 ⬜⬜⬜⬜⬜
1183 _____ **1998. Contemporary Christmas Booklet Issue**
32¢ Traditional wreath .50 .20 ⬜⬜⬜⬜⬜
1184 _____
32¢ Colonial wreath .50 .20 ⬜⬜⬜⬜⬜
1185 _____
32¢ Chili wreath .50 .20 ⬜⬜⬜⬜⬜
1186 _____
32¢ Tropical wreath .50 .20 ⬜⬜⬜⬜⬜
1187 _____
32¢ Traditional wreath .50 .20 ⬜⬜⬜⬜⬜
1188 _____
32¢ Colonial wreath .50 .20 ⬜⬜⬜⬜⬜

	MNHVF	UseVF	

1189 _____
   32¢ **Chili wreath** .50 .20 ☐☐☐☐☐
1190 _____
   32¢ **Tropical wreath** .50 .20 ☐☐☐☐☐
1191 _____ **1998. "H" Make-up Rate, USA White Issue**
   1¢ **multicolored** .25 .20 ☐☐☐☐☐
1192 _____ **1998. "H" Make-Up Rate, USA Light Blue Issue**
   1¢ **multicolored** .25 .20 ☐☐☐☐☐
1193 _____ **1998. Hat "H" First Class Issue**
   33¢ **multicolored** tagged .50 .20 ☐☐☐☐☐
1194 _____ **1998. Hat "H" First Class Coil Issue**
   33¢ **multicolored** tagged .50 .20 ☐☐☐☐☐
1195 _____ **1998. Hat "H" First Class Booklet Issue**
   33¢ **multicolored** tagged .50 .20 ☐☐☐☐☐
1196 _____
   33¢ **multicolored** tagged .50 .20 ☐☐☐☐☐
1197 _____ **1998. Hat "H" First Class Coil Issue**
   33¢ **multicolored** tagged .50 .20 ☐☐☐☐☐

1174

1175, 1176

1178

1179, 1183, 1187
(upper left)
1180, 1184, 1188
(upper right)
1181, 1185, 1189
(lower left)
1182, 1186, 1190
(lower right)

1191

1192

1193-1197

1198, 1199

1200

1201

1202

1203

1206, 1207, 1208
1209, 1210, 1211, 1212

1213

		MNHVF	UseVF

1198 _____ **1998. Uncle Sam Issue**
22¢ **multicolored** tagged — .50 .20 ⬜⬜⬜⬜⬜

1199 _____ **1998. Uncle Sam Coil Issue**
22¢ **multicolored** tagged — .50 .20 ⬜⬜⬜⬜⬜

1200 _____ **1998. Mary Breckinridge Issue**
77¢ **blue** tagged — 1.00 .20 ⬜⬜⬜⬜⬜

1201 _____ **1998. Shuttle Landing Issue**
$3.20 **multicolored** tagged — 4.00 2.75 ⬜⬜⬜⬜⬜

1202 _____ **1998. Shuttle Piggyback Transport Issue**
$11.75 **multicolored** tagged — 14.00 8.00 ⬜⬜⬜⬜⬜

1203 _____ **1998. Hat "H" First Class ATM Vending Issue**
33¢ **multicolored** — .50 .20 ⬜⬜⬜⬜⬜

1204 _____ **1998. Eagle and Shield Coil Issue**
10¢ **multicolored** — .20 .20 ⬜⬜⬜⬜⬜

NOTE: See U.S. Nos. 980 ("Bulk Rate USA"), 1011 and 1012 ("USA Bulk Rate") and 1129 ("USA Bulk Rate").

1205 _____
10¢ **multicolored** — .20 .20 ⬜⬜⬜⬜⬜

1206 _____ **1999. Flag and Skyscrapers Issue**
33¢ **multicolored** — .50 .20 ⬜⬜⬜⬜⬜

1207 _____ **1999. Flag and Skyscrapers Coil Issue**
33¢ **multicolored** — .50 .20 ⬜⬜⬜⬜⬜

1208 _____ **1999. Flag and Skyscrapers Coil Issue**
33¢ **multicolored** — .50 .20 ⬜⬜⬜⬜⬜

1209 _____ **1999. Flag and Skyscrapers Coil Issue**
33¢ **multicolored** — .50 .20 ⬜⬜⬜⬜⬜

1210 _____ **1999. Flag and Skyscrapers Issue**
33¢ **multicolored** — .50 .20 ⬜⬜⬜⬜⬜

1211 _____ **1999. Flag and Skyscrapers Issue**
33¢ **multicolored** — .50 .20 ⬜⬜⬜⬜⬜

1212 _____
33¢ **multicolored** — .50 .20 ⬜⬜⬜⬜⬜

1213 _____ **1999. Flag in Classroom Issue**
33¢ **multicolored** — .50 .20 ⬜⬜⬜⬜⬜

1214 _____ **1999. Fruit Berries Issue**
33¢ Blueberries — .50 .20 ⬜⬜⬜⬜⬜

1215 _____
33¢ Raspberries — .50 .20 ⬜⬜⬜⬜⬜

1216 _____
33¢ Strawberries — .50 .20 ⬜⬜⬜⬜⬜

1217 _____
33¢ Blackberries — .50 .20 ⬜⬜⬜⬜⬜

1218 _____
33¢ Blueberries — .50 .20 ⬜⬜⬜⬜⬜

1219 _____
33¢ Strawberries — .50 .20 ⬜⬜⬜⬜⬜

1220 _____
33¢ Raspberries — .50 .20 ⬜⬜⬜⬜⬜

1221 _____
33¢ Blackberries — .50 .20 ⬜⬜⬜⬜⬜

1222 _____ **1999. Fruit Berries Coil Issue**
33¢ Blackberries — .50 .20 ⬜⬜⬜⬜⬜

1223 _____
33¢ Strawberries — .50 .20 ⬜⬜⬜⬜⬜

1224 _____
33¢ Blueberries — .50 .20 ⬜⬜⬜⬜⬜

	MNHVF	UseVF	

1225 _____
  33¢ Raspberries   .50   .20 ☐☐☐☐☐
1226 _____ **1999. Niagara Falls Issue**
  48¢ **multicolored**   1.00   .20 ☐☐☐☐☐
1227 _____ **1999. Red-headed Woodpecker Issue**
  2¢ **multicolored**   .20   .20 ☐☐☐☐☐
1228 _____ **1999. Justin S. Morrill Issue**
  55¢ **black**   1.00   .20 ☐☐☐☐☐
1229 _____ **1999. American Kestrel Coil Issue**
  1¢ **multicolored**   .20   .20 ☐☐☐☐☐
1230 _____ **1999. Rio Grande Issue**
  40¢ **multicolored**   .75   .20 ☐☐☐☐☐
1231 _____ **1999. Billy Mitchell Issue**
  55¢ **multicolored**   1.00   .40 ☐☐☐☐☐
1232 _____ **1999. Coral Pink Rose Issue**
  33¢ **multicolored**   .50   .20 ☐☐☐☐☐

1214-1217, 1251-1254

1218-1221

1226

1227   1228

1222-1225

1229, 1247   1232, 1255

1230

1233

1231

1234

1235-1238, 1239-1242, 1243-1246

		MNHVF	UseVF	

1233 _____ **1999. Uncle Sam Issue**
22¢ **multicolored**   .50   .20 ☐☐☐☐☐

1234 _____ **1999. Madonna and Child Issue**
33¢ **multicolored**   .50   .20 ☐☐☐☐☐

1235 _____ **1999. Greetings Reindeer Issue**
33¢ **red** background   .50   .20 ☐☐☐☐☐

1236 _____
33¢ **blue** background   .50   .20 ☐☐☐☐☐

1237 _____
33¢ **Violet** background   .50   .20 ☐☐☐☐☐

1238 _____
33¢ **green** background   .50   .20 ☐☐☐☐☐

1239 _____ **1999. Greetings Reindeer Booklet Issue**
33¢ **red** background   .50   .20 ☐☐☐☐☐

1240 _____
33¢ **blue** background   .50   .20 ☐☐☐☐☐

1241 _____
33¢ **violet** background   .50   .20 ☐☐☐☐☐

1242 _____
33¢ **green** background   .50   .20 ☐☐☐☐☐

1243 _____ **1999. Greetings Reindeer Vending Booklet Issue**
33¢ **red** background   .50   .20 ☐☐☐☐☐

1244 _____
33¢ **blue** background   .50   .20 ☐☐☐☐☐

1245 _____
33¢ **violet** background   .50   .20 ☐☐☐☐☐

1246 _____
33¢ **green** background   .50   .20 ☐☐☐☐☐

1247 _____ **1999. American Kestrel Issue**
1¢ **multicolored**   .20   .20 ☐☐☐☐☐

1248 _____ **1999. Ring-necked Pheasant Booklet Issue**
20¢ **multicolored**   .40   .20 ☐☐☐☐☐

1249 _____ **2000. Grand Canyon Issue**
60¢ **multicolored**   1.20   .30 ☐☐☐☐☐

1250 _____ **2000. Eddie Rickenbacker Issue**
60¢ **multicolored**   1.20   .30 ☐☐☐☐☐

1251 _____ **2000. Fruit Berries Issue**
33¢ **multicolored**   1.00   .30 ☐☐☐☐☐

1252 _____
33¢ **multicolored**   1.00   .30 ☐☐☐☐☐

1253 _____
33¢ **multicolored**   1.00   .30 ☐☐☐☐☐

1254 _____
33¢ **multicolored**   1.00   .30 ☐☐☐☐☐

1255 _____ **2000. Coral Pink Rose Issue**
33¢ **multicolored**   .50   .20 ☐☐☐☐☐

1249

1251-1254

	UnFVF	UseFVF

COMMEMORATIVE ISSUES

		UnFVF	UseFVF	
CM1 _____	**1893. Columbian Issues**			
1¢	**deep blue** (449,195,550)	17.50	.35	☐☐☐☐☐
CM2 _____				
2¢	**dull purple** (1,464,588,750)	17.50	.20	☐☐☐☐☐
NOTE: Imperforate 2¢ Columbians are from printer's waste.				
CM3 _____				
3¢	**deep bluish green** (11,501,250)	40.00	11.00	☐☐☐☐☐
CM4 _____				
4¢	**gray blue** (19,181,550)	60.00	5.50	☐☐☐☐☐
CM5 _____				
5¢	**brown** (35,248,250)	65.00	6.00	☐☐☐☐☐
CM6 _____				
6¢	**dark lilac** (4,707,550)	60.00	17.50	☐☐☐☐☐
CM7 _____				
8¢	**brown purple** (10,656,550)	50.00	7.00	☐☐☐☐☐
CM8 _____				
10¢	**black brown** (16,516,950)	95.00	5.50	☐☐☐☐☐
CM9 _____				
15¢	**deep bluish green** (1,576,950)	175.00	50.00	☐☐☐☐☐

CM1

CM2

CM3

CM4

CM5

CM6

CM7

CM8

CM9

CM10

CM11

CM12

		UnFVF	UseFVF	

CM10_____

30¢ **orange brown** (617,250) — 225.00 — 65.00 ☐☐☐☐☐

CM11_____

50¢ **slate black** (243,750) — 350.00 — 125.00 ☐☐☐☐☐

CM12_____

$1 **Venetian red** (55,050) — 1,000.00 — 450.00 ☐☐☐☐☐

CM13_____

$2 **brown red** (45,550) — 1,100.00 — 400.00 ☐☐☐☐☐

CM14_____

$3 **bronze green** (27,650) — 1,700.00 — 725.00 ☐☐☐☐☐

CM15_____

$4 **deep rose** (26,350) — 2,250.00 — 1,000.00 ☐☐☐☐☐

CM16_____

$5 **black** (27,350) — 2,750.00 — 1,600.00 ☐☐☐☐☐

NOTE: For stamps of these designs, but with "1992" instead of "1893" in the top-right corner see Nos. CM1456-61.

CM17_____ **1898. Trans-Mississippi Issue**

1¢ **green** (70,993,400) — 22.50 — 4.75 ☐☐☐☐☐

CM18_____

2¢ **brown red** (159,720,800) — 19.00 — 1.25 ☐☐☐☐☐

CM19_____

4¢ **orange red** (94,924,500) — 100.00 — 17.50 ☐☐☐☐☐

CM20_____

5¢ **deep blue** (7,694,180) — 100.00 — 17.50 ☐☐☐☐☐

CM21_____

8¢ **chocolate** (2,927,200) — 135.00 — 32.50 ☐☐☐☐☐

CM22_____

10¢ **violet black** (4,629,760) — 135.00 — 17.50 ☐☐☐☐☐

CM23_____

50¢ **bronze green** (530,400) — 450.00 — 130.00 ☐☐☐☐☐

CM24_____

$1 **black** (56,900) — 950.00 — 400.00 ☐☐☐☐☐

CM25_____

$2 **red brown** (56,200) — 2,700.00 — 700.00 ☐☐☐☐☐

NOTE: For bicolor versions of the Trans-Mississippi Issue, see Nos. CM1985 and CM1986.

CM26_____ **1901. Pan-American Issue**

1¢ **emerald & black** (91,401,500) — 15.00 — 2.75 ☐☐☐☐☐

CM27_____

2¢ **rose red & black** (209,759,700) — 15.00 — 1.00 ☐☐☐☐☐

CM28_____

4¢ **orange brown & black** (5,737,100) — 70.00 — 12.50 ☐☐☐☐☐

CM29_____

5¢ **gray blue & black** (7,201,300) — 75.00 — 12.50 ☐☐☐☐☐

CM30_____

8¢ **chocolate & black** (4,921,700) — 100.00 — 45.00 ☐☐☐☐☐

CM31_____

10¢ **yellow brown & black** (5,043,700) — 140.00 — 22.50 ☐☐☐☐☐

CM32_____ **1904. Louisiana Purchase Exposition Issue**

1¢ **green** (79,779,200) — 20.00 — 3.50 ☐☐☐☐☐

CM33_____

2¢ **carmine** (192,732,400) — 19.00 — 1.25 ☐☐☐☐☐

CM34_____

3¢ **dark red violet** (4,542,600) — 60.00 — 25.00 ☐☐☐☐☐

CM35_____

5¢ **indigo** (6,926,700) — 75.00 — 17.50 ☐☐☐☐☐

CM13

CM14

CM15

CM16

CM17

CM18

CM19

CM20

CM21

CM22

CM23

CM24

CM25

CM26

CM27

CM28

CM29

CM30

CM31

CM32

CM33

	UnFVF	UseFVF	

CM36_____
  10¢ **red brown** (4,011,200) — 125.00 — 25.00 ☐☐☐☐☐

CM37_____ **1907. Jamestown Issue**
  1¢ **deep bluish green** (77,728,794) — 17.50 — 3.00 ☐☐☐☐☐

CM38_____
  2¢ **rose red** (149,497,994) — 22.50 — 2.75 ☐☐☐☐☐

CM39_____
  5¢ **indigo** (7,980,594) — 85.00 — 22.50 ☐☐☐☐☐
  Perforated 12.

CM40_____ **1909. Lincoln Memorial Centennial Issue**
  2¢ **carmine** (148,387,191) — 5.00 — 1.75 ☐☐☐☐☐
  Imperforate.

CM41_____
  2¢ **carmine** (1,273,900) — 22.50 — 1,750.00 ☐☐☐☐☐
  Bluish gray paper, perforated 12 (Feb. 1909).

CM42_____
  2¢ **carmine** (637,000) — 175.00 — 195.00 ☐☐☐☐☐
  Perforated 12.

CM43_____ **1909. Alaska-Yukon Issue**
  2¢ **carmine** (152,887,311) — 7.00 — 1.50 ☐☐☐☐☐
  Imperforate.

CM44_____
  2¢ **carmine** (525,400) — 30.00 — 22.50 ☐☐☐☐☐
  Perforated 12.

CM45_____ **1909. Hudson-Fulton Issue**
  2¢ **carmine** (72,634,631) — 10.00 — 3.50 ☐☐☐☐☐
  Imperforate.

CM46_____
  2¢ **carmine** (216,480) — 35.00 — 22.50 ☐☐☐☐☐

CM47_____ **1913-15. Panama-Pacific Issue**
  1¢ **green** (334,796,926) — 13.50 — 1.25 ☐☐☐☐☐

CM48_____
  2¢ **rose red** (503,713,086) — 15.00 — .50 ☐☐☐☐☐

CM49_____
  5¢ **blue** (29,088,726) — 55.00 — 8.00 ☐☐☐☐☐

CM50_____
  10¢ **orange yellow** (16,968,365) — 100.00 — 20.00 ☐☐☐☐☐

CM51_____
  10¢ **orange** (16,968,365) (Aug. 1913) — 175.00 — 15.00 ☐☐☐☐☐

CM52_____ **1914-15. Panama-Pacific Issue**
  1¢ **green** — 20.00 — 5.25 ☐☐☐☐☐

CM53_____
  2¢ **rose red** — 60.00 — 1.50 ☐☐☐☐☐

CM54_____
  5¢ **blue** — 125.00 — 13.50 ☐☐☐☐☐

CM55_____
  10¢ **orange** — 750.00 — 55.00 ☐☐☐☐☐

CM56_____ **1919. Victory Issue**
  3¢ **dark lilac** (99,585,200) — 7.50 — 3.00 ☐☐☐☐☐

CM57_____ **1920. Pilgrim Tercentenary Issue**
  1¢ **green** (137,978,207) — 3.50 — 2.50 ☐☐☐☐☐

CM58_____
  2¢ **rose red** (196,037,327) — 5.25 — 1.75 ☐☐☐☐☐

	UnFVF	UseFVF	

CM59_____
5¢   **deep blue** (11,321,607) | | 35.00 | 12.50 ☐☐☐☐☐
Flat plate printing, perforated 11.

CM60_____   **1923. Harding Memorial Issue**
2¢   **black** (1,459,487,085) | | .60 | .20 ☐☐☐☐☐
Flat plate printing, imperforate.

CM61_____
2¢   **black** (770,000) | | 6.50 | 4.50 ☐☐☐☐☐
Rotary press printing, perforated 10.

CM62_____
2¢   **gray black** (99,950,300) | | 15.00 | 1.75 ☐☐☐☐☐
Rotary press printing, perforated 11.

CM63_____
2¢   **gray black** | | | 20,000.00 ☐☐☐☐☐

CM34

CM35

CM36

CM37

CM38

CM39

CM40-42

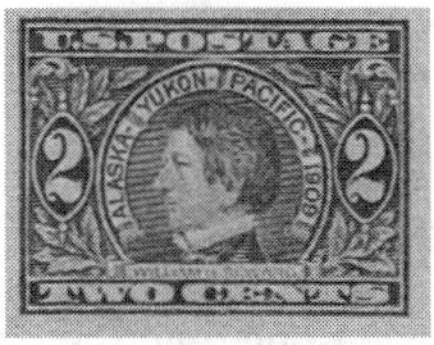

CM43, CM44

CM45

CM47, CM52

CM48, CM53

CM49, CM54

CM50-51, CM55

CM56

CM57

	UnFVF	UseFVF	

CM64_____ **1924. Huguenot-Walloon Issue**
1¢ **green** (51,378,023)   2.75   2.75 □□□□□
CM65_____
2¢ **carmine red** (77,753,423)   5.00   2.00 □□□□□
CM66_____
5¢ **Prussian blue** (5,659,023)   27.50   14.00 □□□□□
CM67_____ **1925. Lexington-Concord Issue**
1¢ **green** (15,615,000)   2.75   2.50 □□□□□
CM68_____
2¢ **carmine red** (26,596,600)   5.00   3.50 □□□□□
CM69_____
5¢ **Prussian blue** (5,348,800)   25.00   14.00 □□□□□
CM70_____ **1925. Norse-American Issue**
2¢ **carmine & black** (9,104,983) 4.00   3.00 □□□□□
CM71_____
5¢ **indigo & black** (1,900,983) 15.00   12.50 □□□□□
CM72_____ **1926. Sesquicentennial Issue**
2¢ **carmine red** (307,731,900)   2.50   .50 □□□□□
CM73_____ **1926. Ericsson Memorial Issue**
5¢ **slate violet** (20,280,500)   6.00   2.50 □□□□□
CM74_____ **1926. White Plains Issue**
2¢ **carmine red** (40,639,485)   2.00   1.50 □□□□□
CM75_____ **1926. White Plains Philatelic Exhibition Issue**
2¢ **carmine red** (107,398)   400.00 425.00 □□□□□
CM76_____ **1927. Vermont Sesquicentennial Issue**
2¢ **carmine red** (39,974,900)   1.25   1.00 □□□□□
CM77_____ **1927. Burgoyne Campaign Issue**
2¢ **carmine red** (25,628,450)   3.50   2.25 □□□□□
CM78_____ **1928. Valley Forge Issue**
2¢ **carmine red** (101,330,328)   1.00   .50 □□□□□
CM79_____ **1928. Hawaiian Sesquicentennial Issue**
2¢ **carmine** (5,519,897)   4.50   4.50 □□□□□
CM80_____
5¢ **blue** (1,459,897)   12.50   12.50 □□□□□
CM81_____ **1928. Molly Pitcher Issue**
2¢ **carmine** (9,779,896)   1.00   1.25 □□□□□
CM82_____ **1928. Aeronautics Conference Issue**
2¢ **carmine red** (51,342,273)   1.25   1.00 □□□□□
CM83_____
5¢ **Prussian blue** (10,319,700) 5.00   3.00 □□□□□
CM84_____ **1929. George Rogers Clark Issue**
2¢ **carmine & black** (16,684,674) .60   .50 □□□□□
Flat press, perforated 11.
CM85_____ **1929. Edison Commemorative Issue**
2¢ **carmine red** (31,679,200)   .75   .75 □□□□□
Rotary press, perforated 11 x 10 1/2.
CM86_____
2¢ **carmine red** (210,119,474)   .75   .25 □□□□□
Rotary press coil, perforated 10 vertically.
CM87_____
2¢ **carmine red** (133,530,000)   12.50   1.50 □□□□□
CM88_____ **1929. Sullivan Expedition Issue**
2¢ **carmine red** (51,451,880)   .75   .75 □□□□□
CM89_____ **1929. Battle of Fallen Timbers Issue**
2¢ **carmine red** (29,338,274)   .75   .75 □□□□□

CM58

CM59

CM60-63

CM64

CM65

CM66

CM67

CM68

CM69

CM70

CM71

CM72

CM73

CM74

CM76

CM77

CM78

CM79

CM75

		UnFVF	UseFVF	

CM90_____ 1929. Ohio River Canalization Issue

2¢	carmine red (32,680,900)	.50	.75	☐☐☐☐☐

CM91_____ 1930. Massachusetts Bay Colony Issue

2¢	carmine red (74,000,774)	.75	.45	☐☐☐☐☐

CM92_____ 1930. Carolina-Charleston Issue

2¢	carmine red (25,215,574)	1.25	1.00	☐☐☐☐☐

CM93_____ 1930. Braddock's Field Issue

2¢	carmine red (25,609,470)	1.00	1.00	☐☐☐☐☐

CM94_____ 1930. Von Steuben Issue

2¢	carmine red (66,487,000)	.50	.50	☐☐☐☐☐

CM95_____ 1931. Pulaski Issue

2¢	carmine red (96,559,400)	.25	.20	☐☐☐☐☐

CM96_____ 1931. Red Cross Issue

2¢	black & scarlet (99,074,600)	.25	.20	☐☐☐☐☐

CM97_____ 1931. Yorktown Issue

2¢	carmine red & black (25,006,400)	.35	.20	☐☐☐☐☐

CM98_____ 1932. Washington Bicentennial Issue

1/2¢	olive brown (87,969,700).	25	.20	☐☐☐☐☐

CM99_____

1¢	yellow green (1,265,555,100)	.25	.20	☐☐☐☐☐

CM100_____

1-1/2¢	yellow brown (304,926,800)	.50	.20	☐☐☐☐☐

CM101_____

2¢	carmine red (4,222,198,300)	.25	.20	☐☐☐☐☐

CM102_____

3¢	slate purple (456,198,500)	.50	.20	☐☐☐☐☐

CM103_____

4¢	yellow brown (151,201,300)	.40	.20	☐☐☐☐☐

CM104_____

5¢	Prussian blue (170,656,100)	1.75	.20	☐☐☐☐☐

CM105_____

6¢	orange (111,739,400)	3.50	.20	☐☐☐☐☐

CM106_____

7¢	black (83,257,400)	.40	.20	☐☐☐☐☐

CM107_____

8¢	bister (96,506,100)	3.00	.75	☐☐☐☐☐

CM108_____

9¢	salmom (75,706,200)	2.50	.20	☐☐☐☐☐

CM109_____

10¢	orange yellow (147,216,000)	12.50	.20	☐☐☐☐☐

CM110_____ 1932. Olympic Winter Games Issue

2¢	carmine red (51,102,800)	.40	.25	☐☐☐☐☐

CM111_____ 1932. Arbor Day Issue

2¢	carmine red (100,869,300)	.25	.20	☐☐☐☐☐

CM112_____ 1932. Olympic Summer Games Issue

3¢	reddish violet (168,885,300)	1.50	.20	☐☐☐☐☐

CM113_____

5¢	blue (52,376,100)	2.25	.30	☐☐☐☐☐

CM114_____ 1932. William Penn Issue

3¢	reddish violet (49,949,000)	.35	.25	☐☐☐☐☐

CM115_____ 1933. Daniel Webster Issue

3¢	reddish violet (49,538,500)	.35	.40	☐☐☐☐☐

CM116_____ 1933. Oglethorpe Issue

3¢	reddish violet (61,719,200)	.35	.25	☐☐☐☐☐

HAWAII
1778 - 1928

CM80

CM81   CM82

CM83   CM84   CM85   CM88

CM89   CM90   CM91   CM92   CM93

CM94   CM95   CM96   CM97

CM98   CM99   CM100   CM101   CM102

CM103   CM104   CM105   CM106   CM107

		UnFVF	UseFVF

CM117_____   **1933. Newburgh Issue**
3¢ **reddish violet** (73,382,400) — .25 — .20 ☐☐☐☐☐
NOTE: For ungummed stamps (Farley Issue), see CM142.

CM118_____   **1933. Century of Progress Issue**
1¢ **yellow green** (348,266,800) — .25 — .20 ☐☐☐☐☐

CM119_____
3¢ **reddish violet** (480,239,300) — .25 — .20 ☐☐☐☐☐

CM120_____   **1933. Century of Progress Souvenir Sheets**
1¢ **yellow green** (456,704) — 35.00 — 32.50 ☐☐☐☐☐

CM121_____
3¢ **reddish violet** (441,172) — 30.00 — 27.50 ☐☐☐☐☐
NOTE: For ungummed stamps (Farley issue) see CM156 & CM157.

CM122_____   **1933. NRA Issue**
3¢ **reddish violet** (1,978,707,300) — .25 — .20 ☐☐☐☐☐

CM123_____   **1933. Byrd Antarctic Issue**
3¢ **blue** (5,735,944) — .75 — .60 ☐☐☐☐☐
NOTE: For ungummed stamps (Farley issue), see CM143.

CM124_____   **1933. Kosciuszko Issue**
5¢ **blue** (45,137,700) — .75 — .35 ☐☐☐☐☐

CM125_____   **1934. Byrd Souvenir Sheet**
3¢ **blue** (811,404) — 17.50 — 16.50 ☐☐☐☐☐
NOTE: For ungummed stamps (Farley issue), see CM158.

CM126_____   **1934. Maryland Tercentenary Issue**
3¢ **carmine red** (46,258,300) — .25 — .20 ☐☐☐☐☐
Rotary press, perforated 11 x 10 1/2.

CM127_____   **1934. Mother's Day Issue**
3¢ **reddish violet** (193,239,100) — .25 — .20 ☐☐☐☐☐
Flat press, perforated 11.

CM128_____
3¢ **reddish violet** (15,432,200) — .25 — .20 ☐☐☐☐☐
NOTE: For ungummed stamps (Farley issue), see CM144.

CM129_____   **1934. Wisconsin Tercentenary Issue**
3¢ **reddish violet** (64,525,400) — .25 — .20 ☐☐☐☐☐
NOTE: For ungummed stamps (Farley issue), see CM145.

CM130_____   **1934. National Parks Issue**
1¢ **green** (84,896,350) — .25 — .20 ☐☐☐☐☐

CM131_____
2¢ **red** (74,400,200) — .25 — .20 ☐☐☐☐☐

CM132_____
3¢ **reddish violet** (95,089,000) — .25 — .20 ☐☐☐☐☐

CM133_____
4¢ **yellow brown** (19,178,650) — .50 — .35 ☐☐☐☐☐

CM134_____
5¢ **light blue** (30,980,100) — 1.00 — .75 ☐☐☐☐☐

CM135_____
6¢ **blue** (16,923,350) — 1.25 — 1.00 ☐☐☐☐☐

CM136_____
7¢ **black** (15,988,250) — 1.00 — .75 ☐☐☐☐☐

CM137_____
8¢ **gray green** (15,288,700) — 2.00 — 1.75 ☐☐☐☐☐

CM138_____
9¢ **orange red** (17,472,600) — 2.00 — .75 ☐☐☐☐☐

CM139_____
10¢ **gray black** (18,874,300) — 3.25 — 1.25 ☐☐☐☐☐
NOTE: For ungummed stamps, (Farley issue), see CM146-CM155.

CM108   CM109   CM110   CM111

CM112   CM113   CM114   CM115   CM116

CM117, CM142   CM118

CM119   CM122

CM123, CM143   CM124

CM120, CM156

CM121, 157

CM125, CM158

		UnFVF	UseFVF

CM140_____ 1934. Trans-Mississippi Philatelic Exposition Issue

1¢ **green,** sheet of 6 (793,551)   14.00   12.50 ❑❑❑❑❑

NOTE: For ungummed stamps, (Farley issue), see CM159.

CM141_____ 1934. American Philatelic Society Issue

3¢ **reddish violet,** sheet of 6 (511,391)   40.00   30.00 ❑❑❑❑❑

NOTE: For ungummed stamps (Farley issue), see CM160.

CM142_____ 1935. Newburgh Farley Issue

3¢ **reddish violet** (3,274,556)   .25   .20 ❑❑❑❑❑

CM143_____ 1935. Byrd Farley Issue

3¢ **blue** (2,040,760)   .50   .45 ❑❑❑❑❑

CM144_____ 1935. Mother's Day Farley Issue

3¢ **reddish violet** (2,389,288)   .60   .60 ❑❑❑❑❑

CM145_____ 1935. Wisconsin Farley Issue

3¢ **reddish violet** (2,294,948)   .60   .60 ❑❑❑❑❑

CM146_____ 1935. National Parks Farley Issue

1¢ **green** (3,217,636)   .25   .20 ❑❑❑❑❑

CM147_____

2¢ **red** (2,746,640)   .25   .20 ❑❑❑❑❑

CM148_____

3¢ **reddish violet** (2,168,088)   .50   .45 ❑❑❑❑❑

CM149_____

4¢ **yellow brown** (1,822,684)   1.25   1.25 ❑❑❑❑❑

CM150_____

5¢ **light blue** (1,724,576)   1.75   1.75 ❑❑❑❑❑

CM151_____

6¢ **blue** (1,647,696)   2.25   2.25 ❑❑❑❑❑

CM152w _____

7¢ **black** (1,682,948)   2.00   1.75 ❑❑❑❑❑

CM153_____

8¢ **gray green** (1,638,644)   2.00   2.00 ❑❑❑❑❑

CM154_____

9¢ **orange red** (1,625,224)   2.00   2.00 ❑❑❑❑❑

CM155_____

10¢ **gray black** (1,644,900)   4.00   3.50 ❑❑❑❑❑

CM156_____ 1935. Century of Progress Souvenir Sheet, Farley Issue

1¢ **yellow green** (2,467,800)   22.50   22.50 ❑❑❑❑❑

CM157_____

3¢ **reddish violet** (2,147,856)   20.00   20.00 ❑❑❑❑❑

CM158_____ 1935. Byrd Souvenir Sheet, Farley Issue

3¢ **blue** (1,603,200)   17.50   12.50 ❑❑❑❑❑

CM159_____ 1935. National Parks Souvenir Sheets, Farley Issue

1¢ **green** (1,679,760)   10.00   9.00 ❑❑❑❑❑

CM160_____

3¢ **reddish violet** (1,295,520)   25.00   20.00 ❑❑❑❑❑

CM161_____ 1935. Airmail Special Delivery Farley Issue

16¢ **blue** (1,370,560)   2.75   2.50 ❑❑❑❑❑

CM162_____ 1935. Connecticut Tercentenary Issue

3¢ **purple** (70,726,800)   .25   .20 ❑❑❑❑❑

NOTE: For imperforates, see No. CM168.

CM163_____ 1935. California-Pacific Issue

3¢ **dark lilac** (100,839,600)   .25   .20 ❑❑❑❑❑

NOTE: For imperforates, see No. CM168.

CM164_____ 1935. Boulder Dam Issue

3¢ **dark lilac** (73,610,650)   .25   .20 ❑❑❑❑❑

CM126

CM129, CM145 ➡️

⬅️ CM127-128, CM144

CM130, CM146

CM131, CM147

CM132, CM148

CM134, CM150

CM133, CM149

CM135, CM151

CM138, CM154

CM139, CM155

CM136, CM152

CM137, CM153

CM141, CM160

CM140, CM159

CM162 ⬅️

CM163

CM164

	UnFVF	UseFVF

CM165_____ 1935. Michigan Centennial Issue
3¢ dark lilac (75,823,900)   .25   .20 ☐☐☐☐☐
NOTE: For imperforates, see No. CM168.

CM166_____ 1936. Texas Centennial Issue
3¢ dark lilac (124,324,500)   .25   .20 ☐☐☐☐☐
NOTE: For imperforates, see No. CM168.

CM167_____ 1936. Rhode Island Tercentenary Issue
3¢ dull purple (67,127,650)   .25   .20 ☐☐☐☐☐

CM168_____ 1936. TIPEX Souvenir Sheet
4x3¢ reddish purple (2,809,039)   2.75   2.50 ☐☐☐☐☐

CM169_____ 1936. Arkansas Centennial Issue
3¢ dark lilac (72,992,650)   .25   .20 ☐☐☐☐☐

CM170_____ 1936. Oregon Territory Centennial Issue
3¢ dark lilac (74,407,450)   .25   .20 ☐☐☐☐☐

CM171_____ 1936. Susan B. Anthony Issue
3¢ reddish purple (269,522,200)   .25   .20 ☐☐☐☐☐

CM172_____ 1936-37. Army Issue
1¢ green (105,196,150)   .25   .20 ☐☐☐☐☐

CM173_____
2¢ rose red (93,848,500)   .25   .20 ☐☐☐☐☐

CM174_____
3¢ dull purple (87,741,150)   .25   .20 ☐☐☐☐☐

CM175_____
4¢ slate (35,794,150)   .50   .20 ☐☐☐☐☐

CM176_____
5¢ gray blue (36,839,250)   .75   .20 ☐☐☐☐☐

CM177_____ 1936-37. Navy Issue
1¢ green (104,773,450)   .25   .20 ☐☐☐☐☐

CM178_____
2¢ rose red (92,054,550)   .25   .20 ☐☐☐☐☐

CM179_____
3¢ dull purple (93,291,650)   .25   .20 ☐☐☐☐☐

CM180_____
4¢ slate (34,521,950)   .50   .20 ☐☐☐☐☐

CM181_____
5¢ gray blue (36,819,050)   .75   .20 ☐☐☐☐☐

CM182_____ 1937. Northwest Ordinance Issue of 1787
3¢ dull purple (84,825,250)   .25   .20 ☐☐☐☐☐

CM183_____ 1937. Virginia Dare Issue
5¢ light slate blue (25,040,400)   .25   .20 ☐☐☐☐☐

CM184_____ 1937. Society of Philatelic Americans Souvenir Sheet
10¢ blue green (5,277,445)   .75   .65 ☐☐☐☐☐

CM185_____ 1937. Constitution Sesquicentennial Issue
3¢ bright purple (99,882,300)   .25   .20 ☐☐☐☐☐

CM186_____ 1937. Hawaii Territory Issue
3¢ violet (78,454,450)   .25   .20 ☐☐☐☐☐

CM187_____ 1937. Alaska Territory Issue
3¢ violet (77,004,200)   .25   .20 ☐☐☐☐☐

CM188_____ 1937. Puerto Rico Territory Issue
3¢ light reddish violet (81,292,450)   .25   .20 ☐☐☐☐☐

CM189_____ 1937. Virgin Islands Issue
3¢ lilac (76, 474,550)   .25   .20 ☐☐☐☐☐

CM190_____ 1938. Constitution Ratification Issue
3¢ violet (73,043,650)   .50   .20 ☐☐☐☐☐

CM165

CM166

CM167

CM168

CM169

CM171

CM170

CM172

CM173

CM174

CM175

CM176

CM177

CM178

CM179

CM180

CM181

CM182

CM183

	UnFVF	UseFVF

CM191_____ **1938. Swedes and Finns Issue**
3¢ **carmine purple** (58,564,368)   .25   .20 ☐☐☐☐☐

CM192_____ **1938. Northwest Territory Issue**
3¢ **light reddish violet** (65,939,500)   .25   .20 ☐☐☐☐☐

CM193_____ **1938. Iowa Territory Issue**
3¢ **violet** (47,064,300)   .25   .20 ☐☐☐☐☐

CM194_____ **1939. Golden Gate Exposition Issue**
3¢ **light reddish violet** (114,439,600)   .25   .20 ☐☐☐☐☐

CM195_____ **1939. New York World's Fair Issue**
3¢ **bluish violet** (101,699,550)   .25   .20 ☐☐☐☐☐

CM196_____ **1939. Washington Inauguration Issue**
3¢ **bright purple** (73,764,550)   .25   .20 ☐☐☐☐☐

CM197_____ **1939. Baseball Centennial Issue**
3¢ **violet** (81,269,600)   2.25   .20 ☐☐☐☐☐

CM198_____ **1939. Panama Canal Issue**
3¢ **deep reddish purple** (67,813,350)   .50   .20 ☐☐☐☐☐

CM199_____ **1939. Printing Tercentenary Issue**
3¢ **violet** (71,394,750)   .25   .20 ☐☐☐☐☐

CM200_____ **1939. Four States Issue**
3¢ **reddish purple** (66,835,000)   .25   .20 ☐☐☐☐☐

CM184

CM185

CM186

CM187

CM188

CM191

CM189

CM190

CM192

CM193

CM197

CM194

CM195

CM196

CM199 ←

CM198

CM200

CM201

CM202

CM203

CM204

CM205

CM206

CM207

CM208

CM209

CM210

CM211

CM212

CM213

CM214

CM215

CM216

CM217

CM218

		MNHVF	UseVF

CM201_____ **1940. Famous Americans Series**

		MNHVF	UseVF	
1¢ **emerald** (56,348,320)		.25	.20	❑❑❑❑❑
CM202_____				
2¢ **carmine** (53,177,110)		.25	.20	❑❑❑❑❑
CM203_____				
3¢ **bright purple** (53,260,270)		.25	.20	❑❑❑❑❑
CM204_____				
5¢ **gray blue** (22,104,950)		.40	.25	❑❑❑❑❑
CM205_____				
10¢ **sepia** (13,201,270)		2.25	1.75	❑❑❑❑❑
CM206_____				
1¢ **emerald** (51,603,580)		.25	.20	❑❑❑❑❑
CM207_____				
2¢ **carmine** (52,100,510)		.25	.20	❑❑❑❑❑
CM208_____				
3¢ **bright purple** (51,666,580)		.25	.20	❑❑❑❑❑
CM209_____				
5¢ **gray blue** (22,207,780)		.45	.25	❑❑❑❑❑
CM210_____				
10¢ **sepia** (11,835,530)		2.25	1.75	❑❑❑❑❑
CM211_____				
1¢ **emerald** (52,471,160)		.25	.20	❑❑❑❑❑
CM212_____				
2¢ **carmine** (52,366,440)		.25	.20	❑❑❑❑❑
CM213_____				
3¢ **bright purple** (51,636,270)		.25	.20	❑❑❑❑❑
CM214_____				
5¢ **gray blue** (20,729,030)		.40	.30	❑❑❑❑❑
CM215_____				
10¢ **sepia** (14,125,580)		2.50	1.75	❑❑❑❑❑
CM216_____				
1¢ **emerald** (59,409,000)		.25	.20	❑❑❑❑❑
CM217_____				
2¢ **carmine** (57,888,600)		.25	.20	❑❑❑❑❑
CM218_____				
3¢ **bright purple** (58,273,180)		.25	.20	❑❑❑❑❑
CM219_____				
5¢ **gray blue** (23,779,000)		.50	.20	❑❑❑❑❑
CM220_____				
10¢ **sepia** (15,112,580)		1.50	1.50	❑❑❑❑❑
CM221_____				
1¢ **emerald** (57,322,790)		.25	.20	❑❑❑❑❑
CM222_____				
2¢ **carmine** (58,281,580)		.25	.20	❑❑❑❑❑
CM223_____				
3¢ **bright purple** (56,398,790)		.25	.20	❑❑❑❑❑
CM224_____				
5¢ **gray blue** (21,147,000)		.75	.30	❑❑❑❑❑
CM225_____				
10¢ **sepia** (13,328,000)		5.00	2.00	❑❑❑❑❑
CM226_____				
1¢ **emerald** (54,389,510)		.25	.20	❑❑❑❑❑
CM227_____				
2¢ **carmine** (53,636,580)		.25	.20	❑❑❑❑❑

CM219

CM220

CM221

CM222

CM223

CM224

CM225

CM226

CM227

CM228

CM229

CM230

CM231

CM232

CM233

CM234

CM235

CM236

CM237

CM238

CM239

CM240

CM241

CM242

CM243

CM244

CM245

	MNHVF	UseVF
CM228_____		
3¢ **bright purple** (55,313,230)	.25	.20
CM229_____		
5¢ **gray blue** (21,720,580)	.75	.30
CM230_____		
10¢ **sepia** (13,600,580)	2.00	1.75
CM231_____		
1¢ **emerald** (47,599,580)	.25	.20
CM232_____		
2¢ **carmine** (53,766,510)	.25	.20
CM233_____		
3¢ **bright purple** (54,193,580)	.25	.20
CM234_____		
5¢ **gray blue** (20,264,580)	1.25	.50
CM235_____		
10¢ **sepia** (13,726,580)	15.00	3.25
CM236_____ **1940. Pony Express Issue**		
3¢ **chestnut** (46,497,400)	.35	.20
CM237_____ **1940. Pan-American Union Issue**		
3¢ **lilac** (47,700,000)	.30	.20
CM238_____ **1940. Idaho Statehood Issue**		
3¢ **light reddish violet** (50,618,150)	.25	.20
CM239_____ **1940. Wyoming Statehood Issue**		
3¢ **purple brown** (50,034,400)	.25	.20
CM240_____ **1940. Coronado Expedition Issue**		
3¢ **reddish lilac** (60,943,700)	.25	.20
CM241_____ **1940. National Defense Issue**		
1¢ **emerald** (6,081,409,300)	.25	.20
CM242_____		
2¢ **rose** (5,211,708,200)	.25	.20
CM243_____		
3¢ **light reddish violet** (8,384,867,600)	.25	.20
CM244_____ **1940. Thirteenth Amendment Issue**		
3¢ **violet** (44,389,550)	.35	.20
CM245_____ **1941. Vermont Statehood Issue**		
3¢ **violet** (54,574,550)	.25	.20
CM246_____ **1942. Kentucky Statehood Issue**		
3¢ **reddish violet** (63,558,400)	.25	.20
CM247_____ **1942. Win the War Issue**		
3¢ **violet** (20,642,793,300)	.25	.20
CM248_____ **1942. Chinese Commemorative Issue**		
5¢ **Prussian blue** (21,272,800)	.60	.30
CM249_____ **1943. Allied Nations Issue**		
2¢ **carmine** (1,671,564,200)	.25	.20
CM250_____ **1943. Four Freedoms Issue**		
1¢ **emerald** (1,227,334,200)	.25	.20
CM251_____ **1943-44. Overrun Countries Issue**		
5¢ **slate violet, scarlet & black** (19,999,646)	.25	.20
CM252_____		
5¢ **slate violet, blue, scarlet & black** (19,999,646)	.25	.20
CM253_____		
5¢ **slate violet, rose red, ultramarine & black** (19,999,616)	.25	.20
CM254_____		
5¢ **slate violet, rose red, light blue & black** (19,999,646)	.25	.20

CM246

CM247

CM248

CM249

CM250

CM251

CM252

CM253

CM254

CM255

CM256

CM257

CM258

CM259

CM260

CM261

CM262

CM263

CM264

	MNHVF	UseVF	

CM255_____

5¢ **slate violet, scarlet, blue & black** (19,999,646)   .25   .20 ☐☐☐☐☐

CM256_____

5¢ **slate violet, scarlet, greenish yellow & black** (19,999,646)   .25   .20 ☐☐☐☐☐

CM257_____

5¢ **slate violet, blue, red & black** (19,999,648)   .25   .20 ☐☐☐☐☐

CM258_____

5¢ **slate violet, pale light blue & black** (14,999,646)   .50   .20 ☐☐☐☐☐

CM259_____

5¢ **slate violet, blue, rose red & black** (14,999,646)   .30   .20 ☐☐☐☐☐

CM260_____

5¢ **slate violet, red & black** (14,999,646)   .30   .20 ☐☐☐☐☐

CM261_____

5¢ **slate violet, red & black** (14,999,646)   .30   .20 ☐☐☐☐☐

CM262_____

5¢ **slate violet, scarlet & black** (14,999,646)   .30   .20 ☐☐☐☐☐

CM263_____

5¢ **slate violet, scarlet, bright blue & gray** (14,999,646)   .30   .20 ☐☐☐☐☐

CM264_____   **1944. Transcontinental Railroad Issue**

3¢ **violet** (61,303,000)   .30   .20 ☐☐☐☐☐

CM265_____   **1944. Steamship Issue**

3¢ **violet** (61,001,450)   .25   .20 ☐☐☐☐☐

CM266_____   **1944. Telegraph Centennial Issue**

3¢ **bright purple** (60,605,000)   .25   .20 ☐☐☐☐☐

CM267_____   **1944. Corregidor Issue**

3¢ **violet** (50,129,350)   .25   .20 ☐☐☐☐☐

CM268_____   **1944. Motion Picture Issue**

3¢ **violet** (53,479,400)   .25   .20 ☐☐☐☐☐

CM269_____   **1945. Florida Centennial Issue**

3¢ **bright purple** (61,617,350)   .25   .20 ☐☐☐☐☐

CM270_____   **1945. United Nations Conference Issue**

5¢ **ultramarine** (75,500,000)   .25   .20 ☐☐☐☐☐

CM271_____   **1945-46. Roosevelt Series**

1¢ **blue green** (128,140,000)   .25   .20 ☐☐☐☐☐

CM265

CM266

CM267

CM268

CM269

CM270

CM271

CM272

CM273

CM274

CM275 ←

CM276

CM277

CM278

CM279

CM280

CM281

CM282

CM283

CM284

CM285

CM286

CM287 ←

CM288

CM289

	MNHVF	UseVF

CM272_____

2¢ **carmine red** (67,255,000) .25 .20 ☐☐☐☐☐

CM273_____

3¢ **lilac** (138,870,000) .25 .20 ☐☐☐☐☐

CM274_____

5¢ **light blue** (76,455,400) .25 .20 ☐☐☐☐☐

CM275_____ **1945. Marine Commemorative**

3¢ **dark yellow green** (137,321,000) .25 .20 ☐☐☐☐☐

CM276_____ **1945. Army Commemorative**

3¢ **brown olive** (128,357,750) .25 .20 ☐☐☐☐☐

CM277_____ **1945. Navy Commemorative**

3¢ **blue** (138,863,000) .25 .20 ☐☐☐☐☐

CM278_____ **1945. Coast Guard Commemorative**

3¢ **blue green** (111,616,700) .25 .20 ☐☐☐☐☐

CM279_____ **1946. Merchant Marine Commemorative**

3¢ **blue green** (135,927,000) .25 .20 ☐☐☐☐☐

CM280_____ **1945. Alfred E. Smith Issue**

3¢ **dark lilac** (308,587,700) .25 .20 ☐☐☐☐☐

CM281_____ **1945. Texas Statehood Issue**

3¢ **Prussian blue** (170,640,000) .25 .20 ☐☐☐☐☐

CM282_____ **1946. Honorable Discharge Stamp**

3¢ **violet** (269,339,100) .25 .20 ☐☐☐☐☐

CM283_____ **1946. Tennessee Statehood Issue**

3¢ **violet** (132,274,500) .25 .20 ☐☐☐☐☐

CM284_____ **1946. Iowa Statehood Issue**

3¢ **Prussian blue** (132,430,000) .25 .20 ☐☐☐☐☐

CM285_____ **1946. Smithsonian Institution Issue**

3¢ **brown purple** (139,209,500) .25 .20 ☐☐☐☐☐

CM286_____ **1946. Kearny Expedition Issue**

3¢ **brown purple** (114,684,450) .25 .20 ☐☐☐☐☐

CM287_____ **1947. Thomas A. Edison Issue**

3¢ **bright purple** (156,540,510) .25 .20 ☐☐☐☐☐

CM288_____ **1947. Joseph Pulitzer Issue**

3¢ **dark lilac** (120,452,600) .25 .20 ☐☐☐☐☐

CM289_____ **1947. Postage Stamp Centenary Issue**

3¢ **blue** (127,104,300) .25 .20 ☐☐☐☐☐

CM290_____ **1947. CIPEX Souvenir Sheet**

15¢ **Complete sheet of 2 stamps** (10,299,600) .75 .65 ☐☐☐☐☐

CM291_____ **1947. The Doctors Issue**

3¢ **brown purple** (132,902,000) .25 .20 ☐☐☐☐☐

CM292_____ **1947. Utah Issue**

3¢ **violet** (131,968,000) .25 .20 ☐☐☐☐☐

CM293_____ **1947. U.S. Frigate Constitution Issue**

3¢ **blue green** (131,488,000) .25 .20 ☐☐☐☐☐

CM294_____ **1947. Everglades National Park Issue**

3¢ **emerald** (122,362,000) .25 .20 ☐☐☐☐☐

CM295_____ **1948. George Washington Carver Issue**

3¢ **bright purple** (121,548,000) .25 .20 ☐☐☐☐☐

CM296_____ **1948. California Gold Centennial Issue**

3¢ **violet** (131,109,500) .25 .20 ☐☐☐☐☐

CM297_____ **1948. Mississippi Territory Issue**

3¢ **brown purple** (122,650,500) .25 .20 ☐☐☐☐☐

CM298_____ **1948. Four Chaplains Issue**

3¢ **black** (121,953,500) .25 .20 ☐☐☐☐☐

CM290

CM291

CM292

CM293

CM294

CM295

CM296

CM297

CM298

CM299

CM300

CM301

CM302
→

CM303

CM304

CM305

	MNHVF	UseVF

CM299_____   1948. Wisconsin Centennial Issue
3¢   violet (115,250,000)   .25   .20 ☐☐☐☐☐

CM300_____   1948. Swedish Pioneers Issue
5¢   blue (64,198,500)   .25   .20 ☐☐☐☐☐

CM301_____   1948. The Progress of Women Issue
3¢   violet (117,642,500)   .25   .20 ☐☐☐☐☐

CM302_____   1948. William Allen White Issue
3¢   bright purple (77,649,000)   .25   .20 ☐☐☐☐☐

CM303_____   1948. United States - Canada Friendship Issue
3¢   blue (113,474,500)   .25   .20 ☐☐☐☐☐

CM304_____   1948. Francis Scott Key Issue
3¢   carmine (120,868,500)   .25   .20 ☐☐☐☐☐

CM305_____   1948. American Youth Issue
3¢   blue (77,800,500)   .25   .20 ☐☐☐☐☐

CM306_____   1948. Oregon Territory Issue
3¢   Venetian red (52,214,000)   .25   .20 ☐☐☐☐☐

CM307_____   1948. Harlan Fiske Stone Issue
3¢   bright purple (53,958,100)   .25   .20 ☐☐☐☐☐

CM308_____   1948. Palomar Mountain Observatory Issue
3¢   blue (61,120,010)   .25   .20 ☐☐☐☐☐

CM309_____   1948. Clara Barton Issue
3¢   carmine (57,823,000)   .25   .20 ☐☐☐☐☐

CM310_____   1948. Poultry Industry Centennial Issue
3¢   sepia (52,975,000)   .25   .20 ☐☐☐☐☐

CM311_____   1948. Gold Star Mothers Issue
3¢   yellow (77,149,000)   .25   .20 ☐☐☐☐☐

CM312_____   1948. Fort Kearny Issue
3¢   violet (58,332,000)   .25   .20 ☐☐☐☐☐

CM313_____   1948. Volunteer Fireman Issue
3¢   rose carmine (56,228,000)   .25   .20 ☐☐☐☐☐

CM314_____   1948. Indian Centennial Issue
3¢   brown (57,832,000)   .25   .20 ☐☐☐☐☐

CM315_____   1948. Rough Riders Issue
3¢   brown purple (53,875,000)   .25   .20 ☐☐☐☐☐

CM316_____   1948. Juliette Low Issue
3¢   blue green (63,834,000)   .25   .20 ☐☐☐☐☐

CM317_____   1948. Will Rogers Issue
3¢   bright purple (67,162,200)   .25   .20 ☐☐☐☐☐

CM318_____   1948. Fort Bliss Centennial Issue
3¢   chestnut (64,561,000)   .35   .20 ☐☐☐☐☐

CM319_____   1948. Moina Michael Issue
3¢   rose carmine (64,079,500)   .25   .20 ☐☐☐☐☐

CM320_____   1948. Gettysburg Address Issue
3¢   light blue (63,388,000)   .25   .20 ☐☐☐☐☐

CM321_____   1948. American Turners Issue
3¢   carmine (62,285,000)   .25   .20 ☐☐☐☐☐

CM322_____   1948. Joel Chandler Harris Issue
3¢   bright purple (57,492,610)   .25   .20 ☐☐☐☐☐

CM323_____   1949. Minnesota Territory Issue
3¢   blue green (99,190,000)   .25   .20 ☐☐☐☐☐

CM324_____   1949. Washington and Lee University Issue
3¢   bright blue (104,790,000)   .25   .20 ☐☐☐☐☐

CM325_____   1949. Puerto Rico Election Issue
3¢   dull green (108,805,000)   .25   .20 ☐☐☐☐☐

CM306

CM307

CM308

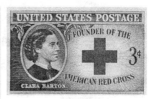

CM309

CM310

CM311

CM312

CM313

CM314

CM315

CM316

CM317

CM318

CM319

CM320

CM321

CM322

CM323

CM324

CM325

CM326

	MNHVF	UseVF

CM326_____   **1949. Annapolis Tercentenary Issue**
3¢ **turquoise green** (107,340,000) — .25 — .20 ☐☐☐☐☐

CM327_____   **1949. GAR Issue**
3¢ **carmine** (117,020,000) — .25 — .20 ☐☐☐☐☐

CM328_____   **1949. Edgar Allan Poe Issue**
3¢ **bright purple** (122,633,000) — .25 — .20 ☐☐☐☐☐

CM329_____   **1950. American Bankers Association Issue**
3¢ **green** (130,960,000) — .25 — .20 ☐☐☐☐☐

CM330_____   **1950. Samuel Gompers Issue**
3¢ **bright purple** (128,478,000) — .25 — .20 ☐☐☐☐☐

CM331_____   **1950. National Capital Sesquicentennial Issue**
3¢ **light blue** (132,090,000) — .25 — .20 ☐☐☐☐☐

CM332_____
3¢ **dull green** (130,050,000) — .25 — .20 ☐☐☐☐☐

CM333_____
3¢ **bluish violet** (131,350,000) — .25 — .20 ☐☐☐☐☐

CM334_____
3¢ **bright purple** (129,980,000) — .25 — .20 ☐☐☐☐☐

CM335_____   **1950. Railroad Engineers Issue**
3¢ **brown purple** (122,315,000) — .25 — .20 ☐☐☐☐☐

CM336_____   **1950. Kansas City Centennial Issue**
3¢ **violet** (122,170,000) — .25 — .20 ☐☐☐☐☐

CM337_____   **1950. Boy Scout Issue**
3¢ **sepia** (131,635,000) — .25 — .20 ☐☐☐☐☐

CM338_____   **1950. Indiana Territory Sesquicentennial Issue**
3¢ **light blue** (121,860,000) — .25 — .20 ☐☐☐☐☐

CM339_____   **1950. California Statehood Centennial Issue**
3¢ **yellow** (121,120,000) — .25 — .20 ☐☐☐☐☐

CM340_____   **1951. Confederate Veterans Issue**
3¢ **gray** (119,120,000) — .25 — .20 ☐☐☐☐☐

CM341_____   **1951. Nevada Centennial Issue**
3¢ **light olive green** (112,125,000) — .25 — .20 ☐☐☐☐☐

CM342_____   **1952. Detroit Issue**
3¢ **light blue** (114,140,000) — .25 — .20 ☐☐☐☐☐

CM343_____   **1951. Colorado Statehood Issue**
3¢ **violet blue** (114,490,000) — .25 — .20 ☐☐☐☐☐

CM344_____   **1951. American Chemical Society Issue**
3¢ **brown purple** (117,200,000) — .25 — .20 ☐☐☐☐☐

CM345_____   **1951. Battle of Brooklyn Issue**
3¢ **violet** (16,130,000) — .25 — .20 ☐☐☐☐☐

CM346_____   **1952. Betsy Ross Issue**
3¢ **carmine red** (116,175,000) — .25 — .20 ☐☐☐☐☐

CM347_____   **1952. 4-H Club Issue**
3¢ **blue green** (115,945,000) — .25 — .20 ☐☐☐☐☐

CM348_____   **1952. American Railroads Issue**
3¢ **light blue** (112,540,000) — .25 — .20 ☐☐☐☐☐

CM349_____   **1952. AAA Issue**
3¢ **blue** (117,415,000) — .25 — .20 ☐☐☐☐☐

CM350_____   **1952. NATO Issue**
3¢ **violet** (2,899,580,000) — .25 — .20 ☐☐☐☐☐

CM351_____   **1952. Grand Coulee Dam Issue**
3¢ **blue green** (114,540,000) — .25 — .20 ☐☐☐☐☐

CM352_____   **1952. Lafayette Issue**
3¢ **bright blue** (113,135,000) — .25 — .20 ☐☐☐☐☐

CM327

CM328

CM329

CM330

CM331

CM332

CM333

CM334

CM335

CM336

CM337

CM338

CM339

CM340

CM341

CM342

CM343

CM344

CM345

	MNHVF	UseVF

CM353_____ **1952. Mount Rushmore Memorial Issue**
3¢ **blue green** (116,255,000) | .25 | .20 ☐☐☐☐☐

CM354_____ **1952. Engineering Centennial Issue**
3¢ **ultramarine** (113,860,000) | .25 | .20 ☐☐☐☐☐

CM355_____ **1952. Service Women Issue**
3¢ **blue** (124,260,000) | .25 | .20 ☐☐☐☐☐

CM356_____ **1952. Gutenberg Bible Issue**
3¢ **violet** (115,735,000) | .25 | .20 ☐☐☐☐☐

CM357_____ **1952. Newspaperboys of America Issue**
3¢ **violet** (115,430,000) | .25 | .20 ☐☐☐☐☐

CM358_____ **1952. International Red Cross Issue**
3¢ **ultramarine & scarlet** (136,220,000) | .25 | .20 ☐☐☐☐☐

CM359_____ **1953. National Guard Issue**
3¢ **light blue** (114,894,600) | .25 | .20 ☐☐☐☐☐

CM360_____ **1953. Ohio Sesquicentennial Issue**
3¢ **sepia** (117,706,000) | .25 | .20 ☐☐☐☐☐

CM361_____ **1953. Washington Territory Issue**
3¢ **blue green** (114,190,000) | .25 | .20 ☐☐☐☐☐

CM362_____ **1953. Louisiana Purchase Issue**
3¢ **brown purple** (113,990,000) | .25 | .20 ☐☐☐☐☐

CM363_____ **1953. Opening of Japan Issue**
5¢ **blue green** (89,289,600) | .25 | .20 ☐☐☐☐☐

CM364_____ **1953. American Bar Association Issue**
3¢ **light reddish violet** (114,865,000) | .25 | .20 ☐☐☐☐☐

CM365_____ **1953. Sagamore Hill Issue**
3¢ **green** (115,780,000) | .25 | .20 ☐☐☐☐☐

CM346

CM347

CM348

CM349

CM350

CM351

CM352

CM353

CM354

CM355

CM356

CM357

CM358

CM359

CM360

CM361

CM362

CM363

CM364

CM365

CM366

CM367

CM368

CM369

CM370

CM371

CM372

	MNHVF	UseVF

CM366_____ **1953. Future Farmers of America Issue**
3¢ bright blue (115,224,600) .25 .20 ☐☐☐☐☐

CM367_____ **1953. Trucking Industry Issue**
3¢ violet (123,709,600) .25 .20 ☐☐☐☐☐

CM368_____ **1953. General Patton Issue**
3¢ bluish violet (114,789,600) .25 .20 ☐☐☐☐☐

CM369_____ **1953. New York City Tercentenary Issue**
3¢ bright purple (115,759,600) .25 .20 ☐☐☐☐☐

CM370_____ **1953. Gadsden Purchase Issue**
3¢ Venetian red (115,759,600) .25 .20 ☐☐☐☐☐

CM371_____ **1953. Columbia University Issue**
3¢ cobalt blue (118,540,000) .25 .20 ☐☐☐☐☐

CM372_____ **1954. Nebraska Territorial Centennial Issue**
3¢ violet (115,810,000) .25 .20 ☐☐☐☐☐

CM373_____ **1954. Kansas Territorial Centennial Issue**
3¢ salmon (113,603,700) .25 .20 ☐☐☐☐☐

CM374_____ **1954. George Eastman Issue**
3¢ brown purple (121,100,000) .25 .20 ☐☐☐☐☐

CM375_____ **1954. Lewis and Clark Expedition Issue**
3¢ brown (116,078,150) .25 .20 ☐☐☐☐☐

CM376_____ **1955. Pennsylvania Academy of Fine Arts Issue**
3¢ brown purple (116,139,800) .25 .20 ☐☐☐☐☐

CM377_____ **1955. First Land-Grant College Issue**
3¢ emerald green (120,484,800) .25 .20 ☐☐☐☐☐

CM378_____ **1955. Rotary International Issue**
8¢ deep blue (53,854,750) .25 .20 ☐☐☐☐☐

CM379_____ **1955. The Armed Forces Reserve Issue**
3¢ bright purple (176,075,000) .25 .20 ☐☐☐☐☐

CM380_____ **1955. Old Man of the Mountains Issue**
3¢ blue green (125,944,400) .25 .20 ☐☐☐☐☐

CM381_____ **1955. Soo Locks Centennial Issue**
3¢ blue (122,284,600) .25 .20 ☐☐☐☐☐

CM382_____ **1955. Atoms for Peace Issue**
3¢ deep blue (133,638,850) .25 .20 ☐☐☐☐☐

CM383_____ **1955. Fort Ticonderoga Bicentennial Issue**
3¢ dark red brown (118,664,600) .25 .20 ☐☐☐☐☐

CM384_____ **1955. Andrew Mellon Issue**
3¢ carmine red (112,434,000) .25 .20 ☐☐☐☐☐

CM385_____ **1956. Franklin 250th Anniversary Issue**
3¢ carmine (129,384,550) .25 .20 ☐☐☐☐☐

CM386_____ **1956. Booker T. Washington Issue**
3¢ deep blue (121,184,600) .25 .20 ☐☐☐☐☐

CM387_____ **1956. FIPEX Issue**
3¢ violet (119,784,200) .25 .20 ☐☐☐☐☐

CM388_____ **1956. Fifth International Philatelic Exhibition (FIPEX) Souvenir Sheet**
11¢ Complete sheet of 2 stamps (9,802,025) 2.50 2.00 ☐☐☐☐☐

CM389_____ **1956. Wild Turkey Issue**
3¢ brown purple (123,159,400) .25 .20 ☐☐☐☐☐

CM390_____ **1956. Pronghorn Antelope Issue**
3¢ sepia (123,138,800) .25 .20 ☐☐☐☐☐

CM391_____ **1956. King Salmon Issue**
3¢ blue green (109,275,000) .25 .20 ☐☐☐☐☐

CM392_____ **1956. Pure Food and Drug Laws Issue**
3¢ blue green (112,932,200) .25 .20 ☐☐☐☐☐

CM373

CM374

CM375

 CM376

CM377

CM378

CM379

CM380

CM381

ATOMS FOR PEACE

CM382

CM383

CM384

CM386

CM385

CENTENNIAL OF BOOKER T. WASHINGTON

CM387

CM388

CM389

	MNHVF	UseVF

CM393_____   **1956. Wheatland Issue**
3¢ **black brown** (125,475,000)   .25   .20 ▢▢▢▢▢

CM394_____   **1956. Labor Day Issue**
3¢ **deep blue** (117,855,000)   .25   .20 ▢▢▢▢▢

CM395_____   **1956. Nassau Hall Issue**
3¢ **black on orange** (122,100,00)   .25   .20 ▢▢▢▢▢

CM396_____   **1956. Devils Tower Issue**
3¢ **lilac** (118,180,000)   .25   .20 ▢▢▢▢▢

CM397_____   **1956. Children's Issue**
3¢ **blue** (100,975,000)   .25   .20 ▢▢▢▢▢

CM398_____   **1957. Alexander Hamilton Bicentennial Issue**
3¢ **rose red** (115,299,450)   .25   .20 ▢▢▢▢▢

CM399_____   **1957. Anti-Polio Issue**
3¢ **bright purple** (186,949,250)   .25   .20 ▢▢▢▢▢

CM400_____   **1957. Coast and Geodetic Survey Issue**
3¢ **deep blue** (115,235,000)   .25   .20 ▢▢▢▢▢

CM401_____   **1957. Architects of America Issue**
3¢ **rose lilac** (106,647,500)   .25   .20 ▢▢▢▢▢

CM402_____   **1957. Steel Industry in America Issue**
3¢ **bright blue** (112,010,000)   .25   .20 ▢▢▢▢▢

CM403_____   **1957. International Naval Review Issue**
3¢ **blue green** (118,399,600)   .25   .20 ▢▢▢▢▢

CM404_____   **1957. Oklahoma Statehood Issue**
3¢ **bright blue** (102,209,500)   .25   .20 ▢▢▢▢▢

CM405_____   **1957. Teachers of America Issue**
3¢ **brown purple** (103,045,000)   .25   .20 ▢▢▢▢▢

CM406_____   **1957. American Flag Issue**
4¢ **deep blue & carmine** (84,054,400)   .25   .20 ▢▢▢▢▢

CM407_____   **1957. Virginia of Sagadahock Issue**
3¢ **violet** (126,266,000)   .25   .20 ▢▢▢▢▢

CM408_____   **1957. Ramon Magsaysay Issue**
8¢ **scarlet, deep ultramarine & ocher** (39,489,600)   .25   .20 ▢▢▢▢▢

CM409_____   **1957. Lafayette Issue**
3¢ **brown purple** (122,990,000)   .25   .20 ▢▢▢▢▢

CM410_____   **1957. Whooping Crane Issue**
3¢ **gray blue, yellow & blue green** (174,372,800)   .25   .20 ▢▢▢▢▢

CM411_____   **1957. Flushing Remonstrance Issue**
3¢ **brown black** (114,365,000)   .25   .20 ▢▢▢▢▢

CM412_____   **1958. Garden and Horticultural Issue**
3¢ **dull green** (122,765,200)   .25   .20 ▢▢▢▢▢

CM413_____   **1958. Brussels Universal and International Exhibition Issue**
3¢ **brown purple** (113,660,200)   .25   .20 ▢▢▢▢▢

CM414_____   **1958. James Monroe Issue**
3¢ **violet** (120,196,580)   .25   .20 ▢▢▢▢▢

CM415_____   **1958. Minnesota Statehood Centennial Issue**
3¢ **emerald green** (120,805,200)   .25   .20 ▢▢▢▢▢

CM416_____   **1958. International Geophysical Year Issue**
3¢ **black & red** (125,815,200)   .25   .20 ▢▢▢▢▢

CM417_____   **1958. Gunston Hall Bicentennial Issue**
3¢ **dull green** (108,415,200)   .25   .20 ▢▢▢▢▢

CM418_____   **1958. Mackinac Straits Bridge Issue**
3¢ **turquoise blue** (107,195,200)   .25   .20 ▢▢▢▢▢

CM419_____   **1958. Simon Bolívar Issue**
4¢ **olive buff** (115,745,280)   .25   .20 ▢▢▢▢▢

CM390

CM391

CM392

CM393

CM394

CM395

CM396

CM397

CM398

CM399

CM400

CM401

CM402

CM403

CM404

CM405

CM406

CM407

	MNHVF	UseVF

CM420_____   **1958. Simon Bolívar Issue**
8¢ scarlet, deep ultramarine & deep ocher (39,743,640)   .25   .20 ❑❑❑❑❑

CM421_____   **1958. Atlantic Cable Centennial Issue**
4¢ red violet (114,570,200)   .25   .20 ❑❑❑❑❑

CM422_____   **1958. Lincoln Douglas Debate Issue**
4¢ brown (114,860,200)   .25   .20 ❑❑❑❑❑

CM423_____   **1958. Lajos Kossuth Issue**
4¢ dull green (120,561,280)   .25   .20 ❑❑❑❑❑

CM424_____
8¢ scarlet, deep ultramarine & deep ochre (44,064,576)   .25   .20 ❑❑❑❑❑

CM425_____   **1958. Journalism and Freedom of the Press Issue**
4¢ gray black (118,390,200)   .25   .20 ❑❑❑❑❑

CM426_____   **1958. Overland Mail Centennial Issue**
4¢ orange red (125,770,200)   .25   .20 ❑❑❑❑❑

CM427_____   **1958. Noah Webster Bicentennial Issue**
4¢ magenta (114,114,280)   .25   .20 ❑❑❑❑❑

CM428_____   **1958. Forest Conservation Issue**
4¢ deep green, yellow & brown (156,600,200)   .25   .20 ❑❑❑❑❑

CM429_____   **1958. Fort Duquesne Bicentennial Issue**
4¢ light blue (124,200,200)   .25   .20 ❑❑❑❑❑

CM430_____   **1959. Lincoln Sesquicentennial Issue**
1¢ deep green (120,400,200)   .25   .20 ❑❑❑❑❑

CM431_____   **1959. Head of Lincoln Issue**
3¢ deep plum (91,160,200)   .25   .20 ❑❑❑❑❑

CM432_____   **1959. Lincoln Statue Issue**
4¢ blue (126,500,000)   .25   .20 ❑❑❑❑❑

CM433_____   **1959. Oregon Statehood Issue**
4¢ blue green (120,740,200)   .25   .20 ❑❑❑❑❑

CM434_____   **1959. José de San Martin Issue**
4¢ blue (113,623,280)   .25   .20 ❑❑❑❑❑

CM435_____
8¢ carmine, blue & ocher (45,569,088)   .25   .20 ❑❑❑❑❑

CM436_____   **1959. NATO Issue**
4¢ blue (122,493,280)   .25   .20 ❑❑❑❑❑

CM437_____   **1959. Arctic Explorations Issue**
4¢ turquoise blue (131,260,200)   .25   .20 ❑❑❑❑❑

CM438_____   **1959. Peace through Trade Issue**
8¢ brown purple (47,125,200)   .25   .20 ❑❑❑❑❑

CM439_____   **1959. Silver Centennial Issue**
4¢ black (123,105,000)   .25   .20 ❑❑❑❑❑

CM440_____   **1959. St. Lawrence Seaway Issue**
4¢ blue & red (126,105,050)   .25   .20 ❑❑❑❑❑

CM441_____   **1959. 49-Star Flag Issue**
4¢ deep blue & carmine (209,170,000)   .25   .20 ❑❑❑❑❑

CM442_____   **1959. Soil Conservation Issue**
4¢ blue green & yellow orange (120,835,000)   .25   .20 ❑❑❑❑❑

CM443_____   **1959. Petroleum Industry Centennial Issue**
4¢ brown (115,715,000)   .25   .20 ❑❑❑❑❑

CM444_____   **1959. Dental Health Issue**
4¢ dark green (118,445,000)   .25   .20 ❑❑❑❑❑

CM445_____   **1959. Ernst Reuter Issue**
4¢ black (111,685,000)   .25   .20 ❑❑❑❑❑

CM446_____
8¢ carmine, blue & ocher (43,099,200)   .25   .20 ❑❑❑❑❑

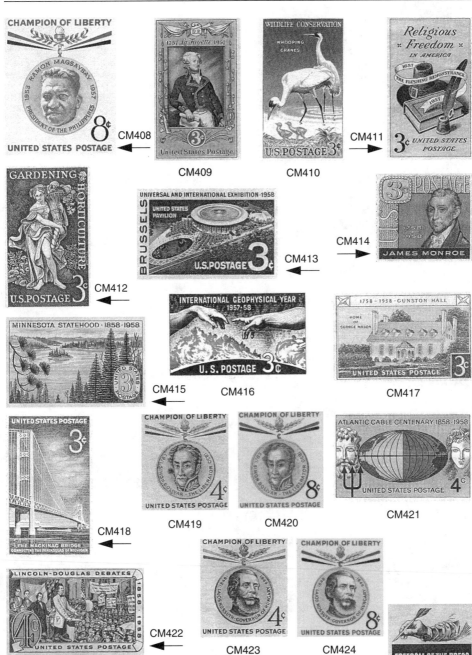

CHAMPION OF LIBERTY
RAMON MAGSAYSAY
PRESIDENT OF THE PHILIPPINES
8¢
UNITED STATES POSTAGE
CM408

1757 La Fayette 1957
3¢
United States Postage
CM409

WILDLIFE CONSERVATION
WHOOPING CRANES
U.S.POSTAGE 3¢
CM410

Religious Freedom IN AMERICA
1657
THE FLUSHING REMONSTRANCE
1957
3¢ UNITED STATES POSTAGE
CM411

GARDENING HORTICULTURE
3¢
U.S.POSTAGE
CM412

UNIVERSAL AND INTERNATIONAL EXHIBITION-1958
UNITED STATES PAVILION
BRUSSELS
U.S.POSTAGE 3¢
CM413

3¢ POSTAGE
1758 1958
JAMES MONROE
CM414

MINNESOTA STATEHOOD · 1858-1958
UNITED STATES POSTAGE 3¢
CM415

INTERNATIONAL GEOPHYSICAL YEAR 1957-58
U. S. POSTAGE 3¢
CM416

1758 - 1958 · GUNSTON HALL
HOME OF GEORGE MASON
UNITED STATES POSTAGE 3¢
CM417

UNITED STATES POSTAGE
3¢
THE MACKINAC BRIDGE
CONNECTING THE PENINSULAS OF MICHIGAN
CM418

CHAMPION OF LIBERTY
SIMON BOLIVAR THE LIBERATOR
4¢
UNITED STATES POSTAGE
CM419

CHAMPION OF LIBERTY
SIMON BOLIVAR THE LIBERATOR
8¢
UNITED STATES POSTAGE
CM420

ATLANTIC CABLE CENTENARY 1858-1958
4¢
UNITED STATES POSTAGE
CM421

LINCOLN-DOUGLAS DEBATES 1858 · 1958
4¢
UNITED STATES POSTAGE
CM422

CHAMPION OF LIBERTY
KOSSUTH-GOVERNOR OF HUNGARY
4¢
UNITED STATES POSTAGE
CM423

CHAMPION OF LIBERTY
KOSSUTH-GOVERNOR OF HUNGARY
8¢
UNITED STATES POSTAGE
CM424

1858 OVERLAND MAIL 1958
U.S.POSTAGE 4¢
CM426

UNITED STATES POSTAGE
NOAH WEBSTER
4¢
CM427

FREEDOM OF THE PRESS
U.S.POSTAGE 4¢
CM425

CM429

CM428 ← → CM430   CM431 →

CM432

CM433

CM434 ←

CM435 ←

CM436 ←

CM437

CM438

CM439

CM440

CM441

CM442

CM443

CM444

CM445

CM446 ←

CM447

CM448

CM449

CM450

CM451

CM452

CM453

CM454

CM455 ➡

CM456 ⬅

CM457 ⬅

CM458 ➡

CM459

CM460

CM461 ➡

CM462 ⬅

CM463

CM464 ➡

	MNHVF	UseVF

CM447_____ **1959. Ephraim McDowell Issue**
4¢ brown purple (115,444,000)   .25   .20 ☐☐☐☐☐

CM448_____ **1960. George Washington Issue**
4¢ deep blue & carmine (126,470,000)   .25   .20 ☐☐☐☐☐

CM449_____ **1960. Benjamin Franklin Issue**
4¢ brown bister & emerald (124,460,000)   .25   .20 ☐☐☐☐☐

CM450_____ **1960. Thomas Jefferson Issue**
4¢ gray & scarlet (115,445,000)   .25   .20 ☐☐☐☐☐

CM451_____ **1960. Francis Scott Key**
4¢ carmine red & deep blue (122,060,000)   .25   .20 ☐☐☐☐☐

CM452_____ **1960. Abraham Lincoln Issue**
4¢ bright purple & green (120,540,000)   .25   .20 ☐☐☐☐☐

CM453_____ **1960. Patrick Henry Issue**
4¢ green & brown (113,075,000)   .25   .20 ☐☐☐☐☐

CM454_____ **1960. Boy Scout Issue**
4¢ red, deep blue & deep ocher (139,325,000)   .25   .20 ☐☐☐☐☐

CM455_____ **1960. Winter Olympic Games Issue**
4¢ turquoise blue (124,445,000)   .25   .20 ☐☐☐☐☐

CM456_____ **1960. Tomas G. Masaryk Issue**
4¢ blue (113,792,000)   .25   .20 ☐☐☐☐☐

CM457_____
8¢ carmine, deep blue & ocher (44,215,200)   .25   .20 ☐☐☐☐☐

CM458_____ **1960. World Refugee Year Issue**
4¢ gray black (113,195,000)   .25   .20 ☐☐☐☐☐

CM459_____ **1960. Water Conservation Issue**
4¢ blue, green & orange brown (120,570,000)   .25   .20 ☐☐☐☐☐

CM460_____ **1960. SEATO Issue**
4¢ blue (115,353,000)   .25   .20 ☐☐☐☐☐

CM461_____ **1960. American Women Issue**
4¢ violet (111,080,000)   .25   .20 ☐☐☐☐☐

CM462_____ **1960. 50-Star Flag Issue**
4¢ deep blue & scarlet (153,025,000)   .25   .20 ☐☐☐☐☐

CM463_____ **1960. Pony Express Centenary Issue**
4¢ sepia (119,665,000)   .25   .20 ☐☐☐☐☐

CM464_____ **1960. Employ the Handicapped Issue**
4¢ blue (117,855,000)   .25   .20 ☐☐☐☐☐

CM465_____ **1960. Fifth World Forestry Congress Issue**
4¢ blue green (118,185,000)   .25   .20 ☐☐☐☐☐

CM466_____ **1960. Mexican Independence Issue**
4¢ deep green & carmine red (112,260,000)   .25   .20 ☐☐☐☐☐

CM467_____ **1960. United States of America-Japan Centennial Issue**
4¢ light blue & carmine (125,010,000)   .25   .20 ☐☐☐☐☐

CM468_____ **1960. Ignace Jan Paderewski Issue**
4¢ blue (119,798,000)   .25   .20 ☐☐☐☐☐

CM469_____
8¢ red, blue & ocher (42,696,000)   .25   .20 ☐☐☐☐☐

CM470_____ **1960. Robert A. Taft Issue**
4¢ violet (115,171,000)   .25   .20 ☐☐☐☐☐

CM471_____ **1960. Wheels of Freedom Issue**
4¢ blue (109,695,000)   .25   .20 ☐☐☐☐☐

CM472_____ **1960. Boys' Club of America Issue**
4¢ deep blue, black & red (123,690,000)   .25   .20 ☐☐☐☐☐

CM473_____ **1960. First Automated Post Office Issue**
4¢ deep blue & scarlet (127,970,000)   .25   .20 ☐☐☐☐☐

CM465

CM466

CM467

CM468

CM469

CM470

CM471

CM472

CM473

CM474

CM475

CM476

CM477

CM478

CM479

CM480

CM481

CM482

CM483

CM484

CM485

	MNHVF	UseVF	

CM474_____ **1960. Baron Karl Gustaf Emil Mannerheim Issue**
4¢ **blue** (124,796,000)   .25   .20 ▢▢▢▢▢

CM475_____
8¢ **red, blue & ocher** (42,076,800)   .25   .20 ▢▢▢▢▢

CM476_____ **1960. Campfire Girls Issue**
4¢ **blue & red** (116,215,000)   .25   .20 ▢▢▢▢▢

CM477_____ **1960. Giuseppe Garibaldi Issue**
4¢ **green** (126,252,000)   .25   .20 ▢▢▢▢▢

CM478_____
8¢ **red, blue & ocher** (42,746,400)   .25   .20 ▢▢▢▢▢

CM479_____ **1960. Walter F. George Issue**
4¢ **violet** (124,117,000)   .25   .20 ▢▢▢▢▢

CM480_____ **1960. John Foster Dulles Issue**
4¢ **violet** (177,187,000)   .25   .20 ▢▢▢▢▢

CM481_____ **1960. Andrew Carnegie Issue**
4¢ **claret** (119,840,000)   .25   .20 ▢▢▢▢▢

CM482_____ **1960. Echo I Satellite Issue**
4¢ **violet** (125,290,000)   .25   .20 ▢▢▢▢▢

CM483_____ **1961. Mahatma Gandhi Issue**
4¢ **red orange** (112,966,000)   .25   .20 ▢▢▢▢▢

CM484_____
8¢ **red, blue & ocher** (41,644,200)   .25   .20 ▢▢▢▢▢

CM485_____ **1961. Range Conservation Issue**
4¢ **blue, orange & indigo** (110,850,000)   .25   .20 ▢▢▢▢▢

CM486_____ **1961. Horace Greeley Issue**
4¢ **violet** (98,616,000)   .25   .20 ▢▢▢▢▢

CM487_____ **1961. Fort Sumter Issue**
4¢ **green** (101,125,000)   .25   .20 ▢▢▢▢▢

CM488_____ **1962. Battle of Shiloh Issue**
4¢ **black on pink** (124,865,000)   .25   .20 ▢▢▢▢▢

CM489_____ **1963. Battle of Gettysburg Issue**
5¢ **gray & blue** (79,905,000)   .25   .20 ▢▢▢▢▢

CM490_____ **1964. Battle of the Wilderness Issue**
5¢ **brown, purple & black** (125,410,000)   .25   .20 ▢▢▢▢▢

CM491_____ **1965. Appomattox Issue**
5¢ **blue & black** (112,845,000)   .25   .20 ▢▢▢▢▢

CM492_____ **1961. Kansas Statehood Centennial Issue**
4¢ **brown, lake & green** on yellow paper (106,210,000)   .25   .20 ▢▢▢▢▢

CM493_____ **1961. George William Norris Issue**
4¢ **blue green** (110,810,000)   .25   .20 ▢▢▢▢▢

CM494_____ **1961. Naval Aviation Issue**
4¢ **blue** (116,995,000)   .25   .20 ▢▢▢▢▢

CM495_____ **1961. Workman's Compensation Issue**
4¢ **ultramarine** on bluish paper (121,015,000)   .25   .20 ▢▢▢▢▢

CM496_____ **1961. Frederic Remington Issue**
4¢ **blue, red & yellow** (111,600,000)   .25   .20 ▢▢▢▢▢

CM497_____ **1961. 50th Anniversary of the Republic of China Issue**
4¢ **blue** (110,620,000)   .25   .20 ▢▢▢▢▢

CM498_____ **1961. Naismith-Basketball Issue**
4¢ **brown** (109,110,000)   .25   .20 ▢▢▢▢▢

CM499_____ **1961. Nursing Issue**
4¢ **blue, black, orange & flesh** (145,350,000)   .25   .20 ▢▢▢▢▢

CM500_____ **1962. New Mexico Statehood Issue**
4¢ **light blue, bister & brown purple** (112,870,000)   .25   .20 ▢▢▢▢▢

CM486

CM487

CM488

CM489

CM490

CM491

CM492

CM493

CM494

CM495

CM496

CM497

CM498

CM499

CM500

CM501

		MNHVF	UseVF

CM501_____ **1962. Arizona Statehood Issue**
4¢ **scarlet, deep blue & green** (121,820,000) — .25 — .20 ☐☐☐☐☐

CM502_____ **1962. Project Mercury Issue**
4¢ **deep blue & yellow** (289,240,000) — .25 — .20 ☐☐☐☐☐

CM503_____ **1962. Malaria Eradication Issue**
4¢ **blue & bister** (120,155,000) — .25 — .20 ☐☐☐☐☐

CM504_____ **1962. Charles Evans Hughes Issue**
4¢ **black** on yellow paper (124,595,000) — .25 — .20 ☐☐☐☐☐

CM505_____ **1962. Seattle World's Fair Issue**
4¢ **red & deep blue** (147,310,000) — .25 — .20 ☐☐☐☐☐

CM506_____ **1962. Louisiana Statehood Commemorative Issue**
4¢ **gray green, blue & vermilion** (118,690,000) — .25 — .20 ☐☐☐☐☐

CM507_____ **1962. Homestead Act Issue**
4¢ **slate blue** (122,730,000) — .25 — .20 ☐☐☐☐☐

CM508_____ **1962. Girl Scouts of America Issue**
4¢ **red** (126,515,000) — .25 — .20 ☐☐☐☐☐

CM509_____ **1962. Brien McMahon Issue**
4¢ **violet** (130,960,000) — .25 — .20 ☐☐☐☐☐

CM510_____ **1962. National Apprenticeship Issue**
4¢ **black,** on buff (120,055,000) — .25 — .20 ☐☐☐☐☐

CM511_____ **1962. Sam Rayburn Issue**
4¢ **brown & blue** (120,715,000) — .25 — .20 ☐☐☐☐☐

CM512_____ **1962. Dag Hammarskjöld Issue**
4¢ **black, brown & yellow** (121,440,000) — .25 — .20 ☐☐☐☐☐

CM513_____ **1962. Dag Hammarskjöld Special Issue**
4¢ **black, brown & yellow** (40,270,000) — .55 — .25 ☐☐☐☐☐

CM514_____ **1962. Higher Education Issue**
4¢ **blue, green & black** (120,035,000) — .25 — .20 ☐☐☐☐☐

CM515_____ **1962. Winslow Homer Issue**
4¢ **multicolored** (117,870,000) — .25 — .20 ☐☐☐☐☐

CM516_____ **1963. Carolina Charter Issue**
5¢ **dark carmine & brown** (129,445,000) — .25 — .20 ☐☐☐☐☐

CM517_____ **1963. Food for Peace Issue**
5¢ **green, yellow & red** (135,620,000) — .25 — .20 ☐☐☐☐☐

CM518_____ **1963. West Virginia Statehood Issue**
5¢ **green, red & black** (137,540,000) — .25 — .20 ☐☐☐☐☐

CM519_____ **1963. Emancipation Proclamation Issue**
5¢ **bright blue, scarlet & indigo** (132,435,000) — .25 — .20 ☐☐☐☐☐

CM520_____ **1963. Alliance for Progress Issue**
5¢ **bright blue & green** (135,520,000) — .25 — .20 ☐☐☐☐☐

CM521_____ **1963. Cordell Hull Issue**
5¢ **blue green** (131,420,000) — .25 — .20 ☐☐☐☐☐

CM522_____ **1963. Eleanor Roosevelt Issue**
5¢ **purple** (133,170,000) — .25 — .20 ☐☐☐☐☐

CM523_____ **1963. National Academy of Science Issue**
5¢ **turquoise, blue & black** (139,195,000) — .25 — .20 ☐☐☐☐☐

CM524_____ **1963. City Mail Delivery Issue**
5¢ **red, gray & blue,** tagged (128,450,000) — .25 — .20 ☐☐☐☐☐

CM525_____ **1963. International Red Cross Issue**
5¢ **deep gray & red** (116,665,000) — .25 — .20 ☐☐☐☐☐

CM526_____ **1963. John James Audubon Issue**
5¢ **multicolored** (175,175,000) — .25 — .20 ☐☐☐☐☐

CM527_____ **1964. Sam Houston Issue**
5¢ **black** (125,995,000) — .25 — .20 ☐☐☐☐☐

CM502

CM503

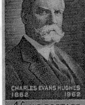

CM504

CM505

CM506

CM507

CM508

CM509

CM510

CM511

CM512

CM513

CM514

CM515

CM516

CM517

CM518

CM519

	MNHVF	UseVF

CM528_____ **1964. Charles M. Russell Issue**
5¢ multicolored (128,025,000) .25 .20 ❑❑❑❑❑

CM529_____ **1964. New York World's Fair Issue**
5¢ green (145,700,000) .25 .20 ❑❑❑❑❑

CM530_____ **1964. John Muir Issue**
5¢ brown, green, brownish gray & olive green (120,310,000) .25 .20 ❑❑❑❑❑

CM531_____ **1964. John F. Kennedy Memorial Issue**
5¢ gray blue (500,000,000) .25 .20 ❑❑❑❑❑

CM532_____ **1964. New Jersey Tercentenary Issue**
5¢ ultramarine (123,845,000) .25 .20 ❑❑❑❑❑

CM533_____ **1964. Nevada Statehood Issue**
5¢ multicolored (122,825,000) .25 .20 ❑❑❑❑❑

CM534_____ **1964. Register and Vote Issue**
5¢ blue & red (325,000,000) .25 .20 ❑❑❑❑❑

CM535_____ **1964. William Shakespeare Issue**
5¢ brown on tan paper (123,245,000) .25 .20 ❑❑❑❑❑

CM536_____ **1964. Doctors Mayo Issue**
5¢ green (123,355,000) .25 .20 ❑❑❑❑❑

CM537_____ **1964. American Music Issue**
5¢ red, gray & blue on granite paper (126,370,000) .25 .20 ❑❑❑❑❑

CM538_____ **1964. Homemakers Issue**
5¢ multicolored on buff (121,250,000) .25 .20 ❑❑❑❑❑

CM539_____ **1964. Verrazano-Narrows Bridge Issue**
5¢ green (125,005,000) .25 .20 ❑❑❑❑❑

CM540_____ **1964. Abstract Art Issue**
5¢ blue, black & red (125,800,000) .25 .20 ❑❑❑❑❑

CM541_____ **1964. Amateur Radio Operators Issue**
5¢ purple (122,230,000) .25 .20 ❑❑❑❑❑

CM542_____ **1965. Battle of New Orleans Issue**
5¢ carmine, blue & slate (115,695,000) .25 .20 ❑❑❑❑❑

CM543_____ **1965. Sokol Centennial - Physical Fitness Issue**
5¢ lake & deep slate (115,095,000) .25 .20 ❑❑❑❑❑

CM544_____ **1965. Crusade Against Cancer Issue**
5¢ reddish violet, black & red (116,560,000) .25 .20 ❑❑❑❑❑

CM545_____ **1965. Winston Churchill Memorial Issue**
5¢ black (125,180,000) .25 .20 ❑❑❑❑❑

CM546_____ **1965. Magna Carta Issue**
5¢ black, yellow & reddish-violet (120,135,000) .25 .20 ❑❑❑❑❑

CM547_____ **1965. UN International Cooperation Year Issue**
5¢ turquoise blue & slate (115,405,000) .25 .20 ❑❑❑❑❑

CM548_____ **1965. Salvation Army Issue**
5¢ red, black & deep blue (115,855,000) .25 .20 ❑❑❑❑❑

CM549_____ **1965. Dante Alighieri Issue**
5¢ carmine red on light venetian red paper (115,340,000) .25 .20 ❑❑❑❑❑

CM550_____ **1965. Herbert Hoover Issue**
5¢ red (114,840,000) .25 .20 ❑❑❑❑❑

CM551_____ **1965. Robert Fulton Issue**
5¢ blue & black (116,140,000) .25 .20 ❑❑❑❑❑

CM552_____ **1965. European Settlement Issue**
5¢ yellow, red & black (116,900,000) .25 .20 ❑❑❑❑❑

CM553_____ **1965. Traffic Safety Issue**
5¢ green, black & red (114,085,000) .25 .20 ❑❑❑❑❑

CM554_____ **1965. John Singleton Copley Issue**
5¢ black & tones of brown & olive (114,880,000) .25 .20 ❑❑❑❑❑

CM520

CM521
➡️

CM522

CM524
⬅️

CM523

CM525

CM526
➡️

CM527

CM528

CM529

CM531

CM532

CM533

CM530
⬅️

CM537

CM534

CM535

CM536

CM538

	MNHVF	UseVF

CM555_____ **1965. International Telecommunication Union Issue**
11¢ yellow, red & black (26,995,000) .25 .20 ⬜⬜⬜⬜⬜

CM556_____ **1965. Adlai Stevenson Issue**
5¢ light blue gray, black, red & blue (128,495,000) .25 .20 ⬜⬜⬜⬜⬜

CM557_____ **1966. Migratory Bird Treaty Issue**
5¢ red, blue & light blue (116,835,000) .25 .20 ⬜⬜⬜⬜⬜

CM558_____ **1966. Humane Treatment of Animals Issue**
5¢ reddish brown & black (117,470,000) .25 .20 ⬜⬜⬜⬜⬜

CM559_____ **1966. Indiana Statehood Issue**
5¢ blue, yellow & brown (123,770,000) .25 .20 ⬜⬜⬜⬜⬜

CM560_____ **1966. American Circus Issue**
5¢ red, blue, pink & black (131,270,000) .25 .20 ⬜⬜⬜⬜⬜

CM561_____ **1966. Sixth International Philatelic Exhibition Issue**
5¢ multicolored (122,285,000) .25 .20 ⬜⬜⬜⬜⬜

CM562_____ **1966. SIPEX Souvenir Sheet**
5¢ multicolored (14,680,000) .30 .25 ⬜⬜⬜⬜⬜

CM563_____ **1966. Bill of Rights Issue**
5¢ red & blue (114,160,000) .25 .20 ⬜⬜⬜⬜⬜

CM564_____ **1966. Polish Millennium Issue**
5¢ red (126,475,000) .25 .20 ⬜⬜⬜⬜⬜

CM565_____ **1966. National Park Service Issue**
5¢ multicolored (119,535,000) .25 .20 ⬜⬜⬜⬜⬜

CM566_____ **1966. Marine Corps Reserve Issue**
5¢ black, olive, red & blue (125,110,000) .25 .20 ⬜⬜⬜⬜⬜

CM567_____ **1966. General Federation of Women's Clubs Issue**
5¢ pink, blue & black (114,853,000) .25 .20 ⬜⬜⬜⬜⬜

CM568_____ **1966. Johnny Appleseed Issue**
5¢ black, red & green (124,290,000) .25 .20 ⬜⬜⬜⬜⬜

CM569_____ **1966. Beautification of America Issue**
5¢ black, green & pink (128,460,000) .25 .20 ⬜⬜⬜⬜⬜

CM570_____ **1966. Great River Road Issue**
5¢ salmon, blue, olive yellow & yellow green (127,585,000) .25 .20 ⬜⬜⬜⬜⬜

CM571_____ **1966. U.S. Savings Bond Issue**
5¢ red, blue & black (115,875,000) .25 .20 ⬜⬜⬜⬜⬜

CM572_____ **1966. Mary Cassatt Issue**
5¢ multicolored (114,015,000) .25 .20 ⬜⬜⬜⬜⬜

CM573_____ **1967. National Grange Issue**
5¢ brownish orange, green, orange & black (121,105,000) .25 .20 ⬜⬜⬜⬜⬜

CM574_____ **1967. Canada Centennial Issue**
5¢ blue, green, dark blue & olive green, tagged (132,045,000) .25 .20 ⬜⬜⬜⬜⬜

CM575_____ **1967. Erie Canal Sesquicentennial Issue**
5¢ dark blue, light blue, black red, tagged (118,780,000) .25 .20 ⬜⬜⬜⬜⬜

CM576_____ **1967. Lions International Issue**
5¢ red, blue & black on granite paper, tagged (121,985,000) .25 .20 ⬜⬜⬜⬜⬜

CM577_____ **1967. Henry David Thoreau Issue**
5¢ red, black & green tagged (111,850,000) .25 .20 ⬜⬜⬜⬜⬜

CM578_____ **1967. Nebraska Statehood Issue**
5¢ yellow, green & brown tagged (117,225,000) .25 .20 ⬜⬜⬜⬜⬜

CM579_____ **1967. Voice of America Issue**
5¢ red, blue & black tagged (111,515,000) .25 .20 ⬜⬜⬜⬜⬜

CM580_____ **1967. Davy Crockett Issue**
5¢ green, black & yellow tagged (114,270,000) .25 .20 ⬜⬜⬜⬜⬜

CM581_____ **1967. Space Twins Issue**
5¢ dark blue, black & red tagged (120,865,000) 1.00 .35 ⬜⬜⬜⬜⬜

CM540

CM542

CM539 ← → CM541

CM546

CM543   CM544   CM545

CM547

CM551

CM548   CM549   CM550

CM553

CM552 ← → CM554   CM556

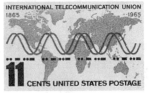

CM555   CM557   CM558

CM559

CM560

CM562

CM563

CM561

CM564 ←

CM565

CM566 →

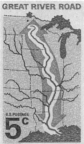

CM567

CM568 →

CM569

CM570 →

CM570 (Great River Road)

CM571

CM572

CM573

CM574

CM575

CM576

CM577 →

CM577

CM578

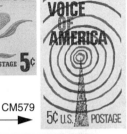

CM579 ➤

CM580

CM583 ➤

CM581-82

Finland
Independence 1917-67

United States 5c

CM584

CM585

ILLINOIS 1818 1968

CM587 ➤

6¢ U.S. POSTAGE

CM586

UNITED STATES POSTAGE 6¢

HEMISFAIR '68

CM588

SUPPORT OUR YOUTH

CM589

CM590 ◄

REGISTER & VOTE U.S. 6

CM591 ◄

LIBERTY

CM592

CM593

AN APPEAL TO HEAVEN

CM594

CM595

CM596

CM597

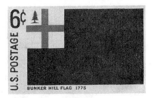

CM598

	MNHVF	UseVF

CM582_____

5¢ **dark blue, red & blue, green** tagged   1.00   .35

CM583_____   **1967. Urban Planning Issue**

5¢ **dark blue, light blue & black** tagged (110,675,000)   .25   .20

CM584_____   **1967. Finland Independence Issue**

5¢ **blue** tagged (110,670,000)   .25   .20

CM585_____   **1967. Thomas Eakins Issue**

5¢ **gold & multicolored** tagged (113,825,000)   .25   .20

CM586_____   **1967. Mississippi Statehood Issue**

5¢ **green blue, blue green & brown** tagged (113,330,000)   .25   .20

CM587_____   **1968. Illinois Statehood Issue**

6¢ **multicolored** tagged (141,350,000)   .25   .20

CM588_____   **1968. Hemisfair '68 Issue**

6¢ **blue, pink, & white** tagged (117,470,600)   .25   .20

CM589_____   **1968. Support Our Youth Issue**

6¢ **red & blue** tagged (147,120,000)   .25   .20

CM590_____   **1968. Law and Order Issue**

6¢ **red, blue & black** tagged (130,125,000)   .25   .20

CM591_____   **1968. Register and Vote Issue**

6¢ **gold and black** tagged (158,070,000)   .25   .20

CM592_____   **1968. Historic Flags Issue**

6¢ **blue** tagged (228,040,000)   .40   .30

CM593_____

6¢ **red & blue** tagged   .40   .30

CM594_____

6¢ **green & blue** tagged   .40   .30

CM595_____

6¢ **red & blue** tagged   .40   .30

CM596_____

6¢ **gold & blue** tagged   .40   .30

CM597_____

6¢ **red & blue** tagged   .40   .30

CM598_____

6¢ **red, green & blue** tagged   .40   .30

CM599_____

6¢ **red & blue** tagged   .40   .30

CM600_____

6¢ **multicolored** tagged   .40   .30

CM601_____

6¢ **red, gold & blue** tagged   .40   .30

CM602_____   **1968. Walt Disney Issue**

6¢ **multicolored** tagged (153,015,000)   .25   .20

CM603_____   **1968. Father Jacques Marquette Issue**

6¢ **black, green & brown** tagged (132,560,000)   .25   .20

CM604_____   **1968. Daniel Boone Issue**

6¢ **red brown, brown, yellow & black** tagged (130,385,000)   .25   .20

CM605_____   **1968. Arkansas River Navigation Issue**

6¢ **blue, black & dark blue** tagged (132,265,000)   .25   .20

CM606_____   **1968. Leif Erikson Issue**

6¢ **brown** (128,710,000)   .25   .20

CM607_____   **1968. Cherokee Strip Issue**

6¢ **brown** tagged (124,775,000)   .25   .20

CM608_____   **1968. John Trumbull Issue**

6¢ **multicolored** tagged (128,295,000)   .25   .20

CM599

CM600

CM601

CM602 ←

CM603

CM604

ARKANSAS RIVER NAVIGATION

CM605

CM607

CM606

CM608

CM609

CM610

CM615

CM611-614

CM616

CM617

	MNHVF	UseVF

CM609_____ **1968. Waterfowl Conservation Issue**

6¢ **multicolored** (142,245,000)   .25   .20 ☐☐☐☐☐

CM610_____ **1968. Chief Joseph Issue**

6¢ **multicolored** tagged (125,100,000)   .25   .20 ☐☐☐☐☐

CM611_____ **1969. Beautification of America Issue**

6¢ **multicolored** tagged (102,570,000)   .30   .25 ☐☐☐☐☐

CM612_____

6¢ **multicolored** tagged   .30   .25 ☐☐☐☐☐

CM613_____

6¢ **multicolored** tagged   .30   .25 ☐☐☐☐☐

CM614_____

6¢ **multicolored** tagged   .30   .25 ☐☐☐☐☐

CM615_____ **1969. American Legion Issue**

6¢ **red, black & blue** tagged (148,770,000)   .25   .20 ☐☐☐☐☐

CM616_____ **1969. Grandma Moses Issue**

6¢ **multicolored** tagged (139,475,000)   .25   .20 ☐☐☐☐☐

CM617_____ **1969. Apollo 8 Issue**

6¢ **gray, deep blue & blue** tagged (187,165,000)   .25   .20 ☐☐☐☐☐

Note: Imperforate varieties, from printer's waste, exist.

CM618_____ **1969. W.C. Handy Issue**

6¢ **multicolored** tagged (125,555,000)   .25   .20 ☐☐☐☐☐

CM619_____ **1969. Settlement of California Issue**

6¢ **multicolored** tagged (144,425,000)   .25   .20 ☐☐☐☐☐

CM620_____ **1969. John Wesley Powell Issue**

6¢ **multicolored** tagged (133,100,000)   .25   .20 ☐☐☐☐☐

CM621_____ **1969. Alabama Statehood Issue**

6¢ **multicolored** tagged (136,900,000)   .25   .20 ☐☐☐☐☐

CM622_____ **1969. 11th International Botanical Congress Issue**

6¢ **multicolored** tagged (158,695,000)   .30   .25 ☐☐☐☐☐

CM623_____

6¢ **multicolored** tagged   .30   .25 ☐☐☐☐☐

CM624_____

6¢ **multicolored** tagged   .30   .25 ☐☐☐☐☐

CM625_____

6¢ **multicolored** tagged   .30   .25 ☐☐☐☐☐

CM626_____ **1969. Dartmouth College Case Issue**

6¢ **green** tagged (124,075,000)   .25   .20 ☐☐☐☐☐

CM627_____ **1969. Professional Baseball Issue**

6¢ **yellow, red, black & green** tagged (129,925,000)   1.25   .20 ☐☐☐☐☐

CM628_____ **1969. Intercollegiate Football Issue**

6¢ **red & green** tagged (129,860,000)   .45   .20 ☐☐☐☐☐

The intaglio portion of CM628 was printed on a rotary press normally used for currency.

CM629_____ **1969. Dwight D. Eisenhower Issue**

6¢ **blue, black & reddish purple** tagged (138,976,000)   .25   .20 ☐☐☐☐☐

CM630_____ **1969. Hope for the Crippled Issue**

6¢ **multicolored** tagged (124,565,000)   .25   .20 ☐☐☐☐☐

CM631_____ **1969. William M. Harnett Issue**

6¢ **multicolored** tagged (124,729,000)   .25   .20 ☐☐☐☐☐

CM632_____ **1970. Natural History Issue**

6¢ **multicolored** tagged (201,794,600)   .25   .20 ☐☐☐☐☐

CM633_____

6¢ **multicolored** tagged   .25   .20 ☐☐☐☐☐

CM634_____

6¢ **multicolored** tagged   .25   .20 ☐☐☐☐☐

CM618

CM619

CM620

CM621

CM622-625

CM626

CM627

CM628

CM629

HOPE
FOR THE CRIPPLED

CM630

CM631

CM636

CM637

CM632-635

CM638

WOMAN SUFFRAGE

50TH ANNIVERSARY

CM639

	MNHVF	UseVF

CM635_____
  6¢ **multicolored** tagged   .25   .20 ☐☐☐☐☐
CM636_____   **1970. Maine Statehood Issue**
  6¢ **multicolored** tagged (171,850,000)   .25   .20 ☐☐☐☐☐
CM637_____   **1970. Wildlife Conservation Issue**
  6¢ **black** on tan (142,205,000)   .25   .20 ☐☐☐☐☐
CM638_____   **1970. Edgar Lee Masters Issue**
  6¢ **black** tagged (137,660,000)   .25   .20 ☐☐☐☐☐
CM639_____   **1970. The 50th Anniversary of Woman Suffrage Issue**
  6¢ **blue** tagged (135,125,000)   .25   .20 ☐☐☐☐☐
CM640_____   **1970. South Carolina Issue**
  6¢ **brown, black & red** tagged (135,895,000)   .25   .20 ☐☐☐☐☐
CM641_____   **1970. Stone Mountain Issue**
  6¢ **gray black** tagged (132,675,000)   .25   .20 ☐☐☐☐☐
CM642_____   **1970. Fort Snelling Sesquicentennial Issue**
  6¢ **multicolored** tagged (134,795,000)   .25   .20 ☐☐☐☐☐
CM643_____   **1970. Anti-Pollution Issue**
  6¢ **multicolored** tagged (161,600,000)   .25   .20 ☐☐☐☐☐
CM644_____
  6¢ **multicolored** tagged   .25   .20 ☐☐☐☐☐
CM645_____
  6¢ **multicolored** tagged   .25   .20 ☐☐☐☐☐
CM646_____
  6¢ **multicolored** tagged   .25   .20 ☐☐☐☐☐
CM647_____   **1970. United Nations Issue**
  6¢ **black, red & blue** tagged (127,610,000)   .25   .20 ☐☐☐☐☐
CM648_____   **1970. Landing of the Pilgrims Issue**
  6¢ **multicolored** tagged (129,785,000)   .25   .20 ☐☐☐☐☐
CM649_____   **1970. U.S. Servicemen Issue**
  6¢ **multicolored** tagged (134,380,000)   .25   .20 ☐☐☐☐☐
CM650_____
  6¢ **dark blue, black & red** tagged   .25   .20 ☐☐☐☐☐
CM651_____   **1971. American Wool Issue**
  6¢ **multicolored** tagged (135,305,000)   .25   .20 ☐☐☐☐☐
CM652_____   **1971. Douglas MacArthur Issue**
  6¢ **red, blue & black** tagged (134,840,000)   .25   .20 ☐☐☐☐☐
CM653_____   **1971. Blood Donors Issue**
  6¢ **red & blue** tagged (130,975,000)   .25   .20 ☐☐☐☐☐
CM654_____   **1971. Missouri Statehood Issue**
  8¢ **multicolored** tagged (161,235,000)   .25   .20 ☐☐☐☐☐
CM655_____   **1971. Wildlife Conservation Issue**
  8¢ **multicolored** tagged (175,680,000)   .25   .20 ☐☐☐☐☐
CM656_____
  8¢ **multicolored** tagged   .25   .20 ☐☐☐☐☐
CM657_____
  8¢ **multicolored** tagged   .25   .20 ☐☐☐☐☐
CM658_____
  8¢ **multicolored** tagged   .25   .20 ☐☐☐☐☐
CM659_____   **1971. Antarctic Treaty Issue**
  8¢ **red & dark blue** tagged (138,700,000)   .25   .20 ☐☐☐☐☐
CM660_____   **1971. American Revolution Bicentennial Issue**
  8¢ **gray, red, blue & black** tagged (138,165,000)   .25   .20 ☐☐☐☐☐
CM661_____   **1971. Space Achievements Decade Issue**
  8¢ **multicolored** tagged (176,295,000)   .25   .20 ☐☐☐☐☐

CM640

CM641

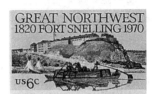

CM642

CM643-646

United Nations 25ᵗʰAnniversary

CM647

CM648

CM649-650

CM651

CM652

CM660

CM653

CM654

CM659

CM655-658

CM663

CM664

	MNHVF	UseVF	

CM662_____
| 8¢ **multicolored** tagged | .25 | .20 | ☐☐☐☐☐ |

CM663_____ **1971. John Sloan Issue**
| 8¢ **multicolored** tagged (152,125,000) | .25 | .20 | ☐☐☐☐☐ |

CM664_____ **1971. Emily Dickinson Issue**
| 8¢ **multicolored** tagged (142,845,000) | .25 | .20 | ☐☐☐☐☐ |

CM665_____ **1971. San Juan Issue**
| 8¢ **multicolored** tagged (148,755,000) | .25 | .20 | ☐☐☐☐☐ |

CM666_____ **1971. Prevent Drug Abuse Issue**
| 8¢ **blue, deep blue & black** tagged (139,080,000) | .25 | .20 | ☐☐☐☐☐ |

CM667_____ **1971. CARE Issue**
| 8¢ **black, blue, violet & red lilac** tagged (130,755,000) | .25 | .20 | ☐☐☐☐☐ |

CM668_____ **1971. Historic Preservation Issue**
| 8¢ **brown & dark beige** on buff, tagged (170,208,000) | .25 | .20 | ☐☐☐☐☐ |

CM669_____
| 8¢ **brown & dark beige** on buff, tagged | .25 | .20 | ☐☐☐☐☐ |

CM670_____
| 8¢ **brown & dark beige** on buff, tagged | .25 | .20 | ☐☐☐☐☐ |

CM671_____
| 8¢ **brown & dark beige** on buff, tagged | .25 | .20 | ☐☐☐☐☐ |

CM672_____ **1972. American Poets Issue**
| 8¢ **black, reddish brown & blue** tagged (137,355,000) | .25 | .20 | ☐☐☐☐☐ |

CM673_____ **1972. Peace Corps Issue**
| 8¢ **dark blue, light blue & red** tagged (150,400,000) | .25 | .20 | ☐☐☐☐☐ |

CM674_____ **1972. Yellowstone Park Issue**
| 8¢ **multicolored** tagged (164,096,000) | .25 | .20 | ☐☐☐☐☐ |

CM675_____ **1972. Cape Hatteras Issue**
| 2¢ **multicolored** tagged (172,730,000) | .25 | .20 | ☐☐☐☐☐ |

CM676_____
| 2¢ **multicolored** tagged | .25 | .20 | ☐☐☐☐☐ |

CM677_____
| 2¢ **multicolored** tagged | .25 | .20 | ☐☐☐☐☐ |

CM678_____
| 2¢ **multicolored** tagged | .25 | .20 | ☐☐☐☐☐ |

CM679_____ **1972. Wolf Trap Farm Issue**
| 6¢ **multicolored** tagged (104,090,000) | .25 | .20 | ☐☐☐☐☐ |

CM680_____ **1972. Mount McKinley Issue**
| 15¢ **multicolored** tagged (53,920,000) | .25 | .20 | ☐☐☐☐☐ |

CM681_____ **1972. Family Planning Issue**
| 8¢ **multicolored** tagged (153,025,000) | .25 | .20 | ☐☐☐☐☐ |

CM682_____ **1972. Colonial Craftsmen Issue**
| 8¢ **deep brown** on buff paper, tagged (201,890,000) | .25 | .20 | ☐☐☐☐☐ |

CM683_____
| 8¢ **deep brown** on buff paper, tagged | .25 | .20 | ☐☐☐☐☐ |

CM684_____
| 8¢ **deep brown** on buff paper, tagged | .25 | .20 | ☐☐☐☐☐ |

CM685_____
| 8¢ **deep brown** on buff paper, tagged | .25 | .20 | ☐☐☐☐☐ |

CM686_____ **1972. Olympic Games Issue**
| 6¢ **multicolored** tagged (67,335,000) | .25 | .20 | ☐☐☐☐☐ |

CM687_____
| 8¢ **multicolored** tagged (96,240,000) | .25 | .20 | ☐☐☐☐☐ |

CM688_____
| 15¢ **multicolored** tagged (46,340,000) | .25 | .20 | ☐☐☐☐☐ |

CM661-662

CM665

CM666

CM667   CM668-671

CM672

CM673

CM675-678

CM679

CM680

CM674

CM681

CM682-685

	MNHVF	UseVF

CM689_____ **1972. Parent Teacher Association Issue**

8¢   **yellow & black** tagged (180,155,000) .25 .20 ☐☐☐☐☐

CM690_____ **1972. Wildlife Conservation Issue**

8¢   **multicolored** tagged (198,364,800) .25 .20 ☐☐☐☐☐

CM691_____

8¢   **multicolored** tagged .25 .20 ☐☐☐☐☐

CM692_____

8¢   **multicolored** tagged .25 .20 ☐☐☐☐☐

CM693_____

8¢   **multicolored** tagged .25 .20 ☐☐☐☐☐

CM694_____ **1972. Mail Order Centennial Issue**

8¢   **multicolored** tagged (185,490,000) .25 .20 ☐☐☐☐☐

Tagging on this issue typically consists of a vertical bar, 10mm wide.

CM695_____ **1972. Osteopathic Medicine Issue**

8¢   **multicolored** tagged (162,335,000) .25 .20 ☐☐☐☐☐

CM696_____ **1972. Tom Sawyer Issue**

8¢   **multicolored** tagged (162,789,950) .25 .20 ☐☐☐☐☐

CM697_____ **1972. Pharmacy Issue**

8¢   **multicolored** tagged (165,895,000) .25 .20 ☐☐☐☐☐

CM698_____ **1972. Stamp Collecting Issue**

8¢   **multicolored** tagged (166,508,000) .25 .20 ☐☐☐☐☐

CM699_____ **1973. Love Issue**

8¢   **red, green, violet & blue** tagged (330,055,000) .25 .20 ☐☐☐☐☐

CM700_____ **1973. Rise of the Spirit of Independence Issue**

8¢   **blue, greenish black & red** tagged (166,005,000) .25 .20 ☐☐☐☐☐

CM701_____

8¢   **black, orange & ultramarine** tagged (163,050,000) .25 .20 ☐☐☐☐☐

CM702_____

8¢   **blue, black, red & green** tagged (159,005,000) .25 .20 ☐☐☐☐☐

CM703_____

8¢   **blue, black, yellow & red** tagged (147,295,000) .25 .20 ☐☐☐☐☐

CM704_____ **1973. George Gershwin Issue**

8¢   **multicolored** (139,152,000) .25 .20 ☐☐☐☐☐

CM705_____ **1973. Nicolaus Copernicus Issue**

8¢   **black & yellow** tagged (159,475,000) .25 .20 ☐☐☐☐☐

CM706_____ **1973. Postal Service Employee Issue**

8¢   **multicolored** tagged (486,020,000) .25 .20 ☐☐☐☐☐

CM707_____

8¢   **multicolored** tagged .25 .20 ☐☐☐☐☐

CM708_____

8¢   **multicolored** tagged .25 .20 ☐☐☐☐☐

CM709_____

8¢   **multicolored** tagged .25 .20 ☐☐☐☐☐

CM710_____

8¢   **multicolored** tagged .25 .20 ☐☐☐☐☐

CM711_____

8¢   **multicolored** tagged .25 .20 ☐☐☐☐☐

CM712_____

8¢   **multicolored** tagged .25 .20 ☐☐☐☐☐

CM713_____

8¢   **multicolored** tagged .25 .20 ☐☐☐☐☐

CM714_____

8¢   **multicolored** tagged .25 .20 ☐☐☐☐☐

XX OLYMPIC SUMMER GAMES-MUNICH 1972

CM686

XI OLYMPIC WINTER GAMES-SAPPORO 1972

CM687

XX OLYMPIC SUMMER GAMES-MUNICH 1972

CM688

CM689

CM690-693 →

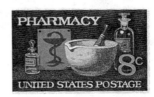

CM695

100ᵗʰ Anniversary of Mail Order

CM694

Tom Sawyer

United States 8c   CM696 ←

PHARMACY

UNITED STATES POSTAGE

CM697

Stamp Collecting U.S. 8c

CM698

CM699

Rise of the Spirit of Independence

CM700

Rise of the Spirit of Independence

CM701

Copernicus 1473-1973

8¢ US

CM705

CM703 →

Rise of the Spirit of Independence

GEORGE GERSHWIN

CM702 ←   CM704

Rise of the Spirit of Independence

	MNHVF	UseVF

CM715_____

  8¢ **multicolored** tagged | .25 | .20 ☐☐☐☐☐

CM716_____   **1973. Harry S. Truman Issue**

  8¢ **red, black & blue** tagged (157,052,800) | .25 | .25 ☐☐☐☐☐

CM717_____   **1973. Boston Tea Party Issue**

  8¢ **multicolored** tagged (196,275,000) | .25 | .20 ☐☐☐☐☐

CM718_____

  8¢ **multicolored** tagged | .25 | .20 ☐☐☐☐☐

CM719_____

  8¢ **multicolored** tagged | .25 | .20 ☐☐☐☐☐

CM720_____

  8¢ **multicolored** tagged | .25 | .20 ☐☐☐☐☐

CM721_____   **1973. Progress in Electronics Issue**

  6¢ **multicolored** tagged (53,005,000) | .25 | .20 ☐☐☐☐☐

CM722_____

  8¢ **multicolored** tagged (159,775,000) | .25 | .20 ☐☐☐☐☐

CM723_____

  15¢ **multicolored** tagged (39,005,000) | .25 | .20 ☐☐☐☐☐

CM724_____   **1973. Robinson Jeffers Issue**

  8¢ **multicolored** tagged (128,048,000) | .25 | .20 ☐☐☐☐☐

CM725_____   **1973. Lyndon B. Johnson Issue**

  8¢ **multicolored** (152,624,000) | .25 | .20 ☐☐☐☐☐

CM726_____   **1973. Henry O. Tanner Issue**

  8¢ **multicolored** tagged (146,008,000) | .25 | .20 ☐☐☐☐☐

CM727_____   **1973. Willa Cather Issue**

  8¢ **multicolored** tagged (139,608,000) | .25 | .20 ☐☐☐☐☐

CM728_____   **1973. Angus Cattle Issue**

  8¢ **multicolored** tagged (145,430,000) | .25 | .20 ☐☐☐☐☐

CM729_____   **1974. Veterans of Foreign Wars Issue**

  10¢ **red & blue** tagged (145,430,000) | .25 | .20 ☐☐☐☐☐

CM730_____   **1974. Robert Frost Issue**

  10¢ **black** tagged (145,235,000) | .25 | .20 ☐☐☐☐☐

CM731_____   **1974. Expo 74 World's Fair Issue**

  10¢ **multicolored** tagged (135,052,000) | .25 | .20 ☐☐☐☐☐

CM732_____   **1974. Horse Racing Issue**

  10¢ **multicolored** tagged (156,750,000) | .25 | .20 ☐☐☐☐☐

CM733_____   **1974. Skylab Project Issue**

  10¢ **multicolored** tagged (164,670,000) | .25 | .20 ☐☐☐☐☐

CM734_____   **1974. Universal Postal Union Issue**

  10¢ **multicolored** tagged (190,154,680) | .25 | .20 ☐☐☐☐☐

CM735_____

  10¢ **multicolored** tagged | .25 | .20 ☐☐☐☐☐

CM736_____

  10¢ **multicolored** tagged | .25 | .20 ☐☐☐☐☐

CM737_____

  10¢ **multicolored** tagged | .25 | .20 ☐☐☐☐☐

CM738_____

  10¢ **multicolored** tagged | .25 | .20 ☐☐☐☐☐

CM739_____

  10¢ **multicolored** tagged | .25 | .20 ☐☐☐☐☐

CM740_____

  10¢ **multicolored** tagged | .25 | .20 ☐☐☐☐☐

CM741_____

  10¢ **multicolored** tagged | .25 | .20 ☐☐☐☐☐

CM706-715

CM716

CM717-720

CM721

CM722

CM723

CM724

CM725

CM726

CM727

CM728

CM729

CM730

		MNHVF	UseVF

CM742_____   **1974. Mineral Heritage Issue**

10¢ **multicolored** tagged (167,212,800)   .25   .20 ☐☐☐☐☐

CM743_____

10¢ **multicolored** tagged   .25   .20 ☐☐☐☐☐

CM744_____

10¢ **multicolored** tagged   .25   .20 ☐☐☐☐☐

CM745_____

10¢ **multicolored** tagged   .25   .20 ☐☐☐☐☐

CM746_____   **1974. Settlement of Kentucky Issue**

10¢ **multicolored** tagged (156,265,000)   .25   .20 ☐☐☐☐☐

CM747_____   **1974. First Continental Congress Issue**

10¢ **dark blue & red** tagged (195,585,000)   .25   .20 ☐☐☐☐☐

CM748_____

10¢ **red & dark blue** tagged   .25   .20 ☐☐☐☐☐

CM749_____

10¢ **gray, dark blue & red** tagged   .25   .20 ☐☐☐☐☐

CM750_____

10¢ **gray, dark blue & red** tagged   .25   .20 ☐☐☐☐☐

CM751_____   **1974. Chautauqua Tent Issue**

10¢ **multicolored** tagged (151,335,000)   .25   .20 ☐☐☐☐☐

CM731

CM732

CM733

CM734-741

CM742-745

CM747-750

CM755

CM756

CM746

CM753

CM758

CM760

CM761

CM751

CM752

CM754

CM757 →

CM759

CM762

	MNHVF	UseVF	

CM752_____ 1974. Winter Wheat and Train Issue

10¢ **multicolored** tagged (141,085,000) .25 .20 ☐☐☐☐☐

CM753_____ 1974. Energy Conservation Issue

10¢ **multicolored** tagged (148,850,000) .25 .20 ☐☐☐☐☐

CM754_____ 1974. Legend of Sleepy Hollow Issue

10¢ **dark blue, black, orange, & yellow** tagged (157,270,000) .25 .20 ☐☐☐☐☐

CM755_____ 1974. Help for Retarded Children Issue

10¢ **light & dark brown** tagged (150,245,000) .25 .20 ☐☐☐☐☐

CM756_____ 1975. Benjamin West Issue

10¢ **multicolored** tagged (156,995,000) .25 .20 ☐☐☐☐☐

CM757_____ 1975. Pioneer Space Issue

10¢ **dark blue, yellow & red** tagged (173,685,000) .25 .20 ☐☐☐☐☐

Imperforate varieties came from printer's waste.

CM758_____ 1975. Collective Bargaining Issue

10¢ **multicolored** tagged (153,355,000) .25 .20 ☐☐☐☐☐

Imperforate varieties came from printer's waste.

CM759_____ 1975. Contributors to the Cause Issue

10¢ **multicolored** tagged (63,205,000) .25 .20 ☐☐☐☐☐

CM760_____

10¢ **multicolored** tagged (157,865,000) .25 .20 ☐☐☐☐☐

CM761_____

10¢ **multicolored** tagged (166,810,000) .25 .20 ☐☐☐☐☐

CM762_____

18¢ **multicolored** tagged (44,825,000) .25 .20 ☐☐☐☐☐

CM763_____ 1975. Mariner Space Issue

10¢ **black, red, ultramarine & bister** tagged (158,600,000) .25 .20 ☐☐☐☐☐

CM764_____ 1975. Lexington and Concord Issue

10¢ **multicolored** tagged (114,028,000) .25 .20 ☐☐☐☐☐

CM765_____ 1975. Paul Laurence Dunbar Issue

10¢ **multicolored** tagged (146,365,000) .25 .20 ☐☐☐☐☐

CM766_____ 1975. D.W. Griffith Issue

10¢ **multicolored** tagged (148,805,000) .25 .20 ☐☐☐☐☐

CM767_____ 1975. Bunker Hill Issue

10¢ **multicolored** tagged (139,928,000) .25 .20 ☐☐☐☐☐

CM768_____ 1975. Military Services Bicentennial Issue

10¢ **multicolored** tagged (179,855,000) .25 .20 ☐☐☐☐☐

CM769_____

10¢ **multicolored** tagged .25 .20 ☐☐☐☐☐

CM770_____

10¢ **multicolored** tagged .25 .20 ☐☐☐☐☐

CM771_____

10¢ **multicolored** tagged .25 .20 ☐☐☐☐☐

CM772_____ 1975. Apollo Soyuz Issue

10¢ **multicolored** tagged (161,863,200) .25 .20 ☐☐☐☐☐

CM773_____

10¢ **multicolored** tagged .25 .20 ☐☐☐☐☐

CM774_____ 1975. World Peace Through Law Issue

10¢ **green, gray blue & brown** tagged (146,615,000) .25 .20 ☐☐☐☐☐

CM775_____ 1975. International Women's Year Issue

10¢ **blue, orange & dark blue** tagged (145,640,000) .25 .20 ☐☐☐☐☐

CM776_____ 1975. U.S. Postal Service Bicentennial Issue

10¢ **multicolored** tagged (168,655,000) .25 .20 ☐☐☐☐☐

CM777_____

10¢ **multicolored** tagged .25 .20 ☐☐☐☐☐

CM763

Lexington & Concord 1775 by Sandham

US Bicentennial IOcents

CM764

Paul Laurence
Dunbar

American poet

CM765 →

10 cents U.S. postage

CM766

CM767 →

Bunker Hill 1775 by Trumbull

US Bicentennial IOc

CM768-771 →

CM772

CM768-771 →

CM774

APOLLO SOYUZ SPACE TEST PROJECT
UNITED STATES · 1975
10c

CM773

USA
10c
INTERNATIONAL WOMEN'S YEAR

CM775

CM776-779

	MNHVF	UseVF

CM778_____
10¢ **multicolored** tagged | .25 | .20 ☐☐☐☐☐

CM779_____
10¢ **multicolored** tagged | .25 | .20 ☐☐☐☐☐

CM780_____   **1975. Banking and Commerce Issue**
10¢ **multicolored** tagged (146,196,000) | .25 | .20 ☐☐☐☐☐

CM781_____
10¢ **multicolored** tagged | .25 | .20 ☐☐☐☐☐

CM782_____   **1976. Spirit of 76 Issue**
13¢ **multicolored** tagged (219,455,000) | .25 | .20 ☐☐☐☐☐

CM783_____
13¢ **multicolored** tagged | .25 | .20 ☐☐☐☐☐

CM784_____
13¢ **multicolored** tagged | .25 | .20 ☐☐☐☐☐

CM785_____   **1976. INTERPHIL Issue**
13¢ **blue, red & ultramarine** tagged (157,825,000) | .25 | .20 ☐☐☐☐☐

CM786_____   **1976. 50-State Flag Issue**
13¢ **Delaware,** tagged (436,005,000) | .55 | .40 ☐☐☐☐☐

CM787_____
13¢ **Pennsylvania,** tagged | .55 | .40 ☐☐☐☐☐

CM788_____
13¢ **New Jersey,** tagged | .55 | .40 ☐☐☐☐☐

CM789_____
13¢ **Georgia,** tagged | .55 | .40 ☐☐☐☐☐

CM790_____
13¢ **Connecticut,** tagged | .55 | .40 ☐☐☐☐☐

CM791_____
13¢ **Massachusetts,** tagged | .55 | .40 ☐☐☐☐☐

CM792_____
13¢ **Maryland,** tagged | .55 | .40 ☐☐☐☐☐

CM793_____
13¢ **South Carolina,** tagged | .55 | .40 ☐☐☐☐☐

CM794_____
13¢ **New Hampshire,** tagged | .55 | .40 ☐☐☐☐☐

CM795_____
13¢ **Virginia,** tagged | .55 | .40 ☐☐☐☐☐

CM796_____
13¢ **New York,** tagged | .55 | .40 ☐☐☐☐☐

CM797_____
13¢ **North Carolina,** tagged | .55 | .40 ☐☐☐☐☐

CM798_____
13¢ **Rhode Island,** tagged | .55 | .40 ☐☐☐☐☐

CM799_____
13¢ **Vermont,** tagged | .55 | .40 ☐☐☐☐☐

CM800_____
13¢ **Kentucky,** tagged | .55 | .40 ☐☐☐☐☐

CM801_____
13¢ **Tennessee,** tagged | .55 | .40 ☐☐☐☐☐

CM802_____
13¢ **Ohio,** tagged | .55 | .40 ☐☐☐☐☐

CM803_____
13¢ **Louisiana,** tagged | .55 | .40 ☐☐☐☐☐

CM804_____
13¢ **Indiana,** tagged | .55 | .40 ☐☐☐☐☐

CM780-781

CM782-784

CM785

CM786-835

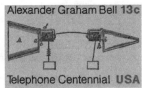

CM836

CM837

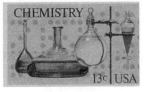

CM838

	MNHVF	UseVF

CM805_____
   13¢ **Mississippi,** tagged | .55 | .40 ☐☐☐☐☐
CM806_____
   13¢ **Illinois,** tagged | .55 | .40 ☐☐☐☐☐
CM807_____
   13¢ **Alabama,** tagged | .55 | .40 ☐☐☐☐☐
CM808_____
   13¢ **Maine,** tagged | .55 | .40 ☐☐☐☐☐
CM809_____
   13¢ **Missouri,** tagged | .55 | .40 ☐☐☐☐☐
CM810_____
   13¢ **Arkansas,** tagged | .55 | .40 ☐☐☐☐☐
CM811_____
   13¢ **Michigan,** tagged | .55 | .40 ☐☐☐☐☐
CM812_____
   13¢ **Florida,** tagged | .55 | .40 ☐☐☐☐☐
CM813_____
   13¢ **Texas,** tagged | .55 | .40 ☐☐☐☐☐
CM814_____
   13¢ **Iowa,** tagged | .55 | .40 ☐☐☐☐☐
CM815_____
   13¢ **Wisconsin,** tagged | .55 | .40 ☐☐☐☐☐
CM816_____
   13¢ **California,** tagged | .55 | .40 ☐☐☐☐☐
CM817_____
   13¢ **Minnesota,** tagged | .55 | .40 ☐☐☐☐☐
CM818_____
   13¢ **Oregon,** tagged | .55 | .40 ☐☐☐☐☐
CM819_____
   13¢ **Kansas,** tagged | .55 | .40 ☐☐☐☐☐
CM820_____
   13¢ **West Virginia,** tagged | .55 | .40 ☐☐☐☐☐
CM821_____
   13¢ **Nevada,** tagged | .55 | .40 ☐☐☐☐☐
CM822_____
   13¢ **Nebraska,** tagged | .55 | .40 ☐☐☐☐☐
CM823_____
   13¢ **Colorado,** tagged | .55 | .40 ☐☐☐☐☐
CM824_____
   13¢ **North Dakota,** tagged | .55 | .40 ☐☐☐☐☐
CM825_____
   13¢ **South Dakota,** tagged | .55 | .40 ☐☐☐☐☐
CM826_____
   13¢ **Montana,** tagged | .55 | .40 ☐☐☐☐☐
CM827_____
   13¢ **Washington,** tagged | .55 | .40 ☐☐☐☐☐
CM828_____
   13¢ **Idaho,** tagged | .55 | .40 ☐☐☐☐☐
CM829_____
   13¢ **Wyoming,** tagged | .55 | .40 ☐☐☐☐☐
CM830_____
   13¢ **Utah,** tagged | .55 | .40 ☐☐☐☐☐
CM831_____
   13¢ **Oklahoma,** tagged | .55 | .40 ☐☐☐☐☐

CM839

CM840

CM841

CM842

CM843

JULY 4,1776 JULY 4,1776 JULY 4,1776 JULY 4,1776

CM844-847

CM848-851

CM852

CM853

	MNHVF	UseVF	

CM832_____

13¢ **New Mexico,** tagged · .55 · .40 ☐☐☐☐☐

CM833_____

13¢ **Arizona,** tagged · .55 · .40 ☐☐☐☐☐

CM834_____

13¢ **Alaska,** tagged · .55 · .40 ☐☐☐☐☐

CM835_____

13¢ **Hawaii,** tagged · .55 · .40 ☐☐☐☐☐

CM836_____ **1976. Telephone Centennial Issue**

13¢ **black, purple & red,** on tan paper, tagged (159,915,000) · .25 · .20 ☐☐☐☐☐

CM837_____ **1976. Commercial Aviation Issue**

13¢ **multicolored** tagged (156,960,000) · .25 · .20 ☐☐☐☐☐

CM838_____ **1976. Chemistry Issue**

13¢ **multicolored** tagged (158,470,000) · .25 · .20 ☐☐☐☐☐

CM839_____ **1976. Bicentennial Souvenir Sheets**

65¢ **multicolored** tagged (1,990,500) · 4.75 · 4.50 ☐☐☐☐☐

CM840_____

90¢ **multicolored** tagged (1,983,000) · 6.00 · 5.75 ☐☐☐☐☐

CM841_____

$1.20 **multicolored** tagged (1,953,000) · 8.25 · 8.00 ☐☐☐☐☐

CM842_____

$1.55 **multicolored** tagged (1,903,000) · 10.75 · 10.50 ☐☐☐☐☐

CM843_____ **1976. Benjamin Franklin Issue**

13¢ **multicolored** tagged (164,890,000) · .25 · .20 ☐☐☐☐☐

CM844_____ **1976. Declaration of Independence Issue**

13¢ **multicolored** tagged (208,035,000) · .25 · .20 ☐☐☐☐☐

CM845_____

13¢ **multicolored** tagged · .25 · .20 ☐☐☐☐☐

CM846_____

13¢ **multicolored** tagged · .25 · .20 ☐☐☐☐☐

CM847_____

13¢ **multicolored** tagged · .25 · .20 ☐☐☐☐☐

CM848_____ **1976. Olympic Games Issue**

13¢ **multicolored** tagged (185,715,000) · .25 · .20 ☐☐☐☐☐

CM849_____

13¢ **multicolored** tagged · .25 · .20 ☐☐☐☐☐

CM850_____

13¢ **multicolored** tagged · .25 · .20 ☐☐☐☐☐

CM851_____

13¢ **multicolored** tagged · .25 · .20 ☐☐☐☐☐

CM852_____ **1976. Clara Maass Issue**

13¢ **multicolored** tagged (130,592,000) · .25 · .20 ☐☐☐☐☐

CM853_____ **1976. Adolph S. Ochs Issue**

13¢ **gray & black** tagged (158,332,800) · .25 · .20 ☐☐☐☐☐

CM854_____ **1977. Washington at Princeton Issue**

13¢ **multicolored** tagged (150,328,000) · .25 · .20 ☐☐☐☐☐

CM855_____ **1977. Sound Recording Issue**

13¢ **multicolored** tagged (176,830,000) · .25 · .20 ☐☐☐☐☐

CM856_____ **1977. Pueblo Indian Art Issue**

13¢ **multicolored** tagged (195,976,000) · .25 · .20 ☐☐☐☐☐

CM857_____

13¢ **multicolored** tagged · .25 · .20 ☐☐☐☐☐

CM858_____

13¢ **multicolored** tagged · .25 · .20 ☐☐☐☐☐

Washington at Princeton 1777 by Peale
US Bicentennial 13c

CM854

CM855

CM861

Pueblo Art USA 13c   Pueblo Art USA 13c
Pueblo Art USA 13c   Pueblo Art USA 13c

CM856-859

USA·13c
50th Anniversary Solo Transatlantic Flight

CM860

Lafayette

CM866   US Bicentennial 13c

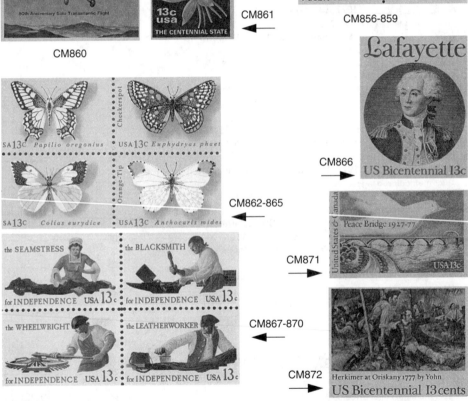

CM862-865

CM871

CM867-870

CM872

Peace Bridge 1927-77   USA 13c

Herkimer at Oriskany 1777 by Yohn
US Bicentennial 13 cents

First Civil Settlement·Alta California·1777

CM873

Drafting the Articles of Confederation
York Town, Pennsylvania 1777 13c USA

CM874

CM875

	MNHVF	UseVF

CM859_____

13¢ **multicolored** tagged .25 .20 ☐☐☐☐☐

CM860_____   **1977. 50th Anniversary of Transatlantic Flight Issue**

13¢ **multicolored** tagged (208,820,000) .25 .20 ☐☐☐☐☐

Privately applied overprints on this stamp have no official status.

CM861_____   **1977. Colorado Statehood Issue**

13¢ **multicolored** tagged (190,005,000) .25 .20 ☐☐☐☐☐

CM862_____   **1977. Butterfly Issue**

13¢ **multicolored** tagged (219,830,000) .25 .20 ☐☐☐☐☐

CM863_____

13¢ **multicolored** tagged .25 .20 ☐☐☐☐☐

CM864_____

13¢ **multicolored** tagged .25 .20 ☐☐☐☐☐

CM865_____

13¢ **multicolored** tagged .25 .20 ☐☐☐☐☐

CM866_____   **1977. Lafayette Issue**

13¢ **blue, black & red** (159,852,000) .25 .20 ☐☐☐☐☐

CM867_____   **1977. Skilled Hands of Independence Issue**

13¢ **multicolored** tagged (188,310,000) .25 .20 ☐☐☐☐☐

CM868_____

13¢ **multicolored** tagged .25 .20 ☐☐☐☐☐

CM869_____

13¢ **multicolored** tagged .25 .20 ☐☐☐☐☐

CM870_____

13¢ **multicolored** tagged .25 .20 ☐☐☐☐☐

CM871_____   **1977. Peace Bridge Issue**

13¢ **blue** tagged (163,625,000) .25 .20 ☐☐☐☐☐

CM872_____   **1977. Herkimer at Oriskany Issue**

13¢ **multicolored** tagged (156,296,000) .25 .20 ☐☐☐☐☐

CM873_____   **1977. Alta California Issue**

13¢ **multicolored** tagged (154,495,000) .25 .20 ☐☐☐☐☐

CM874_____   **1977. Articles of Confederation Issue**

13¢ **red & dark brown** on cream paper, tagged (168,050,000) .25 .20 ☐☐☐☐☐

CM875_____   **1977. Talking Pictures Issue**

13¢ **multicolored** tagged (156,810,000) .25 .20 ☐☐☐☐☐

CM876_____   **1977. Surrender at Saratoga**

13¢ **multicolored** (153,736,000) .25 .20 ☐☐☐☐☐

CM876A _____   **1977. Energy Issue**

13¢ **multicolored** tagged .25 .20 ☐☐☐☐☐

CM876B _____

13¢ **multicolored** tagged .25 .20 ☐☐☐☐☐

CM877_____   **1978. Carl Sandburg Issue**

13¢ **brown & black** tagged (156,560,000) .25 .20 ☐☐☐☐☐

CM878_____   **1978. Captain Cook Issue**

13¢ **blue** tagged (202,155,000) .25 .20 ☐☐☐☐☐

CM879_____

13¢ **green** tagged .25 .20 ☐☐☐☐☐

CM880_____   **1978. Harriet Tubman Issue**

13¢ **multicolored** tagged (156,525,000) .25 .20 ☐☐☐☐☐

CM881_____   **1978. American Quilts Issue**

13¢ **multicolored** tagged (165,182,000) .25 .20 ☐☐☐☐☐

CM882_____

13¢ **multicolored** tagged .25 .20 ☐☐☐☐☐

Surrender at Saratoga 1777 by Trumbull
US Bicentennial 13 cents

CM876

Alaska 1778
Capt.ⁿ JAMES COOK
13c USA

CM878-879

CM876A-876B

Carl Sandburg
USA 13c

CM877

CM881-884

↑

CM890

←

EARLY CANCER DETECTION
PAP TEST
USA 13c
Dr. George Papanicolaou

CM885-888

Harriet Tubman
Black Heritage USA 13c

CM880

French Alliance
1778
US Bicentennial 13c

CM889

JIMMIE RODGERS
Singing Brakeman
Performing Arts USA 13c

CM891 ←

Canadian International Philatelic Exhibition
Toronto

CM892

Photography USA 15c

CM893

	MNHVF	UseVF

CM883_____
13¢ **multicolored** tagged — .25 — .20 ☐☐☐☐☐

CM884_____
13¢ **multicolored** tagged — .25 — .20 ☐☐☐☐☐

CM885_____   **1978. American Dance Issue**
13¢ **multicolored** tagged (157,598,400) — .25 — .20 ☐☐☐☐☐

CM886_____
13¢ **multicolored** tagged — .25 — .20 ☐☐☐☐☐

CM887_____
13¢ **multicolored** tagged — .25 — .20 ☐☐☐☐☐

CM888_____
13¢ **multicolored** tagged — .25 — .20 ☐☐☐☐☐

CM889_____   **1978. French Alliance Issue**
13¢ **blue, black, & red** tagged (102,856,000) — .25 — .20 ☐☐☐☐☐

CM890_____   **1978. George Papanicolaou Issue**
13¢ **brown** tagged (152,270,000) — .25 — .20 ☐☐☐☐☐

CM891_____   **1978. Jimmie Rodgers Issue**
13¢ **multicolored** tagged (94,600,000) — .25 — .20 ☐☐☐☐☐

CM892_____   **1978. Canadian International Philatelic Exhibition**
$1.04 **multicolored** (10,400,000) — 2.75 — 2.00 ☐☐☐☐☐

CM893_____   **1978. Photography Issue**
15¢ **multicolored** tagged (161,228,000) — .30 — .20 ☐☐☐☐☐

CM894_____   **1978. George M. Cohan Issue**
15¢ **multicolored** tagged (151,570,000) — .30 — .20 ☐☐☐☐☐

CM895_____   **1978. Viking Missions Issue**
15¢ **multicolored** tagged (158,880,000) — .30 — .20 ☐☐☐☐☐

CM896_____   **1978. Wildlife Conservation Issue**
15¢ **Great Gray Owl,** tagged (186,550,000) — .30 — .20 ☐☐☐☐☐

CM897_____
15¢ **Saw Whet Owl,** tagged — .30 — .20 ☐☐☐☐☐

CM898_____
15¢ **Barred Owl,** tagged — .30 — .20 ☐☐☐☐☐

CM899_____
15¢ **Great Horned Owl,** tagged — .30 — .20 ☐☐☐☐☐

CM900_____   **1978. American Trees Issue**
15¢ **Giant Sequoia,** tagged (168,136,000) — .30 — .20 ☐☐☐☐☐

CM901_____
15¢ **Eastern White Pine,** tagged — .30 — .20 ☐☐☐☐☐

CM902_____
15¢ **White Oak,** tagged — .30 — .20 ☐☐☐☐☐

CM903_____
15¢ **Gray Birch,** tagged — .30 — .20 ☐☐☐☐☐

CM904_____   **1979. Robert F. Kennedy Issue**
15¢ **blue** tagged (159,297,000) — .30 — .20 ☐☐☐☐☐

CM905_____   **1979. Martin Luther King Jr. Issue**
15¢ **multicolored** tagged (166,435,000) — .30 — .20 ☐☐☐☐☐

CM906_____   **1979. International Year of the Child Issue**
15¢ **light & dark brown** tagged (162,535,000) — .30 — .20 ☐☐☐☐☐

CM907_____   **1979. John Steinbeck Issue**
15¢ **dark blue** tagged (155,000,000) — .30 — .20 ☐☐☐☐☐

CM908_____   **1979. Albert Einstein Issue**
15¢ **brown** tagged (157,310,000) — .30 — .20 ☐☐☐☐☐

CM909_____   **1979. Pennsylvania Toleware Issue**
15¢ **Coffee pot with straight spout** (174,096,000) — .30 — .20 ☐☐☐☐☐

Performing Arts USA 15c

CM894

CM895

CM896-899

CM900-903

CM904

← CM905

CM906

CM907

CM908

CM909-912

CM913-916

CM917-920 →

	MNHVF	UseVF	

CM910_____
| 15¢ **Tea caddy** | .30 | .20 ☐☐☐☐☐ |

CM911_____
| 15¢ **Sugar bowl with lid** | .30 | .20 ☐☐☐☐☐ |

CM912_____
| 15¢ **Coffee pot with gooseneck spout** | .30 | .20 ☐☐☐☐☐ |

CM913_____   **1979. American Architecture Issue**
| 15¢ **University of Virginia Rotunda,** tagged (164,793,000) | .30 | .20 ☐☐☐☐☐ |

CM914_____
| 15¢ **Baltimore Cathedral,** tagged | .30 | .20 ☐☐☐☐☐ |

CM915_____
| 15¢ **Boston State House,** tagged | .30 | .20 ☐☐☐☐☐ |

CM916_____
| 15¢ **Philadelphia Exchange,** tagged | .30 | .20 ☐☐☐☐☐ |

CM917_____   **1979. Endangered Flora Issue**
| 15¢ **Persistent Trillium,** tagged (163,055,000) | .30 | .20 ☐☐☐☐☐ |

CM918_____
| 15¢ **Hawaiian Wild Broadbean,** tagged | .30 | .20 ☐☐☐☐☐ |

CM919_____
| 15¢ **Contra Costa Wallflower,** tagged | .30 | .20 ☐☐☐☐☐ |

CM920_____
| 15¢ **Antioch Dunes Evening Primrose,** tagged | .30 | .20 ☐☐☐☐☐ |

CM921_____   **1979. Seeing Eye Dog Issue**
| 15¢ **multicolored** tagged (161,860,000) | .30 | .20 ☐☐☐☐☐ |

CM922_____   **1979. Special Olympics Issue**
| 15¢ **multicolored** tagged (165,775,000) | .30 | .20 ☐☐☐☐☐ |

CM923_____   **1979. Summer Games Issue**
| 10¢ **multicolored** tagged (67,195,000) | .25 | .25 ☐☐☐☐☐ |

CM924_____   **1979. John Paul Jones Issue**
| 15¢ **multicolored** tagged (160,000,000, all perforation types) | .30 | .20 ☐☐☐☐☐ |

Imperforate errors are from printer's waste.
CM924A _____
| 15¢ **multicolored** tagged, perforated 11 | .75 | .25 ☐☐☐☐☐ |

CM924B _____
| 15¢ **multicolored** tagged, perforated 12 | 2,300.00 | 1,000.00 ☐☐☐☐☐ |

CM925_____   **1979. Summer Games Issue**
| 15¢ **Women runners,** tagged (186,905,000) | .25 | .20 ☐☐☐☐☐ |

CM926_____
| 15¢ **Women swimmers,** tagged | .25 | .20 ☐☐☐☐☐ |

CM927_____
| 15¢ **Pair of rowers,** tagged | .25 | .20 ☐☐☐☐☐ |

CM928_____
| 15¢ **Horse & Rider,** tagged | .25 | .20 ☐☐☐☐☐ |

CM929_____   **1979. Will Rogers Issue**
| 15¢ **multicolored** tagged (161,290,000) | .30 | .20 ☐☐☐☐☐ |

CM930_____   **1979. Vietnam Veterans Issue**
| 15¢ **multicolored** tagged (172,740,000) | .30 | .20 ☐☐☐☐☐ |

CM931_____   **1980. W.C. Fields Issue**
| 15¢ **multicolored** tagged (168,995,000) | .30 | .20 ☐☐☐☐☐ |

CM932_____   **1980. Winter Games Issue**
| 15¢ **Speed skater,** tagged (208,295,000) *(both perforation types)* | .30 | .20 ☐☐☐☐☐ |

CM933_____
| 15¢ **Ski jumper,** tagged | .30 | .20 ☐☐☐☐☐ |

CM921

CM922

CM923

CM924

CM925-928

CM929

CM930

CM931

CM932-935
CM932A-935A

CM936

CM937-942

Frances Perkins
USA 15c

CM943

CM944

	MNHVF	UseVF

CM934_____

   15¢ **Downhill skier,** tagged | .30 | .20 ☐☐☐☐☐

CM935_____

   15¢ **Hockey goaltender,** tagged | .30 | .20 ☐☐☐☐☐

CM935A _____

   15¢ **Speed Skater,** tagged | .80 | .75 ☐☐☐☐☐

CM935B _____

   15¢ **Ski jumper,** tagged | .80 | .75 ☐☐☐☐☐

CM935C _____

   15¢ **Downhill skier,** tagged | .80 | .75 ☐☐☐☐☐

CM935D _____

   15¢ **Hockey goaltender,** tagged | .80 | .75 ☐☐☐☐☐

CM936_____ **1980. Benjamin Banneker Issue**

   15¢ **multicolored** tagged (160,000,000) | .30 | .20 ☐☐☐☐☐

Imperforates with misregistered colors are from printers' waste, have been fraudulently perforated to simulate CM936v. Genuine examples of this error have colors correctly registered. Expert certification recommended.

CM937_____ **1980. National Letter Writing Issue**

   15¢ **"Letters Preserve Memories"** (232,134,000) | .30 | .20 ☐☐☐☐☐

CM938_____

   15¢ **"Write Soon," (purple),** tagged | .30 | .20 ☐☐☐☐☐

CM939_____

   15¢ **"Letters Lift Spirits,"** tagged | .30 | .20 ☐☐☐☐☐

CM940_____

   15¢ **"Write Soon", (green),** tagged | .30 | .20 ☐☐☐☐☐

CM941_____

   15¢ **"Letters Shape Opinions,"** tagged | .30 | .20 ☐☐☐☐☐

CM942_____

   15¢ **"Write Soon," (red),** tagged | .30 | .20 ☐☐☐☐☐

CM943_____ **1980. Frances Perkins Issue**

   15¢ **blue** tagged (163,510,000) | .30 | .20 ☐☐☐☐☐

CM944_____ **1980. Emily Bissell Issue**

   15¢ **black & red** tagged (95,695,000) | .30 | .20 ☐☐☐☐☐

CM945_____ **1980. Helen Keller and Anne Sullivan Issue**

   15¢ **multicolored** tagged (153,975,000) | .30 | .20 ☐☐☐☐☐

CM946_____ **1980. Veterans Administration Issue**

   15¢ **red & dark blue** tagged (160,000,000) | .30 | .20 ☐☐☐☐☐

CM947_____ **1980. Bernardo de Galvez Issue**

   15¢ **multicolored** tagged (103,850,000) | .30 | .20 ☐☐☐☐☐

CM948_____ **1980. Coral Reefs Issue**

   15¢ **Brain Coral,** tagged (204,715,000) | .30 | .20 ☐☐☐☐☐

CM949_____

   15¢ **Elkhorn Coral,** tagged | .30 | .20 ☐☐☐☐☐

CM950_____

   15¢ **Chalice Coral,** tagged | .30 | .20 ☐☐☐☐☐

CM951_____

   15¢ **Finger Coral,** tagged | .30 | .20 ☐☐☐☐☐

CM952_____ **1980. Organized Labor Issue**

   15¢ **multicolored** tagged (166,545,000) | .30 | .20 ☐☐☐☐☐

CM953_____ **1980. Edith Wharton Issue**

   15¢ **purple** tagged (163,310,000) | .30 | .20 ☐☐☐☐☐

CM954_____ **1980. Education in America Issue**

   15¢ **multicolored** tagged (160,000,000) | .30 | .20 ☐☐☐☐☐

CM955_____ **1980. Pacific Northwest Masks Issue**

   15¢ **Heiltsuk Bella Bella mask,** tagged (152,404,000) | .30 | .20 ☐☐☐☐☐

HELEN KELLER
ANNE SULLIVAN

CM945

CM946

Gen. Bernardo de Gálvez
Battle of Mobile 1780

CM947

CM948-951

Organized Labor
Proud and Free
USA 15c

CM952

CM953

Learning
never ends

CM954

Heiltsuk, Bella Bella
Indian Art USA 15c

Chilkat Tlingit
Indian Art USA 15c

CM955-958

Tlingit
Indian Art USA 15c

Bella Coola
Indian Art USA 15c

Architecture USA 15c

CM959-962

Rose USA 18c   Camellia USA 18c

Dahlia USA 18c   Lily USA 18c

CM965-968

USA 15c
Everett Dirksen

CM963

Whitney Moore Young

Black Heritage USA 15c

CM964

	MNHVF	UseVF

CM956_____
15¢ **Chikat Tlingit mask,** tagged — .30 — .20
CM957_____
15¢ **Tlingit mask,** tagged — .30 — .20
CM958_____
15¢ **Bella Coola mask,** tagged — .30 — .20
CM959_____ **1980. American Architecture Issue**
15¢ **Smithsonian Institution,** tagged (152,720,000) — .30 — .20
CM960_____
15¢ **Trinity Church,** tagged — .30 — .20
CM961_____
15¢ **Pennsylvania Academy of the Fine Arts,** tagged — .30 — .20
CM962_____
15¢ **Lyndhurst,** tagged — .30 — .20
CM963_____ **1981. Everett Dirksen Issue**
15¢ **gray** tagged (160,155,000) — .30 — .20
CM964_____ **1981. Whitney Moore Young Issue**
15¢ **multicolored** tagged (159,505,000) — .30 — .20
CM965_____ **1981. Flower Issue**
18¢ **Rose,** tagged (210,633,000) — .30 — .20
CM966_____
18¢ **Camellia,** tagged — .30 — .20
CM967_____
18¢ **Dahlia,** tagged — .30 — .20
CM968_____
18¢ **Lily,** tagged — .30 — .20
CM969_____ **1981. American Red Cross Issue**
18¢ **multicolored** tagged (165,175,000) — .30 — .20
CM970_____ **1981. Savings and Loan Issue**
18¢ **multicolored** tagged (107,240,000) — .30 — .20
CM971_____ **1981. Space Achievement Issue**
18¢ **Astronaut on Moon,** tagged (337,819,000) — .30 — .20
CM972_____
18¢ **Pioneer II & Saturn,** tagged — .30 — .20
CM973_____
18¢ **Skylab & Sun,** tagged — .30 — .20
CM974_____
18¢ **Hubble Space Telescope,** tagged — .30 — .20
CM975_____
18¢ **Space Shuttle in orbit,** tagged — .30 — .20
CM976_____
18¢ **Space Shuttle with arm deployed,** tagged — .30 — .20
CM977_____
18¢ **Space Shuttle at launch,** tagged — .30 — .20
CM978_____
18¢ **Space Shuttle at landing,** tagged — .30 — .20
CM979_____ **1981. Professional Management Issue**
18¢ **blue & black** tagged (99,420,000) — .30 — .20
CM980_____ **1981. Save Wildlife Habitats Issue**
18¢ **Blue heron,** tagged (178,930,000) — .30 — .20
CM981_____
18¢ **Badger,** tagged — .30 — .20
CM982_____
18¢ **Grizzly bear,** tagged — .30 — .20

CM969

CM970

CM971-978

CM979

CM984

CM985

CM980-983

CM986

CM991 →

CM992 →

Architecture USA 18c   Architecture USA 18c
Architecture USA 18c   Architecture USA 18c

CM987-990

	MNHVF	UseVF

CM983_____

| 18¢ **Ruffed grouse**, tagged | .30 | .20 ☐☐☐☐☐ |

CM984_____ **1981. Disabled Persons Issue**

| 18¢ **multicolored** tagged (100,265,000) | .30 | .20 ☐☐☐☐☐ |

CM985_____ **1981. Edna St. Vincent Millay Issue**

| 18¢ **multicolored** tagged (99,615,000) | .30 | .25 ☐☐☐☐☐ |

CM986_____ **1981. Beat Alcoholism Issue**

| 18¢ **blue & black** tagged (97,535,000) | .65 | .20 ☐☐☐☐☐ |

CM987_____ **1981. American Architecture Issue**

| 18¢ **N.Y. University Library**, tagged (167,308,000) | .30 | .20 ☐☐☐☐☐ |

CM988_____

| 18¢ **Biltmore House**, tagged | .30 | .20 ☐☐☐☐☐ |

CM989_____

| 18¢ **Palace of Arts**, tagged | .30 | .20 ☐☐☐☐☐ |

CM990_____

| 18¢ **National Farmers Bank Building**, tagged | .30 | .20 ☐☐☐☐☐ |

CM991_____ **1981. Bobby Jones Issue**

| 18¢ **green** tagged (99,170,000) | .30 | .20 ☐☐☐☐☐ |

CM992_____ **1981. (Mildred) Babe Zaharias Issue**

| 18¢ **light violet** tagged (101,625,000) | .30 | .20 ☐☐☐☐☐ |

CM993_____ **1981. Frederic Remington Issue**

| 18¢ **multicolored** tagged (101,155,000) | .30 | .20 ☐☐☐☐☐ |

CM994_____ **1981. James Hoban Issue**

| 18¢ **multicolored** tagged (101,200,000) | .30 | .20 ☐☐☐☐☐ |

CM995_____

| 20¢ **multicolored** tagged (167,360,000) | .30 | .20 ☐☐☐☐☐ |

CM996_____ **1981. Battle of Yorktown and the Virginia Capes Issue**

| 18¢ **multicolored** tagged (162,420,000) | .30 | .20 ☐☐☐☐☐ |

CM997_____

| 18¢ **multicolored** tagged | .30 | .20 ☐☐☐☐☐ |

CM998_____ **1981. John Hanson Issue**

| 20¢ **multicolored** tagged (167,130,000) | .30 | .20 ☐☐☐☐☐ |

CM999_____ **1981. Desert Plants Issue**

| 20¢ **Barrel cactus**, tagged (191,560,000) | .35 | .20 ☐☐☐☐☐ |

CM1000_____

| 20¢ **Agave**, tagged | .35 | .20 ☐☐☐☐☐ |

CM1001_____

| 20¢ **Beavertail cactus**, tagged | .35 | .20 ☐☐☐☐☐ |

CM1002_____

| 20¢ **Saguaro**, tagged | .35 | .20 ☐☐☐☐☐ |

CM1003_____ **1982. Franklin D. Roosevelt Issue**

| 20¢ **blue** tagged (163,939,200) | .35 | .20 ☐☐☐☐☐ |

CM1004_____ **1982. Love Issue**

| 20¢ **multicolored** tagged | .35 | .20 ☐☐☐☐☐ |

CM1004A _____

| 20¢ **multicolored** tagged, perforated 11 x 10 1/2 | 1.00 | .25 ☐☐☐☐☐ |

CM1005_____ **1982. George Washington Issue**

| 20¢ **multicolored** tagged (180,700,000) | .35 | .20 ☐☐☐☐☐ |

CM1006_____ **1982. State Birds and Flowers**

| 20¢ **Alabama**, **multicolored**, tagged (666,950,000) | 1.00 | .50 ☐☐☐☐☐ |

CM1007_____

| 20¢ **Alaska**, **multicolored**, tagged | 1.00 | .50 ☐☐☐☐☐ |

CM1008_____

| 20¢ **Arizona**, **multicolored**, tagged | 1.00 | .50 ☐☐☐☐☐ |

CM1009 _____			
20¢ **Arkansas, multicolored,** tagged		1.00	.50 ☐☐☐☐☐
CM1010 _____			
20¢ **California, multicolored,** tagged		1.00	.50 ☐☐☐☐☐
CM1011 _____			
20¢ **Colorado, multicolored,** tagged		1.00	.50 ☐☐☐☐☐
CM1012 _____			
20¢ **Connecticut, multicolored,** tagged		1.00	.50 ☐☐☐☐☐
CM1013 _____			
20¢ **Delaware, multicolored,** tagged		1.00	.50 ☐☐☐☐☐

CM993

CM994

CM995

CM996-997

CM998

CM999-1002

CM1003

CM1004

CM1005

	MNHVF	UseVF	

CM1014_____
| 20¢ **Florida, multicolored,** tagged | 1.00 | .50 ☐☐☐☐☐ |

CM1015_____
| 20¢ **Georgia, multicolored,** tagged | 1.00 | .50 ☐☐☐☐☐ |

CM1016_____
| 20¢ **Hawaii, multicolored,** tagged | 1.00 | .50 ☐☐☐☐☐ |

CM1017_____
| 20¢ **Idaho, multicolored,** tagged | 1.00 | .50 ☐☐☐☐☐ |

CM1018_____
| 20¢ **Illinois, multicolored,** tagged | 1.00 | .50 ☐☐☐☐☐ |

CM1019_____
| 20¢ **Indiana, multicolored,** tagged | 1.00 | .50 ☐☐☐☐☐ |

CM1020_____
| 20¢ **Iowa, multicolored,** tagged | 1.00 | .50 ☐☐☐☐☐ |

CM1021_____
| 20¢ **Kansas, multicolored,** tagged | 1.00 | .50 ☐☐☐☐☐ |

CM1022_____
| 20¢ **Kentucky, multicolored,** tagged | 1.00 | .50 ☐☐☐☐☐ |

CM1023_____
| 20¢ **Louisiana, multicolored,** tagged | 1.00 | .50 ☐☐☐☐☐ |

CM1024_____
| 20¢ **Maine, multicolored,** tagged | 1.00 | .50 ☐☐☐☐☐ |

CM1025_____
| 20¢ **Maryland, multicolored,** tagged | 1.00 | .50 ☐☐☐☐☐ |

CM1026_____
| 20¢ **Massachusetts, multicolored,** tagged | 1.00 | .50 ☐☐☐☐☐ |

CM1027_____
| 20¢ **Michigan, multicolored,** tagged | 1.00 | .50 ☐☐☐☐☐ |

CM1028_____
| 20¢ **Minnesota, multicolored,** tagged | 1.00 | .50 ☐☐☐☐☐ |

CM1029_____
| 20¢ **Mississippi, multicolored,** tagged | 1.00 | .50 ☐☐☐☐☐ |

CM1030_____
| 20¢ **Missouri, multicolored,** tagged | 1.00 | .50 ☐☐☐☐☐ |

CM1031_____
| 20¢ **Montana, multicolored,** tagged | 1.00 | .50 ☐☐☐☐☐ |

CM1032_____
| 20¢ **Nebraska, multicolored,** tagged | 1.00 | .50 ☐☐☐☐☐ |

CM1033_____
| 20¢ **Nevada, multicolored,** tagged | 1.00 | .50 ☐☐☐☐☐ |

CM1034_____
| 20¢ **New Hampshire, multicolored,** tagged | 1.00 | .50 ☐☐☐☐☐ |

CM1035_____
| 20¢ **New Jersey, multicolored,** tagged | 1.00 | .50 ☐☐☐☐☐ |

CM1036_____
| 20¢ **New Mexico, multicolored,** tagged | 1.00 | .50 ☐☐☐☐☐ |

CM1037_____
| 20¢ **New York, multicolored,** tagged | 1.00 | .50 ☐☐☐☐☐ |

CM1038_____
| 20¢ **North Carolina, multicolored,** tagged | 1.00 | .50 ☐☐☐☐☐ |

CM1039_____
| 20¢ **North Dakota, multicolored,** tagged | 1.00 | .50 ☐☐☐☐☐ |

CM1040_____
| 20¢ **Ohio, multicolored,** tagged | 1.00 | .50 ☐☐☐☐☐ |

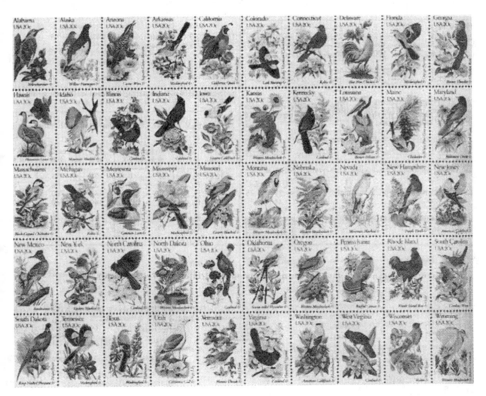

CM1006v-1055v

CM1056

CM1057

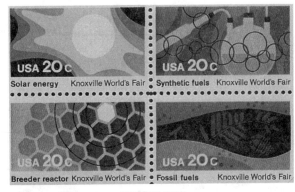

CM1058-1061

CM1062

CM1063

	MNHVF	UseVF	

CM1041_____
20¢ **Oklahoma, multicolored,** tagged — 1.00 / .50 ☐☐☐☐☐

CM1042_____
20¢ **Oregon, multicolored,** tagged — 1.00 / .50 ☐☐☐☐☐

CM1043_____
20¢ **Pennsylvania, multicolored,** tagged — 1.00 / .50 ☐☐☐☐☐

CM1044_____
20¢ **Rhode Island, multicolored,** tagged — 1.00 / .50 ☐☐☐☐☐

CM1045_____
20¢ **South Carolina, multicolored,** tagged — 1.00 / .50 ☐☐☐☐☐

CM1046_____
20¢ **South Dakota, multicolored,** tagged — 1.00 / .50 ☐☐☐☐☐

CM1047_____
20¢ **Tennessee, multicolored,** tagged — 1.00 / .50 ☐☐☐☐☐

CM1048_____
20¢ **Texas multicolored,** tagged — 1.00 / .50 ☐☐☐☐☐

CM1049_____
20¢ **Utah, multicolored,** tagged — 1.00 / .50 ☐☐☐☐☐

CM1050_____
20¢ **Vermont, multicolored,** tagged — 1.00 / .50 ☐☐☐☐☐

CM1051_____
20¢ **Virginia, multicolored,** tagged — 1.00 / .50 ☐☐☐☐☐

CM1052_____
20¢ **Washington, multicolored,** tagged — 1.00 / .50 ☐☐☐☐☐

CM1053_____
20¢ **West Virginia, multicolored,** tagged — 1.00 / .50 ☐☐☐☐☐

CM1054_____
20¢ **Wisconsin, multicolored,** tagged — 1.00 / .50 ☐☐☐☐☐

CM1055_____
20¢ **Wyoming, multicolored,** tagged — 1.00 / .50 ☐☐☐☐☐

NOTE: CM1006-CM1055 exists perforated 11 and 10 1/2 x 11.

CM1056_____ **1982. Netherlands Issue**
20¢ **orange, red, blue & dark gray** tagged (109,245,000) — .35 / .20 ☐☐☐☐☐

CM1057_____ **1982. Library of Congress Issue**
20¢ **black & red** tagged (112,535,000) — .35 / .20 ☐☐☐☐☐

CM1058_____ **1982. Knoxville World's Fair Issue**
20¢ **Solar energy,** tagged (124,640,000) — .35 / .20 ☐☐☐☐☐

CM1059_____
20¢ **Synthetic fuels,** tagged — .35 / .20 ☐☐☐☐☐

CM1060_____
20¢ **Breeder reactor,** tagged — .35 / .20 ☐☐☐☐☐

CM1061_____
20¢ **Fossil fuels,** tagged — .35 / .20 ☐☐☐☐☐

CM1062_____ **1982. Horatio Alger Issue**
20¢ **red & black** on tan paper tagged (107,605,000) — .35 / .20 ☐☐☐☐☐

CM1063_____ **1982. Aging Together Issue**
20¢ **brown** tagged (173,160,000) — .35 / .20 ☐☐☐☐☐

CM1064_____ **1982. Barrymore Family Issue**
20¢ **multicolored** tagged (107,285,000) — .35 / .20 ☐☐☐☐☐

CM1065_____ **1982. Mary Walker Issue**
20¢ **multicolored** tagged (109,040,000) — .35 / .20 ☐☐☐☐☐

CM1066_____ **1982. International Peace Garden Issue**
20¢ **multicolored** tagged (183,270,000) — .35 / .20 ☐☐☐☐☐

	MNHVF	UseVF

CM1067_____ **1982. America's Libraries Issue**
20¢ **red & black** tagged (169,495,000) .35 .20 ⬜⬜⬜⬜⬜
CM1068_____ **1982. Jackie Robinson Issue**
20¢ **multicolored** tagged (164,235,000) 2.50 .20 ⬜⬜⬜⬜⬜
CM1069_____ **1982. Touro Synagogue Issue**
20¢ **multicolored** tagged (110,130,000) .35 .20 ⬜⬜⬜⬜⬜
CM1070_____ **1982. Wolf Trap Farm Issue**
20¢ **multicolored** tagged (110,995,000) .35 .20 ⬜⬜⬜⬜⬜
CM1071_____ **1982. American Architecture Issue**
20¢ **Falling Water,** tagged (165,340,000) .35 .20 ⬜⬜⬜⬜⬜
CM1072_____
20¢ **Illinois Intitute of Technology,** tagged .35 .20 ⬜⬜⬜⬜⬜
CM1073_____
20¢ **Gropius House,** tagged .35 .20 ⬜⬜⬜⬜⬜
CM1074_____
20¢ **Washington International Airport,** tagged .35 .20 ⬜⬜⬜⬜⬜

CM1064

CM1065

CM1066

CM1067

CM1068

CM1069

CM1070

CM1071-1074

CM1075

CM1076

CM1077
→

	MNHVF	UseVF

CM1075_____   **1982. Francis of Assisi Issue**
20¢ **multicolored** tagged (174,180,000) | .35 | .20 ☐☐☐☐☐
CM1076_____   **1982. Ponce de Leon Issue**
20¢ **multicolored** tagged (110,261,000) | .35 | .20 ☐☐☐☐☐
CM1077_____   **1983. Science and Industry Issue**
20¢ **multicolored** tagged (118,555,000) | .35 | .20 ☐☐☐☐☐
CM1078_____   **1983. Sweden Issue**
20¢ **multicolored** tagged (118,225,000) | .30 | .20 ☐☐☐☐☐
CM1079_____   **1983. Ballooning Issue**
20¢ *Intrepid,* tagged (226,128,000) | .35 | .20 ☐☐☐☐☐
CM1080_____
20¢ **Hot air ballooning,** tagged | *.35* | *.20* ☐☐☐☐☐
CM1081_____
20¢ **Hot air ballooning,** tagged | .35 | .20 ☐☐☐☐☐
CM1082_____
20¢ *Explorer II,* tagged | .35 | .20 ☐☐☐☐☐
CM1083_____   **1983. Civilian Conservation Corps Issue**
20¢ **multicolored** tagged (114,290,000) | .35 | .20 ☐☐☐☐☐
CM1084_____   **1983. Joseph Priestly Issue**
20¢ **multicolored** tagged (165,000,000) | .35 | .20 ☐☐☐☐☐
CM1085_____   **1983. Volunteer Issue**
20¢ **red & black** tagged (120,430,000) | .35 | .20 ☐☐☐☐☐
CM1086_____   **1983. German Concord Issue**
20¢ **brown** tagged (117,025,000) | .35 | .20 ☐☐☐☐☐
CM1087_____   **1983. Physical Fitness Issue**
20¢ **multicolored** tagged (111,775,000) | .35 | .20 ☐☐☐☐☐
CM1088_____   **1983. Brooklyn Bridge Issue**
20¢ **blue** tagged (181,700,000) | .35 | .20 ☐☐☐☐☐
CM1089_____   **1983. Tennessee Valley Authority Issue**
20¢ **multicolored** tagged (114,250,000) | .35 | .20 ☐☐☐☐☐
CM1090_____   **1983. Medal of Honor Issue**
20¢ **multicolored** tagged (108,820,000) | .35 | .20 ☐☐☐☐☐
CM1091_____   **1983. Scott Joplin Issue**
20¢ **multicolored** tagged (115,200,000) | .35 | .20 ☐☐☐☐☐
CM1092_____   **1983. Babe Ruth Issue**
20¢ **blue** tagged (184,950,000) | .35 | .20 ☐☐☐☐☐
CM1093_____   **1983. Nathaniel Hawthorne Issue**
20¢ **multicolored** tagged (110,925,000) | .35 | .20 ☐☐☐☐☐
CM1094_____   **1983. 1984 Olympic Issue**
13¢ **Discus,** tagged (395,424,000) | .25 | .20 ☐☐☐☐☐
CM1095_____
13¢ **High jump,** tagged | .25 | .20 ☐☐☐☐☐
CM1096_____
13¢ **Archery,** tagged | .25 | .20 ☐☐☐☐☐
CM1097_____
13¢ **Boxing,** tagged | .25 | .20 ☐☐☐☐☐
CM1098_____   **1983. Treaty of Paris Issue**
20¢ **multicolored** tagged (104,340,000) | .35 | .20 ☐☐☐☐☐
CM1099_____   **1983. Civil Service Issue**
20¢ **beige, blue & red** tagged (114,725,000) | .35 | .20 ☐☐☐☐☐
CM1100_____   **1983. Metropolitan Opera Issue**
20¢ **dark carmine & yellow orange** tagged (112,525,000) | .35 | .20 ☐☐☐☐☐
CM1101_____   **1983. American Inventors Issue**
20¢ **Charles Steinmetz,** tagged (193,055,000) | .35 | .20 ☐☐☐☐☐

CM1078

CM1079-1082

CM1083

CM1085

CM1086

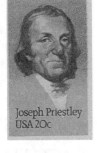

Joseph Priestley
USA 20c

CM1084 ←

Physical Fitness

CM1087 →

CM1088 →

Brooklyn Bridge
1883 1963
USA 20c

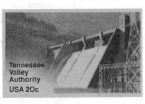

Tennessee
Valley
Authority
USA 20c

CM1089

USA 20c
Medal of Honor

CM1090 ←

CM1091 →

Scott Joplin

Black Heritage USA 20c

CM1092   CM1093

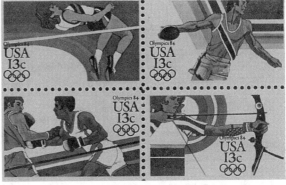

CM1094-1097

	MNHVF	UseVF

CM1102_____
20¢ **Edwin Armstrong,** tagged .35 .20 ☐☐☐☐☐
CM1103_____
20¢ **Nikola Tesla,** tagged .35 .20 ☐☐☐☐☐
CM1104_____
20¢ **Philo T. Farnsworth,** tagged .35 .20 ☐☐☐☐☐
CM1105_____ **1983. Streetcar Issue**
20¢ **NYC's First Horsecar,** tagged .35 .20 ☐☐☐☐☐
CM1106_____
20¢ **Montgomery electric,** tagged .35 .20 ☐☐☐☐☐
CM1107_____
20¢ **"Bobtail" Horse Car,** tagged .35 .20 ☐☐☐☐☐
CM1108_____
20¢ **St. Charles Streetcar,** tagged .35 .20 ☐☐☐☐☐
CM1109_____ **1983. Martin Luther Issue**
20¢ **multicolored** tagged (165,000,000) .35 .20 ☐☐☐☐☐
CM1110_____ **1984. Alaska Statehood Issue**
20¢ **multicolored** tagged (120,000,000) .35 .20 ☐☐☐☐☐
CM1111_____ **1984. Winter Olympics Issue**
20¢ **Ice dancing,** tagged (319,675,000) .35 .20 ☐☐☐☐☐
CM1112_____
20¢ **Alpine skiing,** tagged .35 .20 ☐☐☐☐☐
CM1113_____
20¢ **Cross-country skiing,** tagged **.35** **.20** ☐☐☐☐☐
CM1114_____
20¢ **Ice hockey,** tagged .35 .20 ☐☐☐☐☐
CM1115_____ **1984. Federal Deposit Insurance Corporation Issue**
20¢ **multicolored** tagged (103,975,000) .35 .20 ☐☐☐☐☐
CM1116_____ **1984. Love Issue**
20¢ **multicolored** tagged (554,675,000) .35 .20 ☐☐☐☐☐
CM1117_____ **1984. Carter G. Woodson Issue**
20¢ **multicolored** tagged (120,000,000) .35 .20 ☐☐☐☐☐
CM1118_____ **1984. Soil and Water Conservation Issue**
20¢ **multicolored** tagged (106,975,000) .35 .20 ☐☐☐☐☐
CM1119_____ **1984. Credit Union Act of 1934 Issue**
20¢ **multicolored** tagged (107,325,000) .35 .20 ☐☐☐☐☐
CM1120_____ **1984. Orchids Issue**
20¢ **Wild Pink Orchid,** tagged (306,912,000) .35 .20 ☐☐☐☐☐
CM1121_____
20¢ **Yellow Lady's-Slipper,** tagged .35 .20 ☐☐☐☐☐
CM1122_____
20¢ **Spreading Pogonia,** tagged .35 .20 ☐☐☐☐☐
CM1123_____
20¢ **Pacific Calypso Orchid,** tagged .35 .20 ☐☐☐☐☐
CM1124_____ **1984. Hawaii Statehood Issue**
20¢ **multicolored** tagged (120,000,000) .35 .20 ☐☐☐☐☐
CM1125_____ **1984. National Archives Issue**
20¢ **multicolored** tagged (108,000,000) .35 .20 ☐☐☐☐☐
CM1126_____ **1984. Summer Olympics Issue**
20¢ **Men's diving,** tagged (313,350,000) .35 .20 ☐☐☐☐☐
CM1127_____
20¢ **Women's long jump,** tagged .35 .20 ☐☐☐☐☐
CM1128_____
20¢ **Wrestling,** tagged .35 .20 ☐☐☐☐☐

Treaty of Paris 1783
US Bicentennial 20 cents

CM1098

CM1099

CM1100

CM1101-1104

CM1109

CM1110

CM1105-1108

CM1111-1114

CM1115

CM1116

CM1117

	MNHVF	UseVF

CM1129_____
  20¢ **Women's kayacking,** tagged   .35   .20 ☐☐☐☐☐
CM1130_____   **1984. Louisiana World Exposition Issue**
  20¢ **multicolored** tagged (130,320,000)   .35   .20 ☐☐☐☐☐
CM1131_____   **1984. Health Research Issue**
  20¢ **multicolored** tagged (120,000,000)   .35   .20 ☐☐☐☐☐
CM1132_____   **1984. Douglas Fairbanks Issue**
  20¢ **multicolored** tagged (117,050,000)   .35   .20 ☐☐☐☐☐
CM1133_____   **1984. Jim Thorpe Issue**
  20¢ **dark brown** tagged (115,725,000)   .75   .20 ☐☐☐☐☐
CM1134_____   **1984. John McCormack Issue**
  20¢ **multicolored** tagged (116,600,000)   .35   .20 ☐☐☐☐☐

CM1118

CM1119

CM1120-1123

CM1124

CM1125 ←

CM1130

DOUGLAS FAIRBANKS

Performing Arts USA 20c

CM1132

CM1131

CM1126-1129 →

CM1133

CM1134

CM1135

CM1136

USA 20c

Beagle, Boston Terrier

USA 20c

Chesapeake Bay Retriever, Cocker Spaniel

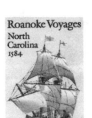

CM1137

CM1138

USA 20c

Alaskan Malamute, Collie

USA 20c

Black and Tan Coonhound, American Foxhound

CM1142-1145

Horace Moses
Founder, Junior Achievement
USA 20c

CM1139

CM1140

CM1141

CM1146

CM1147

CM1148

A Nation of
Readers
USA 20c

CM1149

Hispanic Americans

A Proud Heritage USA 20

CM1150

	MNHVF	UseVF

CM1135_____ **1984. St. Lawrence Seaway Issue**
20¢ **multicolored** tagged (120,000,000) — .35 — .20 ☐☐☐☐☐

CM1136_____ **1984. Wetlands Preservation Issue**
20¢ **blue** tagged (123,575,000) — .35 — .20 ☐☐☐☐☐

CM1137_____ **1984. Roanoke Voyages Issue**
20¢ **multicolored** tagged (120,000,000) — .35 — .20 ☐☐☐☐☐

CM1138_____ **1984. Herman Melville Issue**
20¢ **blue green** tagged (117,125,000) — .35 — .20 ☐☐☐☐☐

CM1139_____ **1984. Horace Moses Issue**
20¢ **orange & dark brown** tagged (117,225,000) — .35 — .20 ☐☐☐☐☐

CM1140_____ **1984. Smokey the Bear Issue**
20¢ **multicolored** tagged (95,525,000) — .35 — .20 ☐☐☐☐☐

CM1141_____ **1984. Roberto Clemente Issue**
20¢ **multicolored** tagged (119,125,000) — 2.75 — .20 ☐☐☐☐☐

CM1142_____ **1984. American Dogs Issue**
20¢ **Beagle & Terrier,** tagged (216,260,000) — .35 — .20 ☐☐☐☐☐

CM1143_____
20¢ **Retriever & Cocker Spaniel,** tagged — **.35** — **.20** ☐☐☐☐☐

CM1144_____
20¢ **Malamute & Collie,** tagged — .35 — .20 ☐☐☐☐☐

CM1145_____
20¢ **Coonhound & Foxhound,** tagged — .35 — .20 ☐☐☐☐☐

CM1146_____ **1984. Crime Prevention Issue**
20¢ **multicolored** tagged (120,000,000) — .35 — .20 ☐☐☐☐☐

CM1147_____ **1984. Family Unity Issue**
20¢ **multicolored** tagged (117,625,000) — .35 — .20 ☐☐☐☐☐

CM1148_____ **1984. Eleanor Roosevelt Issue**
20¢ **blue** tagged (112,896,000) — .35 — .20 ☐☐☐☐☐

CM1149_____ **1984. Nation of Readers Issue**
20¢ **brown & dark red** tagged, (116,500,000) — .35 — .20 ☐☐☐☐☐

CM1150_____ **1984. Hispanic Americans Issue**
20¢ **multicolored** tagged (108,140,000) — .35 — .20 ☐☐☐☐☐

CM1151_____ **1984. Vietnam Veterans Memorial Issue**
20¢ **multicolored** tagged (105,300,000) — .35 — .20 ☐☐☐☐☐

CM1152_____ **1985. Jerome Kern Issue**
22¢ **multicolored** tagged (124,500,000) — .35 — .20 ☐☐☐☐☐

CM1153_____ **1985. Mary McLeod Bethune Issue**
22¢ **multicolored** tagged (120,000,000) — .35 — .20 ☐☐☐☐☐

CM1154_____ **1985. Duck Decoys Issue**
22¢ **Broadbill decoy,** tagged (300,000,000) — .40 — .20 ☐☐☐☐☐

CM1155_____
22¢ **Mallard decoy,** tagged — .40 — .20 ☐☐☐☐☐

CM1156_____
22¢ **Canvasback decoy,** tagged — .40 — .20 ☐☐☐☐☐

CM1157_____
22¢ **Redhead decoy,** tagged — .40 — .20 ☐☐☐☐☐

CM1158_____ **1985. Special Olympics Issue**
22¢ **multicolored** tagged (120,580,000) — .35 — .20 ☐☐☐☐☐

CM1159_____ **1985. Love Issue**
22¢ **multicolored** tagged (729,700,000) — .35 — .20 ☐☐☐☐☐

CM1160_____ **1985. Rural Electrification Administration Issue**
22¢ **multicolored** tagged (124,750,000) — .35 — .20 ☐☐☐☐☐

CM1161_____ **1985. Ameripex 86 Issue**
22¢ **multicolored** tagged (203,496,000) — .35 — .20 ☐☐☐☐☐

Vietnam Veterans Memorial USA 20c

CM1151

Broadbill Decoy

Folk Art USA 22

Mallard Decoy

Folk Art USA 22

Canvasback Decoy

Folk Art USA 22

Redhead Decoy

Folk Art USA 22

CM1154-1157

JEROME KERN

Performing Arts USA

CM1152

Mary McLeod Bethune

Black Heritage USA 22

CM1153

CM1159 →

LOVE US A 22

CM1160 →

22 USA

Rural Electrification Administration 1935 1985

22 USA

Winter Special Olympics

CM1158 →
←

Abigail Adams

USA 22

CM1162 →

CM1163 →

USA 22

F.A. Bartholdi, Statue of Liberty Sculptor

AMERIPEX 86

International Stamp Show, Chicago
May 22 to June 1, 1986

USA 22

CM1161 ←

CM1164 →

Veterans Korea

USA 22

Social Security Act 1935-1985 USA 22

CM1165

Veterans World War I

USA 22

CM1166

USA 22
Quarter horse

USA 22
Morgan

USA 22
Saddlebred

USA 22
Appaloosa

CM1167-1170

	MNHVF	UseVF

CM1162_____   **1985. Abigail Adams Issue**

22¢ **multicolored** tagged (126,325,000)   .35   .20 ☐☐☐☐☐

CM1163_____   **1985. Frederic Auguste Bartholdi Issue**

22¢ **multicolored** tagged (130,000,000)   .35   .20 ☐☐☐☐☐

CM1164_____   **1985. Korean War Veterans Issue**

22¢ **gray green & rose red** tagged (119,975,000)   .35   .20 ☐☐☐☐☐

CM1165_____   **1985. Social Security Act Issue**

22¢ **dark blue & light blue** tagged (120,000,000)   .35   .20 ☐☐☐☐☐

CM1166_____   **1985. World War I Veterans Issue**

22¢ **green & red** tagged (119,975,000)   .35   .20 ☐☐☐☐☐

CM1167_____   **1985. American Horses Issue**

22¢ **Quarter horse,** tagged (147,940,000)   2.75   .20 ☐☐☐☐☐

CM1168_____

22¢ **Morgan,** tagged   2.75   .20 ☐☐☐☐☐

CM1169_____

22¢ **Saddlebred,** tagged   2.75   .20 ☐☐☐☐☐

CM1170_____

22¢ **Appaloosa,** tagged   2.75   .20 ☐☐☐☐☐

CM1171_____   **1985. Public Education Issue**

22¢ **multicolored** tagged (120,000,000)   .35   .20 ☐☐☐☐☐

CM1172_____   **1985. International Youth Year Issue**

22¢ **YMCA youth camping,** tagged (130,000,000)   1.00   .20 ☐☐☐☐☐

CM1173_____

22¢ **Boy Scouts,** tagged   1.00   .20 ☐☐☐☐☐

CM1174_____

22¢ **Big Brothers/Sisters,** tagged   1.00   .20 ☐☐☐☐☐

CM1175_____

22¢ **Camp Fire,** tagged   1.00   .20 ☐☐☐☐☐

CM1176_____   **1985. Help End Hunger Issue**

22¢ **multicolored** tagged (129,000,000)   .35   .20 ☐☐☐☐☐

CM1177_____   **1986. Arkansas Statehood Issue**

22¢ **multicolored** tagged   .35   .20 ☐☐☐☐☐

CM1178_____   **1986. Stamp Collecting Booklet Issue**

22¢ **Covers & handstamp,** tagged (67,996,800)   .40   .20 ☐☐☐☐☐

CM1179_____

22¢ **Youth w/albums,** tagged   .40   .20 ☐☐☐☐☐

CM1180_____

22¢ **Magnifier & stamp,** tagged   .40   .20 ☐☐☐☐☐

CM1181_____

22¢ **AMERIPEX '86 souvenir sheet,** tagged   .40   .20 ☐☐☐☐☐

The complete booklet contains 2 panes.

CM1182_____   **1986. Love Stamp Issue**

22¢ **multicolored** tagged (947,450,000)   .35   .20 ☐☐☐☐☐

CM1183_____   **1986. Sojourner Truth Issue**

22¢ **multicolored** tagged (130,000,000)   .35   .20 ☐☐☐☐☐

CM1184_____   **1986. Republic of Texas Issue**

22¢ **dark blue, dark red & dark gray** tagged (136,500,000)   .35   .20 ☐☐☐☐☐

CM1185_____   **1986. Fish Booklet Issue**

22¢ **Muskellunge,** tagged (219,990,000)   1.75   .20 ☐☐☐☐☐

CM1186_____

22¢ **Atlantic cod,** tagged   1.75   .20 ☐☐☐☐☐

CM1187_____

22¢ **Largemouth bass,** tagged   1.75   .20 ☐☐☐☐☐

CM1171

CM1172-1175 →

Boy Scouts   USA   YMCA Youth Camping   USA

Camp Fire   USA   Big Brothers/Big Sisters   USA

Help End Hunger USA 22

CM1176

STAMP COLLECTING   STAMP COLLECTING   STAMP COLLECTING   STAMP COLLECTING

Ameripex 86

USA 22   USA 22   USA 22   USA 22

CM1178-1181

Arkansas
Statehood
1836-1986
Old State House
Little Rock

USA 22   CM1177 ←

CM1185-1189 →

Muskellunge   22 USA

Atlantic Cod   22 USA

LOVE

USA 22

CM1182

Sojourner Truth
22

Black Heritage USA

CM1183

USA 22

San Jacinto 1836
Republic of Texas

CM1184

Largemouth Bass   22 USA

Bluefin Tuna

USA 22

Public Hospitals USA 22

H

CM1190

Duke
Ellington
22 USA

CM1191 ←

Catfish

USA 22

	MNHVF	UseVF	

CM1188_____
22¢ **Bluefin tuna,** tagged 1.75 .20 ☐☐☐☐☐
CM1189_____
22¢ **Catfish,** tagged 1.75 .20 ☐☐☐☐☐
The complete booklet contains 2 panes.
CM1190_____ **1986. Public Hospitals Issue**
22¢ **multicolored** tagged (130,000,000) .35 .20 ☐☐☐☐☐
CM1191_____ **1986. Duke Ellington Issue**
22¢ **multicolored** tagged (130,000,000) .35 .20 ☐☐☐☐☐
CM1192_____ **1986. Presidents Souvenir Sheets**
$1.98 **Souvenir sheet of 9** (5,825,050) 5.25 4.50 ☐☐☐☐☐
CM1193_____ **1986. Presidents Souvenir Sheets**
$1.98 **Souvenir sheet of 9** (5,825,050) 5.25 4.50 ☐☐☐☐☐
CM1194_____ **1986. Presidents Souvenir Sheets**
$1.98 **Souvenir sheet of 9** (5,825,050) 5.25 4.50 ☐☐☐☐☐
CM1195_____ **1986. Presidents Souvenir Sheets**
$1.98 **Souvenir sheet of 9** (5,825,050) 5.25 4.50 ☐☐☐☐☐
CM1196_____ **1986. Arctic Explorers Issue**
22¢ **E.K. Kane,** (130,000,000) 1.10 .20 ☐☐☐☐☐
CM1197_____
22¢ **A.W. Greely** 1.10 .20 ☐☐☐☐☐
CM1198_____
22¢ **V. Stefansson** 1.10 .20 ☐☐☐☐☐
CM1199_____
22¢ **R.E. Peary & M. Henson** 1.10 .20 ☐☐☐☐☐
CM1200_____ **1986. Statue of Liberty Issue**
22¢ **red & blue** (220,725,000) .35 .20 ☐☐☐☐☐
CM1201_____ **1986. Navajo Art Issue**
22¢ **multicolored** (240,525,000) .40 .20 ☐☐☐☐☐
CM1202_____
22¢ **multicolored** .40 .20 ☐☐☐☐☐
CM1203_____
22¢ **multicolored** .40 .20 ☐☐☐☐☐
CM1204_____
22¢ **multicolored** .40 .20 ☐☐☐☐☐
CM1205_____ **1986. T.S. Eliot Issue**
22¢ **copper red** (131,700,000) .35 .20 ☐☐☐☐☐
CM1206_____ **1986. Woodcarved Figurines Issue**
22¢ **Highlander figure,** tagged (240,000,000) .40 .20 ☐☐☐☐☐
CM1207_____
22¢ **Ship figurehead,** tagged .40 .20 ☐☐☐☐☐
CM1208_____
22¢ **Nautical figure,** tagged .40 .20 ☐☐☐☐☐
CM1209_____
22¢ **Cigar Store figure,** tagged .40 .20 ☐☐☐☐☐
CM1210_____ **1987. Michigan Statehood Issue**
22¢ **multicolored** tagged (167,430,000) .35 .20 ☐☐☐☐☐
CM1211_____ **1987. Pan-American Games Issue**
22¢ **multicolored** tagged (166,555,000) .35 .20 ☐☐☐☐☐
CM1212_____ **1987. Love Stamp Issue**
22¢ **multicolored** tagged (811,560,000) .35 .20 ☐☐☐☐☐
CM1213_____ **1987. Jean-Baptiste du Sable Issue**
22¢ **multicolored** tagged (142,905,000) .35 .20 ☐☐☐☐☐

CM1192

Presidents of
the United States: I

AMERIPEX 86
International
Stamp Show
Chicago, Illinois
May 22-June 1, 1986

Presidents of
the United States: II

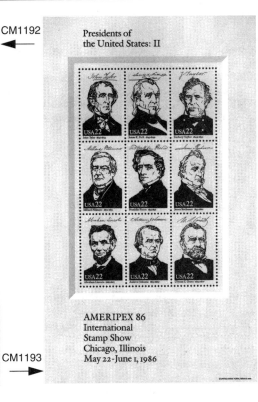

AMERIPEX 86
International
Stamp Show
Chicago, Illinois
May 22-June 1, 1986

CM1193

CM1194

Presidents of
the United States: III

AMERIPEX 86
International
Stamp Show
Chicago, Illinois
May 22-June 1, 1986

Presidents of
the United States: IV

AMERIPEX 86
International
Stamp Show
Chicago, Illinois
May 22-June 1, 1986

CM1195

	MNHVF	UseVF

CM1214_____   **1987. Enrico Caruso Issue**
22¢ **multicolored** tagged (130,000,000) — .35 — .20 ☐☐☐☐☐

CM1215_____   **1987. Girl Scouts Issue**
22¢ **multicolored** tagged (149,980,000) — .35 — .20 ☐☐☐☐☐

CM1216_____   **1987. Special Occasions Issue**
22¢ **Congratulations,** tagged (610,425,000) — 1.75 — .40 ☐☐☐☐☐

CM1217_____
22¢ **Get Well,** tagged — 1.75 — .40 ☐☐☐☐☐

CM1218_____
22¢ **Thank You,** tagged — 1.75 — .40 ☐☐☐☐☐

CM1219_____
22¢ **Love You, Dad,** tagged — 1.75 — .40 ☐☐☐☐☐

CM1220_____
22¢ **Best Wishes,** tagged — 1.75 — .40 ☐☐☐☐☐

CM1221_____
22¢ **Happy Birthday,** tagged — 1.75 — .40 ☐☐☐☐☐

CM1222_____
22¢ **Love You, Mother,** tagged — 1.75 — .40 ☐☐☐☐☐

CM1223_____
22¢ **Keep in Touch,** tagged — 1.75 — .40 ☐☐☐☐☐

Nos. CM1224 and CM1225 are not assigned.

CM1226_____   **1987. United Way Issue**
22¢ **multicolored** tagged (156,995,000) — .35 — .20 ☐☐☐☐☐

CM1227_____   **1987. American Wildlife Issue**
22¢ **Barn Swallow,** tagged — 1.50 — .55 ☐☐☐☐☐

CM1228_____
22¢ **Monarch Butterfly,** tagged — 1.50 — .55 ☐☐☐☐☐

CM1229_____
22¢ **Bighorn Sheep,** tagged — 1.50 — .55 ☐☐☐☐☐

CM1230_____
22¢ **Broad-tailed Hummingbird,** tagged — 1.50 — .55 ☐☐☐☐☐

CM1231_____
22¢ **Cottontail,** tagged — 1.50 — .55 ☐☐☐☐☐

CM1232_____
22¢ **Osprey,** tagged — 1.50 — .55 ☐☐☐☐☐

CM1233_____
22¢ **Mountain Lion,** tagged — 1.50 — .55 ☐☐☐☐☐

CM1234_____
22¢ **Luna Moth,** tagged — 1.50 — .55 ☐☐☐☐☐

CM1235_____
22¢ **Mule Deer,** tagged — 1.50 — .55 ☐☐☐☐☐

CM1236_____
22¢ **Gray Squirrel,** tagged — 1.50 — .55 ☐☐☐☐☐

CM1237_____
22¢ **Armadillo,** tagged — 1.50 — .55 ☐☐☐☐☐

CM1238_____
22¢ **Eastern Chipmunk,** tagged — 1.50 — .55 ☐☐☐☐☐

CM1239_____
22¢ **Moose,** tagged — 1.50 — .55 ☐☐☐☐☐

CM1240_____
22¢ **Black Bear,** tagged — 1.50 — .55 ☐☐☐☐☐

CM1241_____
22¢ **Tiger Swallowtail,** — 1.50 — .55 ☐☐☐☐☐

CM1242_____
22¢ **Bobwhite,** tagged — 1.50 — .55 ☐☐☐☐☐

CM1196-1199

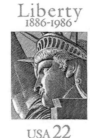

Liberty
1886-1986

USA 22

CM1200

Navajo Art USA 22   Navajo Art USA 22

CM1201-1204 →

Navajo Art USA 22   Navajo Art USA 22

T.S. Eliot

22 USA

CM1205

CM1206-1209 ←

Congratulations! USA

Get Well!   USA 22

USA 22

Thank You!

USA 22

1837-1987
Michigan Statehood

CM1210 ←

Love You, Dad!   USA 22

Best Wishes!   USA 22

Happy Birthday!   USA 22

22 USA

Pan American Games Indianapolis 1987

CM1211

Jean Baptiste
Pointe Du Sable
22

Black Heritage USA

CM1213 ←

LOVE

USA 22

CM1212

Love You, Mother! USA 22

Keep In Touch!   USA 22

Happy Birthday!   USA 22

CM1216-1223 ►

Enrico Caruso
22 USA

CM1214 ←

GIRL SCOUTS USA 22

CM1215 ←

Congratulations! USA 22

	MNHVF	UseVF
CM1243_____		
22¢ **Ringtail,** tagged	1.50	.55 ☐☐☐☐☐
CM1244_____		
22¢ **Red-winged Blackbird,** tagged	1.50	.55 ☐☐☐☐☐
CM1245_____		
22¢ **American Lobster,** tagged	1.50	.55 ☐☐☐☐☐
CM1246_____		
22¢ **Black-tailed Jack Rabbit,** tagged	1.50	.55 ☐☐☐☐☐
CM1247_____		
22¢ **Scarlet Tanager,** tagged	1.50	.55 ☐☐☐☐☐
CM1248_____		
22¢ **Woodchuck,** tagged	1.50	.55 ☐☐☐☐☐
CM1249_____		
22¢ **Roseate Spoonbill,** tagged	1.50	.55 ☐☐☐☐☐
CM1250_____		
22¢ **Bald Eagle,** tagged	1.50	.55 ☐☐☐☐☐
CM1251_____		
22¢ **Alaskan Brown Bear,** tagged	1.50	.55 ☐☐☐☐☐
CM1252_____		
22¢ **Iiwi,** tagged	1.50	.55 ☐☐☐☐☐
CM1253_____		
22¢ **Badger,** tagged	1.50	.55 ☐☐☐☐☐
CM1254_____		
22¢ **Pronghorn,** tagged	1.50	.55 ☐☐☐☐☐
CM1255_____		
22¢ **River Otter,** tagged	1.50	.55 ☐☐☐☐☐
CM1256_____		
22¢ **Ladybug,** tagged	1.50	.55 ☐☐☐☐☐
CM1257_____		
22¢ **Beaver,** tagged	1.50	.55 ☐☐☐☐☐
CM1258_____		
22¢ **White-tailed Deer,** tagged	1.50	.55 ☐☐☐☐☐
CM1259_____		
22¢ **Blue Jay,** tagged	1.50	.55 ☐☐☐☐☐
CM1260_____		
22¢ **Pika,** tagged	1.50	.55 ☐☐☐☐☐
CM1261_____		
22¢ **Bison,** tagged	1.50	.55 ☐☐☐☐☐
CM1262_____		
22¢ **Snowy Egret,** tagged	1.50	.55 ☐☐☐☐☐
CM1263_____		
22¢ **Gray Wolf,** tagged	1.50	.55 ☐☐☐☐☐
CM1264_____		
22¢ **Mountain Goat,** tagged	1.50	.55 ☐☐☐☐☐
CM1265_____		
22¢ **Deer Mouse,** tagged	1.50	.55 ☐☐☐☐☐
CM1266_____		
22¢ **Black-tailed Prairie Dog,** tagged	1.50	.55 ☐☐☐☐☐
CM1267_____		
22¢ **Box Turtle,** tagged	1.50	.55 ☐☐☐☐☐
CM1268_____		
22¢ **Wolverine,** tagged	1.50	.55 ☐☐☐☐☐
CM1269_____		
22¢ **American Elk,** tagged	1.50	.55 ☐☐☐☐☐

	MNHVF	UseVF	

CM1270_____
   22¢ **California Sea Lion**, tagged   1.50   .55 ☐☐☐☐☐

CM1271_____
   22¢ **Mockingbird**, tagged   1.50   .55 ☐☐☐☐☐

CM1272_____
   22¢ **Raccoon**, tagged   1.50   .55 ☐☐☐☐☐

CM1273_____
   22¢ **Bobcat**, tagged   1.50   .55 ☐☐☐☐☐

CM1274_____
   22¢ **Black-footed Ferret**, tagged   1.50   .55 ☐☐☐☐☐

CM1275_____
   22¢ **Canada Goose**, tagged   1.50   .55 ☐☐☐☐☐

CM1276_____
   22¢ **Red Fox**, tagged   1.50   .55 ☐☐☐☐☐

CM1277_____ **1987. Delaware Statehood Issue**
   22¢ **multicolored** tagged (166,725,000)   .35   .20 ☐☐☐☐☐

CM1278_____ **1987. Friendship with Morocco Issue**
   22¢ **red & black** tagged (157,475,000)   .35   .20 ☐☐☐☐☐

CM1279_____ **1987. William Faulkner Issue**
   22¢ **green** tagged (156,225,000)   .35   .20 ☐☐☐☐☐

Note: Imperforate singles are untagged and from printer's waste.

CM1280_____ **1987. Lacemaking Issue**
   22¢ **Squash blossoms**, tagged (163,980,000)   .40   .20 ☐☐☐☐☐

CM1281_____
   22¢ **Floral design**, tagged   .40   .20 ☐☐☐☐☐

CM1282_____
   22¢ **Floral lace design**, tagged   .40   .20 ☐☐☐☐☐

CM1283_____
   22¢ **Dogwood blossoms**, tagged   .40   .20 ☐☐☐☐☐

CM1284_____ **1987. Pennsylvania Statehood Issue**
   22¢ **multicolored** tagged (186,575,000)   .35   .20 ☐☐☐☐☐

CM1285_____ **1987. Constitution Bicentennial Issue**
   22¢ **The Bicentennial...**, tagged (584,340,000)   .75   .25 ☐☐☐☐☐

CM1286_____
   22¢ **We the people...**, tagged   .75   .25 ☐☐☐☐☐

CM1287_____
   22¢ **Establish justice...**, tagged   .75   .25 ☐☐☐☐☐

CM1288_____
   22¢ **And secure... liberty...**, tagged   .75   .25 ☐☐☐☐☐

CM1289_____
   22¢ **Do ordain...**, tagged   .75   .25 ☐☐☐☐☐

CM1290_____ **1987. New Jersey Statehood Issue**
   22¢ **multicolored** tagged (184,325,000)   .35   .20 ☐☐☐☐☐

CM1291_____ **1987. Constitution Bicentennial Issue**
   22¢ **multicolored** tagged (168,995,000)   .35   .20 ☐☐☐☐☐

CM1292_____ **1987. Certified Public Accountants Issue**
   22¢ **multicolored** tagged (163,120,000)   .35   .20 ☐☐☐☐☐

CM1293_____ **1987. Steam Locomotive Issue**
   22¢ *Stourbridge Lion,* tagged   .75   .25 ☐☐☐☐☐

CM1294_____
   22¢ *Best Friend of Charleston,* tagged   .75   .25 ☐☐☐☐☐

CM1295_____
   22¢ *John Bull,* tagged   .75   .25 ☐☐☐☐☐

	MNHVF	UseVF

CM1296_____
22¢ *Brother Jonathan,* tagged — .75 / .25 ☐☐☐☐☐

CM1297_____
22¢ *Gowan & Marx,* tagged — .75 / .25 ☐☐☐☐☐

CM1298_____   **1988. Georgia Statehood Issue**
22¢ **multicolored** tagged (165,845,000) — .35 / .20 ☐☐☐☐☐

CM1299_____   **1988. Connecticut Statehood Issue**
22¢ **multicolored** tagged (155,170,000) — .35 / .20 ☐☐☐☐☐

CM1300_____   **1988. Winter Olympics Issue**
22¢ **multicolored** tagged (158,870,000) — .35 / .20 ☐☐☐☐☐

CM1301_____   **1988. Australia Bicentennial Issue**
22¢ **multicolored** tagged (145,560,000) — .35 / .20 ☐☐☐☐☐

CM1302_____   **1988. James Weldon Johnson Issue**
22¢ **multicolored** tagged (97,300,000) — .35 / .20 ☐☐☐☐☐

CM1303_____   **1988. Cats Issue**
22¢ **Siamese, Exotic Shorthair,** tagged (158,556,000) — 1.00 / .20 ☐☐☐☐☐

CM1304_____
22¢ **Abyssinian, Himalayan,** tagged — 1.00 / .20 ☐☐☐☐☐

CM1305_____
22¢ **Maine Coon Cat, Burmese,** tagged — 1.00 / .20 ☐☐☐☐☐

CM1306_____
22¢ **American Shorthair, Persian,** tagged — 1.00 / .20 ☐☐☐☐☐

CM1307_____   **1988. Massachusetts Statehood Issue**
22¢ **dark blue & dark red** tagged (102,100,000) — .35 / .20 ☐☐☐☐☐

CM1308_____   **1988. Maryland Statehood Issue**
22¢ **multicolored** tagged (103,325,000) — .35 / .20 ☐☐☐☐☐

CM1309_____   **1988. Knute Rockne Issue**
22¢ **multicolored** tagged (97,300,000) — .35 / .20 ☐☐☐☐☐

CM1310_____   **1988. South Carolina Statehood Issue**
25¢ **multicolored** tagged (162,045,000) — .40 / .20 ☐☐☐☐☐

CM1311_____   **1988. Francis Ouimet Issue**
25¢ **multicolored** tagged (153,045,000) — .40 / .20 ☐☐☐☐☐

CM1312_____   **1988. New Hampshire Statehood Issue**
25¢ **multicolored** tagged (153,295,000) — .40 / .20 ☐☐☐☐☐

CM1313_____   **1988. Virginia Statehood Issue**
25¢ **multicolored** tagged (153,295,000) — .40 / .20 ☐☐☐☐☐

CM1314_____   **1988. Love Issue**
25¢ **multicolored** tagged (841,240,000) — .40 / .20 ☐☐☐☐☐

CM1315_____   **1988. New York Statehood Issue**
25¢ **multicolored** tagged (183,290,000) — .40 / .20 ☐☐☐☐☐

CM1316_____   **1988. Love Issue**
45¢ **multicolored** tagged (169,765,000) — 1.35 / .20 ☐☐☐☐☐

CM1317_____   **1988. Summer Olympic Games Issue**
25¢ **multicolored** tagged (157,215,000) — .40 / .20 ☐☐☐☐☐

CM1318_____   **1988. Classic Cars Issue**
25¢ **Locomobile,** tagged (635,238,000) — 2.00 / .50 ☐☐☐☐☐

CM1319_____
25¢ **Pierce-Arrow,** tagged — 2.00 / .50 ☐☐☐☐☐

CM1320_____
25¢ **Cord,** tagged — 2.00 / .50 ☐☐☐☐☐

CM1321_____
25¢ **Packard,** tagged — 2.00 / .50 ☐☐☐☐☐

CM1322_____
25¢ **Duesenberg,** tagged — 2.00 / .50 ☐☐☐☐☐

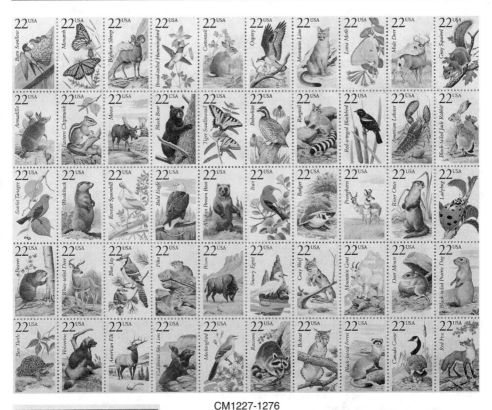

CM1227-1276

CM1226

Dec 7,1787 USA
Delaware 22

CM1277

Friendship
with Morocco
1787-1987

CM1278 ←

USA 22

CM1279

Lacemaking USA 22 : Lacemaking USA 22

CM1280-1283
→ Lacemaking USA 22 : Lacemaking USA 22

Dec 12,1787
Pennsylvania

CM1284

CM1285-1289

	MNHVF	UseVF

CM1323_____   **1988. Antarctic Explorers Issue**

25¢ **Nathaniel Palmer,** tagged (162,142,500) — 1.00 — .20 ☐☐☐☐☐

CM1324_____

25¢ **Lt. Charles Wilkes,** tagged — 1.00 — .20 ☐☐☐☐☐

CM1325_____

25¢ **Richard E. Byrd,** tagged — 1.00 — .20 ☐☐☐☐☐

CM1326_____

25¢ **Lincoln Ellsworth,** tagged — 1.00 — .20 ☐☐☐☐☐

CM1327_____   **1988. Carousel Animal Issue**

25¢ **Deer,** tagged (305,015,000) — 1.00 — .20 ☐☐☐☐☐

CM1328_____

25¢ **Horse,** tagged — 1.00 — .20 ☐☐☐☐☐

CM1329_____

25¢ **Camel,** tagged — 1.00 — .20 ☐☐☐☐☐

CM1330_____

25¢ **Goat,** tagged — 1.00 — .20 ☐☐☐☐☐

CM1331_____   **1988. Special Occasions Issue**

25¢ **multicolored** tagged (480,000,000) — 1.00 — .20 ☐☐☐☐☐

CM1332_____

25¢ **multicolored** tagged — 1.00 — .20 ☐☐☐☐☐

CM1333_____

25¢ **multicolored** tagged — 1.00 — .20 ☐☐☐☐☐

CM1334_____

25¢ **multicolored** tagged — 1.00 — .20 ☐☐☐☐☐

CM1335_____   **1989. Montana Statehood Issue**

25¢ **multicolored** tagged — .40 — .20 ☐☐☐☐☐

CM1336_____   **1989. A. Philip Randolph Issue**

25¢ **multicolored** tagged (151,675,000) — .40 — .20 ☐☐☐☐☐

CM1337_____   **1989. North Dakota Statehood Issue**

25¢ **multicolored** tagged (163,000,000) — .40 — .20 ☐☐☐☐☐

CM1338_____   **1989. Washington Statehood Issue**

25¢ **multicolored** tagged (264,625,000) — .75 — .20 ☐☐☐☐☐

CM1339_____   **1989. Steamboats Issue**

25¢ **Experiment,** tagged (204,984,000) — .75 — .20 ☐☐☐☐☐

CM1340_____

25¢ **Phoenix,** tagged — .75 — .20 ☐☐☐☐☐

CM1341_____

25¢ **New Orleans,** tagged — .75 — .20 ☐☐☐☐☐

CM1342_____

25¢ **Washington,** tagged — .75 — .20 ☐☐☐☐☐

CM1343_____

25¢ **Walk in the Water,** tagged — .75 — .20 ☐☐☐☐☐

CM1344_____   **1989. World Stamp Expo 89 Issue**

25¢ **red, gray & black** (103,835,000) — .40 — .20 ☐☐☐☐☐

CM1345_____   **1989. Arturo Toscanini Issue**

25¢ **multicolored** tagged (152,250,000) — .40 — .20 ☐☐☐☐☐

CM1346_____   **1989. House of Representatives Issue**

25¢ **multicolored** tagged (138,760,000) — .40 — .20 ☐☐☐☐☐

CM1347_____   **1989. Senate Issue**

25¢ **multicolored** tagged (137,985,000) — .40 — .20 ☐☐☐☐☐

CM1348_____   **1989. Executive Branch Issue**

25¢ **multicolored** tagged (138,580,000) — .40 — .20 ☐☐☐☐☐

CM1349_____   **1989. South Dakota Statehood Issue**

25¢ **multicolored** tagged (164,680,000) — .40 — .20 ☐☐☐☐☐

Dec 18, 1787   USA
New Jersey 22

CM1290

CM1291

CM1292

CM1293-1297

January 2, 1788
Georgia

CM1298

January 9, 1788
Connecticut

CM1299

CM1300

CM1301

James Weldon
Johnson 22

Lift ev-'ry voice and sing
Black Heritage USA

CM1302

Feb 6, 1788
Massachusetts

CM1307

April 28, 1788   USA
Maryland   22

CM1308

USA 22   Siamese Cat, Exotic Shorthair Cat

USA 22   Abyssinian Cat, Himalayan Cat

USA 22   Maine Coon Cat, Burmese Cat

USA 22   American Shorthair Cat, Persian Cat

CM1303-1306

22 USA
KNUTE ROCKNE

CM1309

25 USA

May 23, 1788
South Carolina

CM1310

	MNHVF	UseVF

CM1350_____ **1989. Lou Gehrig Issue**

25¢ **multicolored** tagged (138,760,000) — 1.10 — .20 ☐☐☐☐☐

CM1351_____ **1989. Ernest Hemingway Issue**

25¢ **multicolored** tagged (191,755,000) — .40 — .20 ☐☐☐☐☐

CM1352_____ **1989. Moon Landing Anniversary Issue**

$2.40**multicolored** tagged — 6.00 — 2.25 ☐☐☐☐☐

CM1353_____ **1989. North Carolina Statehood Issue**

25¢ **multicolored** tagged (179,800,000) — .40 — .20 ☐☐☐☐☐

CM1354_____ **1989. Letter Carriers Issue**

25¢ **multicolored** tagged (188,400,000) — .40 — .20 ☐☐☐☐☐

CM1355_____ **1989. Bill of Rights Issue**

25¢ **multicolored** tagged (191,860,000) — .40 — .20 ☐☐☐☐☐

CM1356_____ **1989. Dinosaurs Issue**

25¢ **Tyrannosaurus,** tagged — 1.25 — .20 ☐☐☐☐☐

CM1357_____

25¢ **Pteranodon,** tagged — 1.25 — .20 ☐☐☐☐☐

CM1358_____

25¢ **Stegosaurus,** tagged — 1.25 — .20 ☐☐☐☐☐

CM1359_____

25¢ **Apatosaurus,** tagged — 1.25 — .20 ☐☐☐☐☐

CM1360_____ **1989. America Issue**

25¢ **multicolored** tagged (137,410,000) — .40 — .20 ☐☐☐☐☐

CM1361_____ **1989. World Stamp Expo 89 Souvenir Sheet**

$3.60**Souvenir sheet of 4** (2,017,225) — 20.00 — 13.50 ☐☐☐☐☐

CM1362_____ **1989. Classic Mail Transportation Issue**

25¢ **Stagecoach,** tagged (163,824,000) — .75 — .20 ☐☐☐☐☐

CM1363_____

25¢ **Steamboat,** tagged — .75 — .20 ☐☐☐☐☐

CM1364_____

25¢ **Biplane,** tagged — .75 — .20 ☐☐☐☐☐

CM1365_____

25¢ **Early automobile,** tagged — .75 — .20 ☐☐☐☐☐

CM1366_____ **1989. Classic Mail Transportation Souvenir Sheet Issue**

$1 **multicolored Souvenir sheet,** tagged — 5.00 — 4.00 ☐☐☐☐☐

CM1367_____ **1990. Idaho Statehood Issue**

25¢ **multicolored** tagged — .40 — .20 ☐☐☐☐☐

CM1368_____ **1990. Love Issue**

25¢ **multicolored** tagged perforated 12 x 13 — .40 — .20 ☐☐☐☐☐

CM1369_____

25¢ **multicolored** tagged perforated 11 1/2 on 2 or 3 sides — .40 — .20 ☐☐☐☐☐

CM1370_____ **1990. Ida B. Wells Issue**

25¢ **multicolored** tagged — .40 — .20 ☐☐☐☐☐

CM1371_____ **1990. Supreme Court Issue**

25¢ **multicolored** tagged — .40 — .20 ☐☐☐☐☐

CM1372_____ **1990. Wyoming Statehood Issue**

25¢ **multicolored** tagged — .40 — .20 ☐☐☐☐☐

CM1373_____ **1990. Classic Films Issue**

25¢ *Wizard of Oz,* tagged — 2.00 — .20 ☐☐☐☐☐

CM1374_____

25¢ *Gone with The Wind,* tagged — 2.00 — .20 ☐☐☐☐☐

CM1375_____

25¢ *Beau Geste,* tagged — 2.00 — .20 ☐☐☐☐☐

CM1376_____

25¢ *Stagecoach,* tagged — 2.00 — .20 ☐☐☐☐☐

CM1311

June 21, 1788
NewHampshire

CM1312

June 25, 1788 USA
Virginia 25

CM1313

CM1314

July 26, 1788 USA
NewYork 25

CM1315

CM1316

CM1317

1928 Locomobile

1929 Pierce-Arrow

1931 Cord

1932 Packard

1935 Duesenberg

CM1318-1322 →

CM1323-1326 ←

CM1327-1330

Happy Birthday 25 USA

CM1331

Best Wishes 25 USA

CM1332

CM1333

CM1334 →

	MNHVF	UseVF

CM1377_____ 1990. Marianne Moore Issue
25¢ **multicolored** tagged — .40 — .20 ☐☐☐☐☐

CM1378_____ 1990. American Lighthouses Issue
25¢ **Admiralty Head,** tagged — .40 — .20 ☐☐☐☐☐

CM1379_____
25¢ **Cape Hatteras,** tagged — .40 — .20 ☐☐☐☐☐

CM1380_____
25¢ **West Quoddy Head,** tagged — .40 — .20 ☐☐☐☐☐

CM1381_____
25¢ **American Shoals,** tagged — .40 — .20 ☐☐☐☐☐

CM1382_____
25¢ **Sandy Hook,** tagged — .40 — .20 ☐☐☐☐☐

CM1383_____ 1990. Rhode Island Statehood Issue
25¢ **multicolored** tagged — .40 — .20 ☐☐☐☐☐

CM1384_____ 1990. Olympic Athletes Issue
25¢ **Jesse Owens,** tagged — .40 — .20 ☐☐☐☐☐

CM1385_____
25¢ **Ray Ewry,** tagged — .40 — .20 ☐☐☐☐☐

CM1386_____
25¢ **Hazel Wightman,** tagged — .40 — .20 ☐☐☐☐☐

CM1387_____
25¢ **Eddie Eagan,** tagged — .40 — .20 ☐☐☐☐☐

CM1388_____
25¢ **Helene Madison,** tagged — .40 — .20 ☐☐☐☐☐

CM1389_____ 1990. American Indian Headdresses Issue
25¢ **Assiniboine,** tagged — .40 — .20 ☐☐☐☐☐

CM1390_____
25¢ **Cheyenne,** tagged — .40 — .20 ☐☐☐☐☐

CM1391_____
25¢ **Commanche,** tagged — .40 — .20 ☐☐☐☐☐

CM1392_____
25¢ **Flathead,** tagged — .40 — .20 ☐☐☐☐☐

CM1393_____
25¢ **Shoshone,** tagged — .40 — .20 ☐☐☐☐☐

CM1394_____ 1990. Micronesia and Marshall Islands Issue
25¢ **Micronesia,** tagged — .40 — .20 ☐☐☐☐☐

CM1395_____
25¢ **Marshall Islands,** tagged — .40 — .20 ☐☐☐☐☐

CM1396_____ 1990. Sea Mammals Issue
25¢ **Killer Whale,** tagged (278,264,000) — .75 — .20 ☐☐☐☐☐

CM1397_____
25¢ **Northern Sea Lion,** tagged — .75 — .20 ☐☐☐☐☐

CM1398_____
25¢ **Sea Otter,** tagged — .75 — .20 ☐☐☐☐☐

CM1399_____
25¢ **Dolphin,** tagged — .75 — .20 ☐☐☐☐☐

CM1400_____ 1990. America Issue
25¢ **multicolored** tagged (143,995,000) — .40 — .20 ☐☐☐☐☐

CM1401_____ 1990. Dwight D. Eisenhower Issue
25¢ **multicolored** tagged (142,692,000) — .45 — .20 ☐☐☐☐☐

CM1402_____ 1991. Switzerland 700th Anniversary Issue
50¢ **multicolored** tagged (103,648,000) — .75 — .35 ☐☐☐☐☐

CM1403_____ 1991. Vermont Statehood Issue
29¢ **multicolored** tagged (179,990,000) — .45 — .20 ☐☐☐☐☐

CM1335

CM1336

North Dakota 1889

CM1337

CM1338

CM1344

Experiment 1788-1790

Phoenix 1809

CM1345

New Orleans 1812

CM1346   CM1347

Washington 1816

Walk in the Water 1818

CM1339-1343

CM1348

CM1349

CM1350

CM1351

CM1352

CM1353

		MNHVF	UseVF

CM1404_____   **1991. U.S. Savings Bond Issue**
29¢ **multicolored** tagged (150,560,000)   .45   .20 ☐☐☐☐☐
CM1405_____   **1991. Love Issue**
29¢ **multicolored** tagged, perforated 12 1/2 x 13   .45   .20 ☐☐☐☐☐
CM1405A _____
29¢ **multicolored** tagged, perforated 11   .45   .20 ☐☐☐☐☐
CM1406_____
29¢ **multicolored** tagged, perforated 11 on 2 or 3 sides   .45   .20 ☐☐☐☐☐
CM1407_____
52¢ **multicolored** tagged   .75   .35 ☐☐☐☐☐
CM1408_____   **1991. William Saroyan Issue**
29¢ **multicolored** tagged (161,498,000)   .45   .20 ☐☐☐☐☐
CM1409_____   **1991. Fishing Flies Issue**
29¢ **Royal Wulff,** tagged (744,918,000)   .45   .20 ☐☐☐☐☐
CM1410_____
29¢ **Jack Scott,** tagged   .45   .20 ☐☐☐☐☐

CM1354

CM1355

CM1356-1359

CM1360

WORLD STAMP EXPO'89℠

The classic 1869 U.S. Abraham Lincoln stamp is reborn in these four larger versions commemorating World Stamp Expo'89, held in Washington, D.C. during the 20th Universal Postal Congress of the UPU. These stamps show the issued colors and three of the trial proof color combinations.
©USPS 1988

CM1361

CM1362, 1366a (upper left)
CM1363, 1366b (upper right)
CM1364, 1366c (lower left)
CM1365, 1366d (lower right)

20th Universal Postal Congress

A review of historical methods of delivering the mail in the United States is the theme of these four stamps issued in commemoration of the convening of the 20th Universal Postal Congress in Washington, D.C. from November 13 through December 14, 1989. The United States, as host nation to the Congress for the first time in ninety-two years, welcomed more than 1,000 delegates from most of the member nations of the Universal Postal Union to the major international event.
©USPS 1989

CM1366

CM1367

CM1368-1369

CM1372

Black Heritage USA
25

CM1370

Chief Justice John Marshall

CM1371

CM1373-1376

American Poet 1887-1972

CM1377

CM1378-1382

May 29, 1790
Rhode Island

CM1383

CM1384-1388

CM1389-1393

	MNHVF	UseVF

CM1411_____
29¢ **Apte Tarpon,** tagged .45 .20 ☐☐☐☐☐
CM1412_____
29¢ **Lefty's Deceiver,** tagged .45 .20 ☐☐☐☐☐
CM1413_____
29¢ **Muddler Minnow,** tagged .45 .20 ☐☐☐☐☐
CM1414_____ **1991. Cole Porter Issue**
29¢ **multicolored** tagged (149,848,000) .45 .20 ☐☐☐☐☐
CM1415_____ **1991. Desert Shield-Desert Storm Issue**
29¢ **multicolored** tagged (200,003,000) .45 .20 ☐☐☐☐☐
CM1416_____ **1991. Desert Shield-Desert Storm Booklet Issue**
29¢ **multicolored** tagged (200,000,000) .45 .20 ☐☐☐☐☐
CM1417_____ **1991. Olympic Track and Field Issue**
29¢ **Pole vault,** tagged (170,025,000) .45 .20 ☐☐☐☐☐
CM1418_____
29¢ **Discus,** tagged .45 .20 ☐☐☐☐☐
CM1419_____
29¢ **Women's sprint,** tagged .45 .20 ☐☐☐☐☐
CM1420_____
29¢ **Javelin,** tagged .45 .20 ☐☐☐☐☐
CM1421_____
29¢ **Women's hurdles,** tagged .45 .20 ☐☐☐☐☐
CM1422_____ **1991. Numismatics Issue**
29¢ **multicolored** tagged (150,310,000) .45 .20 ☐☐☐☐☐
CM1423_____ **1991. Basketball Centennial Issue**
29¢ **multicolored** tagged (149,810,000) .45 .20 ☐☐☐☐☐
CM1424_____ **1991. American Comedians Issue**
29¢ **Laurel & Hardy,** tagged (699,978,000) .45 .20 ☐☐☐☐☐
CM1425_____
29¢ **Bergen & McCarthy,** tagged .45 .20 ☐☐☐☐☐
CM1426_____
29¢ **Jack Benny,** tagged .45 .20 ☐☐☐☐☐
CM1427_____
29¢ **Fanny Brice,** tagged .45 .20 ☐☐☐☐☐
CM1428_____
29¢ **Abbott & Costello,** tagged .45 .20 ☐☐☐☐☐
CM1429_____ **1991. 1941: A World At War Issue**
$2.90 **Commemorative pane of 10** 9.00 5.00 ☐☐☐☐☐
CM1430_____ **1991. District of Columbia Bicentennial Issue**
29¢ **multicolored** tagged (699,978,000) .45 .20 ☐☐☐☐☐
CM1431_____ **1991. Jan E. Matzeliger Issue**
29¢ **multicolored** tagged (148,973,000) .45 .20 ☐☐☐☐☐
CM1432_____ **1991. Space Exploration Issue**
29¢ **Mercury,** tagged (333,948,000) .45 .20 ☐☐☐☐☐
CM1433_____
29¢ **Venus,** tagged .45 .20 ☐☐☐☐☐
CM1434_____
29¢ **Earth,** tagged .45 .20 ☐☐☐☐☐
CM1435_____
29¢ **Moon,** tagged .45 .20 ☐☐☐☐☐
CM1436_____
29¢ **Mars,** tagged .45 .20 ☐☐☐☐☐
CM1437_____
29¢ **Jupiter,** tagged .45 .20 ☐☐☐☐☐

CM1394-1395

CM1396-1399

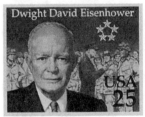
CM1400

CM1401

CM1402

CM1403

CM1404

CM1405-1406

NUMISMATICS
CM1422

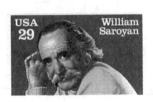
CM1408

CM1407

CM1409-1413

CM1423

CM1414

CM1415-1416

CM1417-1421

	MNHVF	UseVF

CM1438_____
29¢ **Saturn**, tagged — .45 — .20 ☐☐☐☐☐

CM1439_____
29¢ **Uranus**, tagged — .45 — .20 ☐☐☐☐☐

CM1440_____
29¢ **Neptune**, tagged — .45 — .20 ☐☐☐☐☐

CM1441_____
29¢ **Pluto**, tagged — .45 — .20 ☐☐☐☐☐

CM1442_____ **1992. Winter Olympics Issue**
29¢ **multicolored** tagged — .45 — .20 ☐☐☐☐☐

CM1443_____
29¢ **multicolored** tagged — .45 — .20 ☐☐☐☐☐

CM1444_____
29¢ **multicolored** tagged — .45 — .20 ☐☐☐☐☐

CM1445_____
29¢ **multicolored** tagged — .45 — .20 ☐☐☐☐☐

CM1446_____
29¢ **multicolored** tagged — .45 — .20 ☐☐☐☐☐

CM1447_____ **1992. World Columbian Stamp Expo '92 Issue**
29¢ **multicolored** tagged — .45 — .20 ☐☐☐☐☐

CM1448_____ **1992. W.E.B. Du Bois Issue**
29¢ **multicolored** tagged — .45 — .20 ☐☐☐☐☐

CM1449_____ **1992. Love Issue**
29¢ **multicolored** tagged — .45 — .20 ☐☐☐☐☐

CM1450_____ **1992. Olympic Baseball Issue**
29¢ **multicolored** tagged — 1.00 — .20 ☐☐☐☐☐

CM1451_____ **1992. Voyage of Columbus Issue**
29¢ **Seeking Support,** tagged — 1.00 — .20 ☐☐☐☐☐

CM1452_____
29¢ **Atlantic Crossing,** tagged — 1.00 — .20 ☐☐☐☐☐

CM1453_____
29¢ **Approaching Land,** tagged — 1.00 — .20 ☐☐☐☐☐

CM1454_____
29¢ **Coming Ashore,** tagged — 1.00 — .20 ☐☐☐☐☐

CM1455_____ **1992. New York Stock Exchange Issue**
29¢ **multicolored** tagged — .45 — .20 ☐☐☐☐☐

CM1456_____ **1992. Columbian Souvenir Sheets**
85¢ **Sheet of three** — 3.00 — ☐☐☐☐☐

NOTE: *Imperforate souvenir sheets are very probably the result of printer's waste.*
CM1457_____
$1.05 **Sheet of three** — 2.50 — ☐☐☐☐☐

CM1458_____
$2.25 **Sheet of three** — 5.00 — ☐☐☐☐☐

CM1459_____
$3.14 **Sheet of three** — 8.50 — ☐☐☐☐☐

CM1460_____
$4.07 **Sheet of three** — 9.00 — ☐☐☐☐☐

CM1461_____
$5 **Sheet of one, black** like CM15 — 12.00 — 8.50 ☐☐☐☐☐

CM1462_____ **1992. Space Achievements Issue**
29¢ **Space Shuttle,** tagged — 1.00 — .20 ☐☐☐☐☐

CM1463_____
29¢ **Space station,** tagged — 1.00 — .20 ☐☐☐☐☐

CM1424-1428

CM1430 →

District of Columbia Bicentennial

Pennsylvania Avenue, circa 1903

Burma Road, 717-mile lifeline to China / America's first peacetime draft, 1940 / U.S. supports allies with Lend-Lease Act / Atlantic Charter sets war aims of allies / America becomes "arsenal of democracy"

1941: A World at War

Destroyer Reuben James sunk October 31 / Civil Defense mobilizes Americans at home / First Liberty ship delivered December 30 / Japanese bomb Pearl Harbor, December 7 / U.S. declares war on Japan, December 8

CM1429

Jan E. Matzeliger

Black Heritage USA

CM1431

CM1442

CM1443

MERCURY MARINER 10 / VENUS MARINER 2 / EARTH LANDSAT / MOON LUNAR ORBITER

JUPITER PIONEER 11 / SATURN VOYAGER 2 / URANUS VOYAGER 2 / NEPTUNE VOYAGER 2

CM1432-1441

	MNHVF	UseVF	

CM1464_____
29¢ **Apollo & Vostok craft,** tagged | 1.00 | .20 ☐☐☐☐☐
CM1465_____
29¢ **Soyuz, Mercury & Gemini craft,** tagged | 1.00 | .20 ☐☐☐☐☐
CM1466_____ **1992. Alaska Highway Issue**
29¢ **multicolored** tagged | .45 | .20 ☐☐☐☐☐
CM1467_____ **1992. Kentucky Statehood Issue**
29¢ **multicolored** tagged | .45 | .20 ☐☐☐☐☐
CM1468_____ **1992. Summer Olympic Games Issue**
29¢ **Soccer,** tagged | .45 | .20 ☐☐☐☐☐
CM1469_____
29¢ **Gymnastics,** tagged | .45 | .20 ☐☐☐☐☐
CM1470_____
29¢ **Vollyball,** tagged | .45 | .20 ☐☐☐☐☐
CM1471_____
29¢ **Boxing,** tagged | .45 | .20 ☐☐☐☐☐
CM1472_____
29¢ **Swimming,** tagged | .45 | .20 ☐☐☐☐☐
CM1473_____ **1992. Hummingbirds Issue**
29¢ **Ruby-throated,** tagged | .45 | .20 ☐☐☐☐☐
CM1474_____
29¢ **Broad-billed,** tagged | .45 | .20 ☐☐☐☐☐
CM1475_____
29¢ **Costa's,** tagged | .45 | .20 ☐☐☐☐☐
CM1476_____
29¢ **Rufous,** tagged | .45 | .20 ☐☐☐☐☐
CM1477_____
29¢ **Calliope,** tagged | .45 | .20 ☐☐☐☐☐
CM1478_____ **1992. Wildflowers Issue**
29¢ **Indian Paintbrush,** tagged | .95 | .60 ☐☐☐☐☐
CM1479_____
29¢ **Fragrant Water Lily,** tagged | .95 | .60 ☐☐☐☐☐
CM1480_____
29¢ **Meadow Beauty,** tagged | .95 | .60 ☐☐☐☐☐

CM1444

CM1445

CM1446

 CM1447

 CM1448

CM1449

CM1450

CM1455

CM1451-1454

CM1456

CM1457

CM1458

CM1459

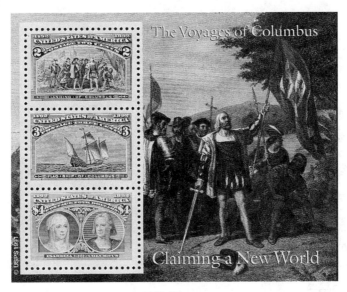

CM1460

CM1461

	MNHVF	UseVF
CM1481_____		
29¢ **Jack-in-the-Pulpit,** tagged	.95	.60 ☐☐☐☐☐
CM1482_____		
29¢ **California Poppy,** tagged	.95	.60 ☐☐☐☐☐
CM1483_____		
29¢ **Large-Flowered Trillium,** tagged	.95	.60 ☐☐☐☐☐
CM1484_____		
29¢ **Tickseed,** tagged	.95	.60 ☐☐☐☐☐
CM1485_____		
29¢ **Shooting Star,** tagged	.95	.60 ☐☐☐☐☐
CM1486_____		
29¢ **Stream Violet,** tagged	.95	.60 ☐☐☐☐☐
CM1487_____		
29¢ **Bluets,** tagged	.95	.60 ☐☐☐☐☐
CM1488_____		
29¢ **Herb Robert,** tagged	.95	.60 ☐☐☐☐☐
CM1489_____		
29¢ **Marsh Marigold,** tagged	.95	.60 ☐☐☐☐☐
CM1490_____		
29¢ **Sweet White Violet,** tagged	.95	.60 ☐☐☐☐☐
CM1491_____		
29¢ **Claret Cup Cactus,** tagged	.95	.60 ☐☐☐☐☐
CM1492_____		
29¢ **White Mountain Avens,** tagged	.95	.60 ☐☐☐☐☐
CM1493_____		
29¢ **Sessile Bellwort,** tagged	.95	.60 ☐☐☐☐☐
CM1494_____		
29¢ **Blue Flag,** tagged	.95	.60 ☐☐☐☐☐
CM1495_____		
29¢ **Harlequin Lupine,** tagged	.95	.60 ☐☐☐☐☐
CM1496_____		
29¢ **Twinflower,** tagged	.95	.60 ☐☐☐☐☐
CM1497_____		
29¢ **Common Sunflower,** tagged	.95	.60 ☐☐☐☐☐
CM1498_____		
29¢ **Sego Lily,** tagged	.95	.60 ☐☐☐☐☐
CM1499_____		
29¢ **Virginia Bluebells,** tagged	.95	.60 ☐☐☐☐☐
CM1500_____		
29¢ **Ohi'a Lehua,** tagged	.95	.60 ☐☐☐☐☐
CM1501_____		
29¢ **Rosebud Orchid,** tagged	.95	.60 ☐☐☐☐☐
CM1502_____		
29¢ **Showy Evening Primrose,** tagged	.95	.60 ☐☐☐☐☐
CM1503_____		
29¢ **Fringed Gentian,** tagged	.95	.60 ☐☐☐☐☐
CM1504_____		
29¢ **Yellow Lady's Slipper,** tagged	.95	.60 ☐☐☐☐☐
CM1505_____		
29¢ **Passionflower,** tagged	.95	.60 ☐☐☐☐☐
CM1506_____		
29¢ **Bunchberry,** tagged	.95	.60 ☐☐☐☐☐
CM1507_____		
29¢ **Pasqueflower,** tagged	.95	.60 ☐☐☐☐☐

CM1462-1465

CM1467

CM1466

CM1468-1472

CM1473-1477

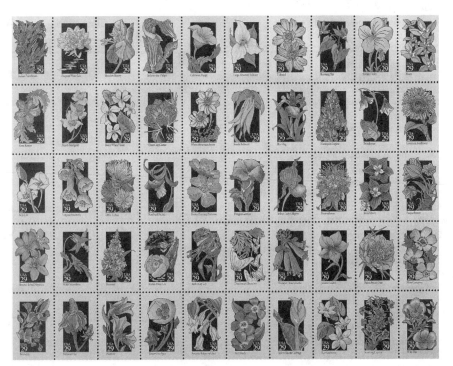

CM1478-1527

	MNHVF	UseVF

CM1508_____
29¢ **Round-Lobed Hepatica,** tagged | .95 | .60 ☐☐☐☐☐
CM1509_____
29¢ **Wild Columbine,** tagged | .95 | .60 ☐☐☐☐☐
CM1510_____
29¢ **Fireweed,** tagged | .95 | .60 ☐☐☐☐☐
CM1511_____
29¢ **Indian Pond Lily,** tagged | .95 | .60 ☐☐☐☐☐
CM1512_____
29¢ **Turk's Cap Lily,** tagged | .95 | .60 ☐☐☐☐☐
CM1513_____
29¢ **Dutchman's Breeches,** tagged | .95 | .60 ☐☐☐☐☐
CM1514_____
29¢ **Trumpet Honeysuckle,** tagged | .95 | .60 ☐☐☐☐☐
CM1515_____
29¢ **Jacob's Ladder,** tagged | .95 | .60 ☐☐☐☐☐
CM1516_____
29¢ **Plains Prickly Pear,** tagged | .95 | .60 ☐☐☐☐☐
CM1517_____
29¢ **Moss Campion,** tagged | .95 | .60 ☐☐☐☐☐
CM1518_____
29¢ **Bearberry,** tagged | .95 | .60 ☐☐☐☐☐
CM1519_____
29¢ **Mexican Hat,** tagged | .95 | .60 ☐☐☐☐☐
CM1520_____
29¢ **Harebell,** tagged | .95 | .60 ☐☐☐☐☐
CM1521_____
29¢ **Desert Five Spot,** tagged | .95 | .60 ☐☐☐☐☐
CM1522_____
29¢ **Smooth Solomon's Seal,** tagged | .95 | .60 ☐☐☐☐☐
CM1523_____
29¢ **Red Maids,** tagged | .95 | .60 ☐☐☐☐☐
CM1524_____
29¢ **Yellow Skunk Cabbage,** tagged | .95 | .60 ☐☐☐☐☐
CM1525_____
29¢ **Rue Anemone,** tagged | .95 | .60 ☐☐☐☐☐
CM1526_____
29¢ **Standing Cypress,** tagged | .95 | .60 ☐☐☐☐☐
CM1527_____
29¢ **Wild Flax,** tagged | .95 | .60 ☐☐☐☐☐

CM1528_____   **1992. 1942: Into The Battle Issue**
$2.90 **Sheet of 10** | 9.00 | 5.00 ☐☐☐☐☐

CM1529_____   **1992. Dorothy Parker Issue**
29¢ **multicolored** tagged | .45 | .20 ☐☐☐☐☐

CM1530_____   **1992. Theodore von Kármán Issue**
29¢ **multicolored** tagged | .45 | .20 ☐☐☐☐☐

CM1531_____   **1992. Minerals Issue**
29¢ **Azurite,** tagged | .45 | .20 ☐☐☐☐☐
CM1532_____
29¢ **Copper,** tagged | .45 | .20 ☐☐☐☐☐
CM1533_____
29¢ **Variscite,** tagged | .45 | .20 ☐☐☐☐☐
CM1534_____
29¢ **Wulfenite,** tagged | .45 | .20 ☐☐☐☐☐

	MNHVF	UseVF

CM1535_____ **1992. Juan Rodríguez Cabrillo Issue**
29¢ multicolored tagged — .45 — .20 ☐☐☐☐☐

CM1536_____ **1992. Wild Animals Issue**
29¢ **Giraffe,** tagged — .45 — .20 ☐☐☐☐☐

CM1537_____
29¢ **Giant Panda,** tagged — .45 — .20 ☐☐☐☐☐

CM1538_____
29¢ **Flamingo,** tagged — .45 — .20 ☐☐☐☐☐

CM1539_____
29¢ **King Penquins,** tagged — .45 — .20 ☐☐☐☐☐

CM1540_____
29¢ **White Bengal Tiger,** tagged — .45 — .20 ☐☐☐☐☐

CM1541_____ **1992. New Year Issue**
29¢ multicolored tagged — .45 — .20 ☐☐☐☐☐

CM1542_____ **1993. Elvis Presley Issue**
29¢ multicolored tagged — .45 — .20 ☐☐☐☐☐

CM1543_____ **1993. Space Fantasy Issue**
29¢ **Saturn Rings,** tagged — .45 — .20 ☐☐☐☐☐

CM1544_____
29¢ **Two oval crafts,** tagged — .45 — .20 ☐☐☐☐☐

CM1545_____
29¢ **Spacemen & Jet Pack,** tagged — .45 — .20 ☐☐☐☐☐

CM1546_____
29¢ **Craft & lights,** tagged — .45 — .20 ☐☐☐☐☐

CM1547_____
29¢ **Three craft,** tagged — .45 — .20 ☐☐☐☐☐

CM1548_____ **1993. Percy Lavon Julian Issue**
29¢ multicolored tagged — .45 — .20 ☐☐☐☐☐

CM1549_____ **1993. Oregon Trail Issue**
29¢ multicolored tagged — .45 — .20 ☐☐☐☐☐

CM1550_____ **1993. World University Games Issue**
29¢ multicolored tagged — .45 — .20 ☐☐☐☐☐

CM1551_____ **1993. Grace Kelly Issue**
29¢ blue tagged — .45 — .20 ☐☐☐☐☐

CM1552_____ **1993. Oklahoma! Issue**
29¢ multicolored tagged — .45 — .20 ☐☐☐☐☐

CM1553_____ **1993. Circus Issue**
29¢ **Trapeze Artist,** tagged — .45 — .20 ☐☐☐☐☐

CM1554_____
29¢ **Elephant,** tagged — .45 — .20 ☐☐☐☐☐

CM1555_____
29¢ **Clown,** tagged — .45 — .20 ☐☐☐☐☐

CM1556_____
29¢ **Ringmaster,** tagged — .45 — .20 ☐☐☐☐☐

CM1557_____ **1993. Cherokee Strip Land Run Centennial Issue**
29¢ multicolored tagged — .45 — .20 ☐☐☐☐☐

CM1558_____ **1993. Dean Acheson Issue**
29¢ multicolored tagged — .45 — .20 ☐☐☐☐☐

CM1559_____ **1993. Sporting Horses Issue**
29¢ **Steeplechase,** tagged — .45 — .20 ☐☐☐☐☐

CM1560_____
29¢ **Thoroughbred racing,** tagged — .45 — .20 ☐☐☐☐☐

CM1561_____
29¢ **Harness racing,** tagged — .45 — .20 ☐☐☐☐☐

		MNHVF	UseVF

CM1562_____

   29¢ **Polo,** tagged   .45   .20 ❑❑❑❑❑

CM1563_____ **1993. Garden Flowers Issue**

   29¢ **Hyacinth,** tagged   .45   .20 ❑❑❑❑❑

CM1564_____

   29¢ **Daffodil,** tagged   .45   .20 ❑❑❑❑❑

CM1565_____

   29¢ **Tulip,** tagged   .45   .20 ❑❑❑❑❑

CM1566_____

   29¢ **Iris,** tagged   .45   .20 ❑❑❑❑❑

CM1567_____

   29¢ **Lilac,** tagged   .45   .20 ❑❑❑❑❑

CM1568_____ **1993. 1943: Turning The Tide Issue**

   $2.90 **Commemorative pane of 10**   8.75   7.00 ❑❑❑❑❑

CM1569_____ **1993. Hank Williams Issue**

   29¢ **multicolored** tagged   .45   .20 ❑❑❑❑❑

CM1570_____ **1993. Rock 'n Roll - Rhythm & Blues Issue**

   29¢ **Elvis Presley,** tagged   .45   .20 ❑❑❑❑❑

CM1571_____

   29¢ **Buddy Holly,** tagged   .45   .20 ❑❑❑❑❑

CM1572_____

   29¢ **Richie Valens,** tagged   .45   .20 ❑❑❑❑❑

CM1573_____

   29¢ **Bill Haley,** tagged   .45   .20 ❑❑❑❑❑

CM1574_____

   29¢ **Dinah Washington,** tagged   .45   .20 ❑❑❑❑❑

CM1575_____

   29¢ **Otis Redding,** tagged   .45   .20 ❑❑❑❑❑

CM1576_____

   29¢ **Clyde McPhatter,** tagged   .45   .20 ❑❑❑❑❑

29 USA — *B-25s take off to raid Tokyo April 18, 1942*

29 USA — *Food and other commodities rationed, 1942*

29 USA — *U.S. wins Battle of the Coral Sea May 1942*

29 USA — *Corregidor falls to Japanese May 6, 1942*

29 USA — *Japan invades Aleutian Islands June 1942*

1942: Into the Battle

29 USA — *Allies decipher secret enemy codes, 1942*

29 USA — *Yorktown lost, U.S. wins at Midway, 1942*

29 USA — *Millions of women join war effort, 1942*

29 USA — *Marines land on Guadalcanal Aug. 7, 1942*

29 USA — *Allies land in North Africa November 1942*

CM1529

CM1530

CM1531-1534

CM1535

Giraffe

Giant Panda

Flamingo

King Penguins

White Bengal Tiger

CM1536-1540

CM1541

Elvis

CM1542

CM1543-1547

CM1548

CM1549 ←

CM1550 ←

CM1551 →

Grace Kelly

CM1552

	MNHVF	UseVF

CM1577_____
29¢ **multicolored** tagged .45 .20 ☐☐☐☐☐
CM1578_____
29¢ **multicolored** tagged .45 .20 ☐☐☐☐☐
CM1579_____
29¢ **multicolored** tagged .45 .20 ☐☐☐☐☐
CM1580_____
29¢ **multicolored** tagged .45 .20 ☐☐☐☐☐
CM1581_____
29¢ **multicolored** tagged .45 .20 ☐☐☐☐☐
CM1582_____
29¢ **multicolored** tagged .45 .20 ☐☐☐☐☐
CM1583_____
29¢ **multicolored** tagged .45 .20 ☐☐☐☐☐

The vertically oriented pane of eight consists of the following stamps, from top to bottom: CM1577, CM1578, CM1579, CM1580, CM1581, CM1582, CM1583, CM1577. The vertically oriented pane of four consists of the following stamps, from top to bottom: CM1581, CM1582, CM1583, CM1584. A complete booklet consists of two panes of eight and one pane of four.

CM1584_____ **1993. Joe Louis Issue**
29¢ **multicolored** tagged .45 .20 ☐☐☐☐☐
CM1585_____ **1993. Broadway Musicals Issue**
29¢ *Show Boat,* tagged .45 .20 ☐☐☐☐☐
CM1586_____
29¢ *Porgy & Bess,* tagged .45 .20 ☐☐☐☐☐
CM1587_____
29¢ *Oklahoma!,* tagged .45 .20 ☐☐☐☐☐
CM1588_____
29¢ *My Fair Lady,* tagged .45 .20 ☐☐☐☐☐
CM1589_____ **1993. National Postal Museum Issue**
29¢ **Benjamin Franklin,** tagged .45 .20 ☐☐☐☐☐
CM1590_____
29¢ **Civil War soldier writing letter** .45 .20 ☐☐☐☐☐
CM1591_____
29¢ **Charles Lindbergh,** tagged .45 .20 ☐☐☐☐☐
CM1592_____
29¢ **Letters & date stamp,** tagged .45 .20 ☐☐☐☐☐
CM1593_____ **1993. Recognizing Deafness/American Sign Language Issue**
29¢ **Mother and child,** tagged .45 .20 ☐☐☐☐☐
CM1594_____
29¢ **Sign "I love you"** .45 .20 ☐☐☐☐☐
CM1595_____ **1993. Country Music Issue**
29¢ **Hank Williams,** tagged .45 .20 ☐☐☐☐☐
CM1596_____
29¢ **The Carter Family,** tagged .45 .20 ☐☐☐☐☐
CM1597_____
29¢ **Patsy Cline,** tagged .45 .20 ☐☐☐☐☐
CM1598_____
29¢ **Bob Wills,** tagged .45 .20 ☐☐☐☐☐

Gravure by American Bank Note Co., perforated 11 on 1 or 2 sides, from booklet panes.

CM1599_____
29¢ **Hank Williams,** tagged .45 .20 ☐☐☐☐☐
CM1600_____
29¢ **The Carter Family,** tagged .45 .20 ☐☐☐☐☐
CM1601_____
29¢ **Patsy Cline,** tagged .45 .20 ☐☐☐☐☐

CM1557

CM1558 →

CM1559-1562 ←

CM1553-1556

CM1563-1567 ↓

CM1569 ↓

Allied forces battle German U-boats, 1943   *Military medics treat the wounded, 1943*   *Sicily attacked by Allied forces, July 1943*   *B-24s hit Ploesti refineries, August 1943*   *V-mail delivers letters from home, 1943*

1943: Turning the Tide

Italy invaded by Allies, September 1943   *Bonds and stamps help war effort, 1943*   *"Willie and Joe" keep spirits high, 1943*   *Gold Stars mark World War II losses, 1943*   *Marines assault Tarawa, November 1943*

CM1568

	MNHVF	UseVF

CM1602_____

29¢ **Bob Wills,** tagged .45 .20 ☐☐☐☐☐

CM1603_____ **1993. Youth Classics Issue**

29¢ *Rebecca,* tagged .45 .20 ☐☐☐☐☐

CM1604_____

29¢ *Little House,* tagged .45 .20 ☐☐☐☐☐

CM1605_____

29¢ *Huck Finn,* tagged .45 .20 ☐☐☐☐☐

CM1606_____

29¢ *Little Women,* tagged .45 .20 ☐☐☐☐☐

CM1607_____ **1993. Commonwealth of the Northern Mariana Islands Issue**

29¢ multicolored tagged .45 .20 ☐☐☐☐☐

CM1608_____ **1993. Columbus Landing in Puerto Rico Issue**

29¢ multicolored tagged .45 .20 ☐☐☐☐☐

CM1609_____ **1993. AIDS Awareness Issue**

29¢ **red & black** tagged .45 .20 ☐☐☐☐☐

CM1610_____ **1994. Winter Olympics Issue**

29¢ **Downhill skiing,** tagged .45 .20 ☐☐☐☐☐

CM1611_____

29¢ **Luge,** tagged .45 .20 ☐☐☐☐☐

CM1612_____

29¢ **Figure skating,** tagged .45 .20 ☐☐☐☐☐

CM1613_____

29¢ **Cross-country skiing,** tagged .45 .20 ☐☐☐☐☐

CM1614_____

29¢ **Hockey,** tagged .45 .20 ☐☐☐☐☐

CM1615_____ **1994. Edward R. Murrow Issue**

29¢ **brown** tagged .45 .20 ☐☐☐☐☐

CM1616_____ **1994. Love Issue**

29¢ multicolored tagged .45 .20 ☐☐☐☐☐

CM1617_____ **1994. Dr. Allison Davis Issue**

29¢ **red brown & brown** tagged .45 .20 ☐☐☐☐☐

CM1618_____ **1994. New Year Issue**

29¢ multicolored tagged .45 .20 ☐☐☐☐☐

CM1619_____ **1994. Love Issues**

29¢ multicolored tagged .45 .20 ☐☐☐☐☐

CM1620_____

52¢ multicolored tagged 1.50 .35 ☐☐☐☐☐

CM1621_____ **1994. Buffalo Soldiers Issue**

29¢ multicolored tagged .45 .20 ☐☐☐☐☐

CM1622_____ **1994. Silent Screen Stars Issue**

29¢ **Rudolph Valentino,** tagged .45 .20 ☐☐☐☐☐

CM1623_____

29¢ **Clara Bow,** tagged .45 .20 ☐☐☐☐☐

CM1624_____

29¢ **Charlie Chaplin,** tagged .45 .20 ☐☐☐☐☐

CM1625_____

29¢ **Lon Chaney,** tagged .45 .20 ☐☐☐☐☐

CM1626_____

29¢ **John Gilbert,** tagged .45 .20 ☐☐☐☐☐

CM1627_____

29¢ **Zasu Pitts,** tagged .45 .20 ☐☐☐☐☐

CM1628_____

29¢ **Harold Lloyd,** tagged .45 .20 ☐☐☐☐☐

CM1584

CM1570, CM1577
(first stamp)
CM1571, CM1582
(second stamp)
CM1572, CM1580
(third stamp)
CM1573, CM1578
(fourth stamp)
CM1574, CM1583
(fifth stamp)
CM1575, CM1581
(sixth stamp)
CM1576, CM1579
(seventh stamp)

CM1585-1588

CM1595, CM 1599
(first stamp)
CM1596, CM1600
(second stamp)
CM1597, CM1601
(third stamp)
CM1598, CM1602
(fourth stamp)

CM1589-1592

CM1603-1606

CM1593-1594

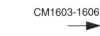

	MNHVF	UseVF

CM1629_____
29¢ **Keystone Cops**, tagged .45 .20 ☐☐☐☐☐

CM1630_____
29¢ **Theda Bara**, tagged .45 .20 ☐☐☐☐☐

CM1631_____
29¢ **Buster Keaton**, tagged .45 .20 ☐☐☐☐☐

CM1632_____ **1994. Garden Flowers Issue**
29¢ **multicolored,** tagged .45 .20 ☐☐☐☐☐

CM1633_____
29¢ **multicolored** tagged .45 .20 ☐☐☐☐☐

CM1634_____
29¢ **multicolored** tagged .45 .20 ☐☐☐☐☐

CM1635_____
29¢ **multicolored** tagged .45 .20 ☐☐☐☐☐

CM1636_____
29¢ **multicolored** tagged .45 .20 ☐☐☐☐☐

CM1637_____ **1994. World Cup Soccer Championship Issue**
29¢ **multicolored** phosphored paper .75 .20 ☐☐☐☐☐

CM1638_____
40¢ **multicolored** phosphored paper 1.00 .35 ☐☐☐☐☐

CM1639_____
50¢ **multicolored** phosphored paper 1.50 .50 ☐☐☐☐☐

CM1640_____
$1.19 **Souvenir Sheet** 3.75 3.00 ☐☐☐☐☐

CM1641_____ **1994. 1944: Road to Victory Issue**
$2.90 **Commemorative pane of 10,** tagged 8.75 7.00 ☐☐☐☐☐

CM1642_____ **1994. Love Issue**
29¢ **multicolored** tagged .50 .20 ☐☐☐☐☐

CM1643_____ **1994. Norman Rockwell Issue**
29¢ **multicolored** tagged .50 .20 ☐☐☐☐☐

CM1644_____
$2 **multicolored** tagged 6.00 5.00 ☐☐☐☐☐

CM1645_____ **1994. Moon Landing Anniversary Issue**
29¢ **multicolored** tagged .50 .25 ☐☐☐☐☐

CM1646_____ **1994. Locomotives Issue**
29¢ **Hudson's General,** tagged .75 .50 ☐☐☐☐☐

CM1647_____
29¢ **McQueen's Jupiter,** tagged .75 .50 ☐☐☐☐☐

CM1648_____
29¢ **Eddy's No. 242,** tagged .75 .50 ☐☐☐☐☐

CM1649_____
29¢ **Ely's No. 10,** tagged .75 .50 ☐☐☐☐☐

CM1650_____
29¢ **Buchannan's No. 999,** tagged .75 .50 ☐☐☐☐☐

CM1651_____ **1994. George Meany Issue**
29¢ **blue** tagged .50 .20 ☐☐☐☐☐

CM1652_____ **1994. Popular Singers Issue**
29¢ **Al Jolson,** tagged .75 .50 ☐☐☐☐☐

CM1653_____
29¢ **Bing Crosby,** tagged .75 .50 ☐☐☐☐☐

CM1654_____
29¢ **Ethel Waters,** tagged .75 .50 ☐☐☐☐☐

CM1655_____
29¢ **Nat "King" Cole,** tagged .47 .50 ☐☐☐☐☐

	MNHVF	UseVF

CM1656_____
   29¢ **Ethel Merman,** tagged   .75   .50 ☐☐☐☐☐
CM1657_____   **1994. James Thurber Issue**
   29¢ **multicolored** tagged   .50   .20 ☐☐☐☐☐

CM1607

CM1608

CM1609

CM1615

CM1610-1614

CM1616

BLACK HERITAGE

CM1618

CM1619

CM1620

DR. ALLISON DAVIS

CM1617

CM1621

CM1622-1631

	MNHVF	UseVF

CM1658_____   1994. Blues and Jazz Singers Issue

29¢ **Bessie Smith,** tagged	.50	.25 ☐☐☐☐☐
CM1659_____		
29¢ **Muddy Waters,** tagged	.50	.25 ☐☐☐☐☐
CM1660_____		
29¢ **Billie Holiday,** tagged	.50	.25 ☐☐☐☐☐
CM1661_____		
29¢ **Robert Johnson,** tagged	.50	.25 ☐☐☐☐☐
CM1662_____		
29¢ **Jimmy Rushing,** tagged	.50	.25 ☐☐☐☐☐
CM1663_____		
29¢ **"Ma" Rainy,** tagged	.50	.25 ☐☐☐☐☐
CM1664_____		
29¢ **Mildred Bailey,** tagged	.50	.25 ☐☐☐☐☐
CM1665_____		
29¢ **Howlin' Wolf,** tagged	.50	.25 ☐☐☐☐☐

CM1666_____   1994. Wonders of the Seas Issue

29¢ **Porcupine fish,** tagged	.75	.25 ☐☐☐☐☐
CM1667_____		
29¢ **Dolphin,** tagged	.75	.25 ☐☐☐☐☐
CM1668_____		
29¢ **Nautilus & ship's wheel,** tagged	.75	.25 ☐☐☐☐☐

CM1632-1636

CM1642

CM1643

From our doughboys in WWI to our astronauts striding across the moon, Norman Rockwell's artwork has captured America's traditional values along with the characteristic optimism of its people. Rockwell loved people, and people loved him. He was an enormously skilled technician and, according to several new reassessments, a true artist. He had a genius for capturing the emotional content of the commonplace. © USPS — 1993

CM1644a-1644d

CM1645

First Moon Landing, 1969

CM1640

CM1641

	MNHVF	UseVF

CM1669 _____
  29¢ **Fish & coral,** tagged   .75   .25

CM1670 _____   **1994. Cranes Issue**
  29¢ **Black-necked crane,** tagged   .45   .20

CM1671 _____
  29¢ **Whooping crane,** tagged   .45   .20

CM1671A _____   **1993-1994. Legends of the West Issue**
  $5.80 **Legends of the West commemorative pane,** tagged, *(earliest known use Dec. 14, 1993)*
                                                              195.00

CM1672 _____   **1994. Revised Legends of the West Issue**
  29¢ **Home on the Range,** tagged   .45   .20

CM1646-1650

CM1651

CM1657

CM1652-1656

CM1658-1665

	MNHVF	UseVF	
CM1673_____			
29¢ **Buffalo Bill,** tagged	.45	.20 ☐☐☐☐☐
CM1674_____			
29¢ **Jim Bridger,** tagged	.45	.20 ☐☐☐☐☐
CM1675_____			
29¢ **Annie Oakley,** tagged	.45	.20 ☐☐☐☐☐
CM1676_____			
29¢ **Native American Culture,** tagged	.45	.20 ☐☐☐☐☐

CM1666-1669

CM1670-1671

CM1671A

	MNHVF	UseVF

CM1677_____

29¢ **Chief Joseph,** tagged   .45   .20 ☐☐☐☐☐

CM1678_____

29¢ **Bill Pickett,** tagged   .45   .20 ☐☐☐☐☐

CM1679_____

29¢ **Bat Masterson,** tagged   .45   .20 ☐☐☐☐☐

CM1680_____

29¢ **John Fremont,** tagged   .45   .20 ☐☐☐☐☐

CM1681_____

29¢ **Wyatt Earp,** tagged   .45   .20 ☐☐☐☐☐

CM1682_____

29¢ **Nellie Cashman,** tagged   .45   .20 ☐☐☐☐☐

CM1683_____

29¢ **Charles Goodnight,** tagged   .45   .20 ☐☐☐☐☐

CM1684_____

29¢ **Geronimo,** tagged   .45   .20 ☐☐☐☐☐

CM1685_____

29¢ **Kit Carson,** tagged   .45   .20 ☐☐☐☐☐

CM1686_____

29¢ **Wild Bill Hickok,** tagged   .45   .20 ☐☐☐☐☐

CM1687_____

29¢ **Western Wildlife,** tagged   .45   .20 ☐☐☐☐☐

CM1688_____

29¢ **Jim Beckwourth,** tagged   .45   .20 ☐☐☐☐☐

CM1689_____

29¢ **Bill Tilghman,** tagged   .45   .20 ☐☐☐☐☐

CM1690_____

29¢ **Sacagawea,** tagged   .45   .20 ☐☐☐☐☐

CM1691_____

29¢ **Overland Mail,** tagged   .45   .20 ☐☐☐☐☐

Because this issue also was made available to collectors in full six-pane printing sheets, gutter pairs and blocks and cross-gutter multiples also exist.

CM1692_____   **1994. Bureau of Engraving and Printing Centennial Souvenir Issue**

$8   **multicolored** tagged, **(Nov. 3, 1994)**   20.00   14.50 ☐☐☐☐☐

Listings for minor double transfers refer to any of approximately 10 different ones that are known.

CM1693_____   **1994. New Year Issue**

29¢ **multicolored** tagged   .50   .20 ☐☐☐☐☐

CM1694_____   **1995. Love Cherub Issue**

32¢ **multicolored** phosphored paper   .50   .20 ☐☐☐☐☐

Self-adhesive booklet, offset and intaglio by Banknote Corp. of America, imperforate (die cut).

CM1695_____

32¢ **multicolored** phosphored paper   .50   .20 ☐☐☐☐☐

CM1696_____   **1995. Florida Sesquicentennial Issue**

32¢ **multicolored** phosphored paper   .50   .20 ☐☐☐☐☐

CM1697_____   **1995. Earth Day Issue**

32¢ **Clean Earth,** phosphored paper   .50   .20 ☐☐☐☐☐

CM1698_____

32¢ **Solar Power,** phosphored paper   .50   .20 ☐☐☐☐☐

CM1699_____

32¢ **Tree Planting,** phosphored paper   .50   .20 ☐☐☐☐☐

CM1700_____

32¢ **Clean Beaches,** phosphored paper   .50   .20 ☐☐☐☐☐

CM1701_____   **1995. Richard M. Nixon Issue**

32¢ **multicolored** phosphored paper   .50   .20 ☐☐☐☐☐

CM1693

CM1694

CM1695

CM1691y

CM1692

CM1697-1700

CM1696

CM1701 →

Richard Nixon

CM1702 →

BLACK HERITAGE

BESSIE COLEMAN

	MNHVF	UseVF

CM1702_____   **1995. Bessie Coleman Issue**
32¢ **red & black** phosphored paper ... .50 ... .20 □□□□□

CM1703_____   **1995. Love Cherub Issue**
32¢ **multicolored** phosphored paper ... .50 ... .20 □□□□□

CM1704_____   **1995. Love Cherub Booklet Issue**
32¢ **multicolored** phosphored paper ... .50 ... .20 □□□□□

CM1705_____
55¢ **multicolored** phosphored paper ... 1.00 ... .35 □□□□□

CM1706_____   **1995. Love Cherub Self-Adhesive Booklet Issue**
55¢ **multicolored** phosphored paper ... 1.00 ... .35 □□□□□

CM1707_____   **1995. Recreational Sports Issue**
32¢ **Bowling,** phosphored paper ... .50 ... .20 □□□□□

CM1708_____
32¢ **Tennis,** phosphored paper ... .50 ... .20 □□□□□

CM1709_____
32¢ **Golf,** phosphored paper ... .50 ... .20 □□□□□

CM1710_____
32¢ **Volleyball,** phosphored paper ... .50 ... .20 □□□□□

CM1711_____
32¢ **Baseball,** phosphored paper ... .50 ... .20 □□□□□

CM1712_____   **1995. POW & MIA Issue**
32¢ **multicolored** phosphored paper ... .50 ... .20 □□□□□

CM1713_____   **1995. Marilyn Monroe Issue**
32¢ **multicolored** block tagged ... .75 ... .20 □□□□□

Because this issue also was made available to collectors in full six-pane printing sheets, gutter pairs and blocks and cross-gutter multiples also exist.

CM1714_____   **1995. Texas Sesquicentennial Issue**
32¢ **multicolored** phosphored paper ... .50 ... .20 □□□□□

CM1715_____   **1995. Lighthouses Issue**
32¢ **Split Rock,** phosphored paper ... .50 ... .20 □□□□□

CM1716_____
32¢ **St. Joseph,** phosphored paper ... .50 ... .20 □□□□□

CM1717_____
32¢ **Spectacle Reef,** phosphored paper ... .50 ... .20 □□□□□

CM1718_____
32¢ **Marblehead,** phosphored paper ... .50 ... .20 □□□□□

CM1719_____
32¢ **Thirty Mile Point,** phosphored paper ... .50 ... .20 □□□□□

CM1720_____   **1995. United Nations Issue**
32¢ **blue** phosphored paper ... .50 ... .20 □□□□□

CM1721_____   **1995. Civil War Issue**
32¢ *Monitor and Virginia* ... .75 ... .50 □□□□□

CM1722_____
32¢ **Robert E. Lee** ... .75 ... .50 □□□□□

CM1723_____
32¢ **Clara Barton** ... .75 ... .50 □□□□□

CM1724_____
32¢ **Ulysses S. Grant** ... .75 ... .50 □□□□□

CM1725_____
32¢ **Battle of Shiloh** ... .75 ... .50 □□□□□

CM1726_____
32¢ **Jefferson Davis** ... .75 ... .50 □□□□□

CM1727_____
32¢ **David Farragut** ... .75 ... .50 □□□□□

CM1703

CM1704

CM1705

CM1706

CM1707-1711

CM1712

CM1714

CM1715-1719

CM1713

CM1720

CM1721-1740

	MNHVF	UseVF	

CM1728_____
    32¢ **Frederick Douglass**   .75   .50 ☐☐☐☐☐

CM1729_____
    32¢ **Raphael Semmes**   .75   .50 ☐☐☐☐☐

CM1730_____
    32¢ **Abraham Lincoln**   .75   .50 ☐☐☐☐☐

CM1731_____
    32¢ **Harriet Tubman**   .75   .50 ☐☐☐☐☐

CM1732_____
    32¢ **Stand Watie**   .75   .50 ☐☐☐☐☐

CM1733_____
    32¢ **Joseph E. Johnston**   .75   .50 ☐☐☐☐☐

CM1734_____
    32¢ **Winfield Hancock**   .75   .50 ☐☐☐☐☐

CM1735_____
    32¢ **Mary Chesnut**   .75   .50 ☐☐☐☐☐

CM1736_____
    32¢ **Battle of Chancellorsville**   .75   .50 ☐☐☐☐☐

CM1737_____
    32¢ **William T. Sherman**   .75   .50 ☐☐☐☐☐

CM1738_____
    32¢ **Phoebe Pember**   .75   .50 ☐☐☐☐☐

CM1739_____
    32¢ **"Stonewall" Jackson**   .75   .50 ☐☐☐☐☐

CM1740_____
    32¢ **Battle of Gettysburg**   .75   .50 ☐☐☐☐☐

Because this issue also was made available to collectors in full six-pane printing sheets, gutter pairs and blocks and cross-gutter multiples also exist.

CM1741_____   **1995. Carousel Horses Issue**
    32¢ **Golden horse,** phosphored paper   .50   .20 ☐☐☐☐☐

CM1742_____
    32¢ **Black horse,** phosphored paper   .50   .20 ☐☐☐☐☐

CM1743_____
    32¢ **Armored horse,** phosphored paper   .50   .20 ☐☐☐☐☐

CM1744_____
    32¢ **Brown horse,** phosphored paper   .50   .20 ☐☐☐☐☐

CM1741-1744

CM1745

CM1746

	MNHVF	UseVF	

CM1745_____   **1995. Woman Suffrage Issue**
32¢ **multicolored,** phosphored paper   .50   .20 ☐☐☐☐☐

CM1746_____   **1995. Louis Armstrong Issue**
32¢ **multicolored,** phosphored paper   .50   .20 ☐☐☐☐☐
For a similar design with "32" in black, see CM1749.

CM1747_____   **1995. 1945: Victory at Last Issue**
$3.20 **Commemortive pane of 10,** overall tagged   9.00   8.00 ☐☐☐☐☐

CM1748_____   **1995. Jazz Musicians Issue**
32¢ **Coleman Hawkins,** phosphored paper   .50   .20 ☐☐☐☐☐

CM1749_____
32¢ **Louis Armstrong,** phosphored paper   .50   .20 ☐☐☐☐☐

CM1750_____
32¢ **James P. Johnson,** phosphored paper   .50   .20 ☐☐☐☐☐

CM1751_____
32¢ **"Jelly Roll" Morton,** phosphored paper   .50   .20 ☐☐☐☐☐

CM1752_____
32¢ **Charles Parker,** phosphored paper   .50   .20 ☐☐☐☐☐

CM1753_____
32¢ **Eubie Blake,** phosphored paper   .50   .20 ☐☐☐☐☐

CM1754_____
32¢ **Charlie Mingus,** phosphored paper   .50   .20 ☐☐☐☐☐

CM1755_____
32¢ **Thelonious Monk,** phosphored paper   .50   .20 ☐☐☐☐☐

CM1756_____
32¢ **John Coltrane,** phosphored paper   .50   .20 ☐☐☐☐☐

CM1757_____
32¢ **Erroll Garner,** phosphored paper   .50   .20 ☐☐☐☐☐

CM1758_____   **1995. Garden Flowers Issue**
32¢ **Aster,** overall tagged   .50   .20 ☐☐☐☐☐

CM1759_____
32¢ **Chrysanthemum,** overall tagged   .50   .20 ☐☐☐☐☐

CM1747

	MNHVF	UseVF	

CM1760_____

32¢ **Dahlia,** overall tagged .50 .20 ☐☐☐☐☐

CM1761_____

32¢ **Hydrangea,** overall tagged .50 .20 ☐☐☐☐☐

CM1762_____

32¢ **Rudbeckia,** overall tagged .50 .20 ☐☐☐☐☐

CM1763_____ **1995. Republic of Palau Issue**

32¢ **multicolored** phosphored paper .50 .20 ☐☐☐☐☐

CM1764_____ **1995. Comic Strip Classics Issue**

32¢ **The Yellow Kid** .75 .50 ☐☐☐☐☐

CM1765_____

32¢ **Katzenjammer Kids** .75 .50 ☐☐☐☐☐

CM1766_____

32¢ **Little Nemo in Slumberland** .75 .50 ☐☐☐☐☐

CM1767_____

32¢ **Bringing Up Father** .75 .50 ☐☐☐☐☐

CM1768_____

32¢ **Krazy Kat** .75 .50 ☐☐☐☐☐

CM1769_____

32¢ **Rube Goldberg's Inventions** .75 .50 ☐☐☐☐☐

CM1770_____

32¢ **Toonerville Folks** .75 .50 ☐☐☐☐☐

CM1748-1757

CM1758-1762

CM1763

CM1764-1783

CM1784

CM1785

CM1786

	MNHVF	UseVF	

CM1771_____
   32¢ **Gasoline Alley** .75 .50 ☐☐☐☐☐
CM1772_____
   32¢ **Barney Google** .75 .50 ☐☐☐☐☐
CM1773_____
   32¢ **Little Orphan Annie** .75 .50 ☐☐☐☐☐
CM1774_____
   32¢ **Popeye** .75 .50 ☐☐☐☐☐
CM1775_____
   32¢ **Blondie** .75 .50 ☐☐☐☐☐
CM1776_____
   32¢ **Dick Tracy** .75 .50 ☐☐☐☐☐
CM1777_____
   32¢ **Alley Oop** .75 .50 ☐☐☐☐☐
CM1778_____
   32¢ **Nancy** .75 .50 ☐☐☐☐☐
CM1779_____
   32¢ **Flash Gordon** .75 .50 ☐☐☐☐☐
CM1780_____
   32¢ **Li'l Abner** .75 .50 ☐☐☐☐☐
CM1781_____
   32¢ **Terry & the Pirates** .75 .50 ☐☐☐☐☐
CM1782_____
   32¢ **Prince Valiant** .75 .50 ☐☐☐☐☐
CM1783_____
   32¢ **Brenda Starr** .75 .50 ☐☐☐☐☐

Because this issue also was made available to collectors in full six-pane printing sheets, gutter pairs and blocks and cross-gutter multiples also exist.

CM1784_____ **1995. U.S. Naval Academy Issue**
   32¢ **multicolored** phosphored paper .50 .20 ☐☐☐☐☐
CM1785_____ **1995. Tennessee Williams Issue**
   32¢ **multicolored** phosphored paper .50 .20 ☐☐☐☐☐
CM1786_____ **1995. James K. Polk Issue**
   32¢ **reddish brown** phosphored paper .50 .20 ☐☐☐☐☐
CM1787_____ **1995. Antique Automobiles Issue**
   32¢ **Duryea,** phosphored paper .75 .50 ☐☐☐☐☐
CM1788_____
   32¢ **Haynes,** phosphored paper .75 .50 ☐☐☐☐☐
CM1789_____
   32¢ **Columbia,** phosphored paper .75 .50 ☐☐☐☐☐
CM1790_____
   32¢ **Winton,** phosphored paper .75 .50 ☐☐☐☐☐
CM1791_____
   32¢ **White,** phosphored paper .75 .50 ☐☐☐☐☐
CM1792_____ **1996. Utah Centennial Issue**
   32¢ **multicolored** tagged (120,000,000) .50 .20 ☐☐☐☐☐
CM1793_____ **1996. Garden Flowers Issue**
   32¢ **Crocus,** phosphored paper (160,000,000) .50 .20 ☐☐☐☐☐
CM1794_____
   32¢ **Winter Aconite,** phosphored paper .50 .20 ☐☐☐☐☐
CM1795_____
   32¢ **Pansy,** phosphored paper .50 .20 ☐☐☐☐☐
CM1796_____
   32¢ **Snowdrop,** phosphored paper .50 .20 ☐☐☐☐☐

	MNHVF	UseVF

CM1797_____
    32¢ **Anemone,** phosphored paper   .50   .20 ☐☐☐☐☐

CM1798_____   **1996. Love Cherub Issue**
    32¢ **multicolored** tagged (2,550,000,000)   .50   .20 ☐☐☐☐☐

CM1799_____   **1996. Ernest E. Just Issue**
    32¢ **black & gray** tagged (92,100,000)   .50   .20 ☐☐☐☐☐

CM1800_____   **1996. Smithsonian Institution Sesquicentennial Issue**
    32¢ **multicolored** tagged (115,600,000)   .50   .20 ☐☐☐☐☐

CM1801_____   **1996. New Years Issue**
    32¢ **multicolored** tagged (93,150,000)   .50   .20 ☐☐☐☐☐

CM1802_____   **1996. Pioneers of Communications Issue**
    32¢ **Eadweard Muybridge,** phosphored paper (23,292,500)   .50   .20 ☐☐☐☐☐

CM1803_____
    32¢ **Ottmar Mergenthaler,** phosphored paper   .50   .20 ☐☐☐☐☐

CM1804_____
    32¢ **Frederic E. Ives,** phosphored paper   .50   .20 ☐☐☐☐☐

CM1805_____
    32¢ **William Dickson,** phosphored paper   .50   .20 ☐☐☐☐☐

CM1806_____   **1996. Fulbright Scholarships Issue**
    32¢ **multicolored** tagged (111,000,000)   .50   .20 ☐☐☐☐☐

CM1807_____   **1996. Marathon Issue**
    32¢ **multicolored** tagged (209,450,000)   .50   .20 ☐☐☐☐☐

CM1792

CM1798

CM1799

CM1787-1791

CM1793-1797

CM1800

CM1801

	MNHVF	UseVF

CM1808_____   **1996. Atlanta 1996 Centennial Olympic Games Issue**

32¢ Javelin	.75	.50 ☐☐☐☐☐

CM1809_____

32¢ Whitewater canoeing	.75	.50 ☐☐☐☐☐

CM1810_____

32¢ Women's running	.75	.50 ☐☐☐☐☐

CM1811_____

32¢ Women's platform diving	.75	.50 ☐☐☐☐☐

CM1812_____

32¢ Men's cycling	.75	.50 ☐☐☐☐☐

CM1813_____

32¢ Freestyle wrestling	.75	.50 ☐☐☐☐☐

CM1814_____

32¢ Women's gymnastics	.75	.50 ☐☐☐☐☐

CM1815_____

32¢ Women's sailboarding	.75	.50 ☐☐☐☐☐

CM1816_____

32¢ Men's shot put	.75	.50 ☐☐☐☐☐

CM1817_____

32¢ Women's soccer	.75	.50 ☐☐☐☐☐

CM1818_____

32¢ Beach volleyball	.75	.50 ☐☐☐☐☐

CM1819_____

32¢ Men's rowing	.75	.50 ☐☐☐☐☐

CM1820_____

32¢ Men's sprinting events	.75	.50 ☐☐☐☐☐

CM1821_____

32¢ Women's swimming	.75	.50 ☐☐☐☐☐

CM1822_____

32¢ Women's softball	.75	.50 ☐☐☐☐☐

CM1823_____

32¢ Men's hurdles	.75	.50 ☐☐☐☐☐

CM1824_____

32¢ Men's swimming (backstroke)	.75	.50 ☐☐☐☐☐

CM1825_____

32¢ Men's gymnastics (pommel Horse)	.75	.50 ☐☐☐☐☐

CM1826_____

32¢ Equestrian events	.75	.50 ☐☐☐☐☐

CM1827_____

32¢ Men's basketball	.75	.50 ☐☐☐☐☐

Because this issue also was made available to collectors in full six-pane printing sheets, gutter pairs and blocks and cross-gutter multiples also exist.

CM1828_____   **1996. Georgia O'Keeffe Issue**

32¢ multicolored tagged (156,300,000)	.50	.20 ☐☐☐☐☐

CM1829_____   **1996. Tennessee Bicentennial Issue**

32¢ multicolored tagged (100,000,000)	.50	.20 ☐☐☐☐☐

CM1830_____   **1996. Tennessee Bicentennial Booklet Issue**

32¢ multicolored tagged (60,120,000)	.75	.20 ☐☐☐☐☐

CM1831_____   **1996. American Indian Dances Issue**

32¢ Fancy Dance, tagged (27,850,000)	.75	.50 ☐☐☐☐☐

CM1832_____

32¢ Butterfly Dance, tagged	.75	.50 ☐☐☐☐☐

CM1833_____

32¢ Traditional Dance, tagged	.75	.50 ☐☐☐☐☐

CM1802-1805

CM1806

CM1807

CM1808-1827

	MNHVF	UseVF

CM1834_____
32¢ **Raven Dance,** tagged .75 .50 ☐☐☐☐☐
CM1835_____
32¢ **Hoop Dance,** tagged .75 .50 ☐☐☐☐☐
CM1836_____ **1996. Prehistoric Animals Issue**
32¢ **Eohippus,** tagged (22,218,000) .75 .50 ☐☐☐☐☐
CM1837_____
32¢ **Woolly Mammoth,** tagged .75 .50 ☐☐☐☐☐
CM1838_____
32¢ **Mastodon,** tagged .75 .50 ☐☐☐☐☐
CM1839_____
32¢ **Saber-tooth Cat,** tagged .75 .50 ☐☐☐☐☐
CM1840_____ **1996. Breast Cancer Awareness Issue**
32¢ **multicolored** tagged (95,600,000) .50 .20 ☐☐☐☐☐
CM1841_____ **1996. James Dean Issue**
32¢ **multicolored** tagged (300,000,000) .50 .20 ☐☐☐☐☐

Because this issue also was made available to collectors in full six-pane printing sheets, gutter pairs and blocks and cross-gutter multiples also exist.

CM1842_____ **1996. Folk Heroes Issue**
32¢ **Mighty Casey,** tagged (23,681,250) .50 .20 ☐☐☐☐☐
CM1843_____
32¢ **Paul Bunyan,** tagged .50 .20 ☐☐☐☐☐
CM1844_____
32¢ **John Henry,** tagged .50 .20 ☐☐☐☐☐
CM1845_____
32¢ **Pecos Bill,** tagged .50 .20 ☐☐☐☐☐
CM1846_____ **1996. Olympic Games Centennial Issue**
32¢ **brown** tagged (133,613,000) .50 .20 ☐☐☐☐☐
CM1847_____ **1996. Iowa Sesquicentennial Issue**
32¢ **multicolored** tagged (103,400,000) .50 .20 ☐☐☐☐☐
CM1848_____ **1996. Iowa Sesquicentennial Self Adhesive Issue**
32¢ **multicolored** tagged (60,000,000) .75 .30 ☐☐☐☐☐
CM1849_____ **1996. Rural Free Delivery Centennial Issue**
32¢ **multicolored** tagged (134,000,000) .50 .20 ☐☐☐☐☐
CM1850_____ **1996. Riverboats Issue**
32¢ *Robt. E. Lee,* tagged (32,000,000) .75 .50 ☐☐☐☐☐
CM1851_____
32¢ *Sylvan Dell,* tagged .75 .50 ☐☐☐☐☐
CM1852_____
32¢ *Far West,* tagged .75 .50 ☐☐☐☐☐
CM1853_____
32¢ *Rebecca Everingham,* tagged .75 .50 ☐☐☐☐☐
CM1854_____
32¢ *Bailey Gatzert,* tagged .75 .50 ☐☐☐☐☐
CM1855_____ **1996. Big Band Leaders Issue**
32¢ **Count Basie,** tagged (23,025,000) .50 .20 ☐☐☐☐☐
CM1856_____
32¢ **Tommy & Jimmy Dorsey,** tagged .50 .20 ☐☐☐☐☐
CM1857_____
32¢ **Glenn Miller,** tagged .50 .20 ☐☐☐☐☐
CM1858_____
32¢ **Benny Goodman,** tagged .50 .20 ☐☐☐☐☐
CM1859_____ **1996. Songwriters Issue**
32¢ **Harold Arlen,** tagged (23,025,000) .50 .20 ☐☐☐☐☐

CM1828

CM1829-1830

CM1836-1839

CM1831-1835

CM1840 →

CM1841

CM1842-1845 →

CM1846

CM1850-1854

CM1847, CM1848

CM1849

	MNHVF	UseVF

CM1860_____
  32¢ **Johnny Mercer,** tagged .50 .20 ☐☐☐☐☐
CM1861_____
  32¢ **Dorothy Fields,** tagged .50 .20 ☐☐☐☐☐
CM1862_____
  32¢ **Hoagy Carmichael,** tagged .50 .20 ☐☐☐☐☐
CM1863_____ **1996. F. Scott Fitzgerald Issue**
  23¢ **multicolored** tagged (300,000,000) .50 .20 ☐☐☐☐☐
CM1864_____ **1996. Endangered Species Issue**
  32¢ **Black-footed ferret** .50 .20 ☐☐☐☐☐
CM1865_____
  32¢ **Thick-billed parrot** .50 .20 ☐☐☐☐☐
CM1866_____
  32¢ **Hawaiian Monk seal** .50 .20 ☐☐☐☐☐
CM1867_____
  32¢ **American crocodile** .50 .20 ☐☐☐☐☐

CM1855-1858 ◄

CM1859-1862 ►

CM1863

CM1879

CM1880

National Stamp Collecting Month 1996 highlights these 15 species to promote awareness of endangered wildlife. Each generation must work to protect the delicate balance of nature, so that future generations may share a sound and healthy planet.

CM1864-1878

	MNHVF	UseVF	

CM1868_____
32¢ **Ocelot** .50 .20 ☐☐☐☐☐

CM1869_____
32¢ **Schaus swallowtail butterfly** .50 .20 ☐☐☐☐☐

CM1870_____
32¢ **Wyoming toad** .50 .20 ☐☐☐☐☐

CM1871_____
32¢ **Brown pelican** .50 .20 ☐☐☐☐☐

CM1872_____
32¢ **California condor** .50 .20 ☐☐☐☐☐

CM1873_____
32¢ **Gila trout** .50 .20 ☐☐☐☐☐

CM1874_____
32¢ **San Francisco garter snake** .50 .20 ☐☐☐☐☐

CM1875_____
32¢ **Woodland caribou** .50 .20 ☐☐☐☐☐

CM1876_____
32¢ **Florida panther** .50 .20 ☐☐☐☐☐

CM1877_____
32¢ **Piping plover** .50 .20 ☐☐☐☐☐

CM1878_____
32¢ **Florida manatee** .50 .20 ☐☐☐☐☐

CM1879_____ **1996. Computer Technology Issue**
32¢ **multicolored** tagged (93,612,000) .50 .20 ☐☐☐☐☐

CM1880_____ **1996. Hanukkah Issue**
32¢ **multicolored** tagged (103,520,000) .75 .20 ☐☐☐☐☐

CM1881_____ **1996. Cycling Souvenir Sheet**
50¢ **multicolored** tagged (20,000,000) 2.50 1.00 ☐☐☐☐☐

CM1882_____ **1997. New Years Issue**
32¢ **multicolored** tagged (160,000,000) .50 .20 ☐☐☐☐☐

CM1883_____ **1997. Benjamin O. Davis Issue**
32¢ **gray, green & black** phosphored paper (112,000,000) .50 .20 ☐☐☐☐☐

CM1884_____ **1997. Love Issue**
32¢ **multicolored** tagged .50 .20 ☐☐☐☐☐

CM1885_____
55¢ **multicolored** tagged 1.00 .30 ☐☐☐☐☐

CM1886_____ **1997. Helping Children Learn Issue**
32¢ **multicolored** tagged .50 .20 ☐☐☐☐☐

CM1887_____ **1997. Pacific 97 Issue**
32¢ **red** phosphored paper (65,000,000) .50 .20 ☐☐☐☐☐

CM1888_____
32¢ **blue** phosphored paper .50 .20 ☐☐☐☐☐

Because this issue also was made available in full 96-subject printing sheets of six 16-stamp panes, gutter pairs and blocks and cross-gutter multiples also exist.

CM1889_____ **1997. Thornton Wilder Issue**
32¢ **multicolored** tagged (97,500,000) .50 .20 ☐☐☐☐☐

CM1890_____ **1997. Raoul Wallenberg Issue**
32¢ **multicolored** tagged (96,000,000) .50 .20 ☐☐☐☐☐

CM1891_____ **1997. The World of Dinosaurs Issue**
$4.80 **Sheet of 15,** tagged (14,600,000) 15.00 9.50 ☐☐☐☐☐

CM1892_____ **1997. Bugs Bunny Issue**
$3.20 **Pane of 10,** tagged 7.50 ☐☐☐☐☐

Serpentine die cut 11 through stamps and backing.

CM1883

CM1881 ←

CM1882

CM1884

CM1885

CM1886

CM1887

CM1888

CM1889

CM1890

CM1892 ←

	MNHVF	UseVF

CM1893_____

$3.20 **Pane of 10,** tagged .... 200.00 ☐☐☐☐☐

This issue also was made available in top and bottom half printing sheets of six 10-stamp panes each. A single plate number, trimmed away on individual panes, appears adjacent to the bottom-left pane in the bottom half of the printing sheet only. Value of plate number half is $225.

A gummed, non-denominated, untagged item similar to CM1893n on the same backing paper as the normal stamps lacks Bugs' "autograph" and single stamp, the latter of which is replaced by "32 USA" as on the issued stamp. Though printed for the USPS, this item was an advertising piece and was not postally valid.

CM1894_____   **1997. Pacific 97 U.S. Stamp Sesquicentennial Issue**

$6   **Pane of 12,** tagged .... 11.50   9.00 ☐☐☐☐☐

CM1895_____   **1997. Pacific 97 U.S. Stamp Sesquicentennial Issue**

$7.20 **Pane of 12,** tagged .... 12.50   10.00 ☐☐☐☐☐

Because this issue also was made available to collectors in full six-pane printing sheets, gutter pairs and blocks and cross-gutter multiples also exist.

CM1896_____   **1997. Marshall Plan 50th Anniversary Issue**

32¢ **multicolored** tagged (45,250,000) .... .50   .20 ☐☐☐☐☐

CM1897_____   **1997. Classic American Aircraft Issue**

32¢ **North American P-51 Mustang fighter** .... .75   .50 ☐☐☐☐☐

CM1898_____

32¢ **Wright Model B Flyer** .... .75   .50 ☐☐☐☐☐

CM1899_____

32¢ **Piper J-3 Cub** .... .75   .50 ☐☐☐☐☐

CM1900_____

32¢ **Lockheed Vega** .... .75   .50 ☐☐☐☐☐

CM1891

	MNHVF	UseVF	

CM1901_____
    32¢ *Northrop Alpha* — .75 — .50 ☐☐☐☐☐

CM1902_____
    32¢ **Martin B-10 bomber** — .75 — .50 ☐☐☐☐☐

CM1903_____
    32¢ **Chance Vought Corsair F4U fighter** — .75 — .50 ☐☐☐☐☐

CM1904_____
    32¢ **Boeing B-47 Stratojet bomber** — .75 — .50 ☐☐☐☐☐

CM1905_____
    32¢ **Gee Bee Super-Sportster** — .75 — .50 ☐☐☐☐☐

CM1906_____
    32¢ **Beech Model C17L Staggerwing** — .75 — .50 ☐☐☐☐☐

CM1907_____
    32¢ **Boeing B-17 Flying Fortress bomber** — .75 — .50 ☐☐☐☐☐

CM1908_____
    32¢ **Stearman PT-13 training aircraft** — .75 — .50 ☐☐☐☐☐

CM1909_____
    32¢ **Lockheed Constellation** — .75 — .50 ☐☐☐☐☐

CM1910_____
    32¢ **Lockheed P-38 Lightning fighter** — .75 — .50 ☐☐☐☐☐

CM1911_____
    32¢ **Boeing P-26 Peashooter fighter** — .75 — .50 ☐☐☐☐☐

CM1896

CM1894

CM1895

	MNHVF	UseVF
CM1912_____		
32¢ **Ford Tri-Motor**	.75	.50 ▢▢▢▢▢
CM1913_____		
32¢ **Douglas DC-3 passenger plane**	.75	.50 ▢▢▢▢▢
CM1914_____		
32¢ **Boeing 314 Clipper flying boat**	.75	.50 ▢▢▢▢▢
CM1915_____		
32¢ **Curtiss JN-4 Jenny training aircraft**	.75	.50 ▢▢▢▢▢
CM1916_____		
32¢ **Grumman F4F Wildcat fighter**	.75	.50 ▢▢▢▢▢

Because this issue also was made available to collectors in full six-pane printing sheets, gutter pairs and blocks and cross-gutter multiples also exist.

CM1917_____ 1997. Legendary Football Coaches Issue

32¢ **Paul "Bear" Bryant,** tagged (22,500,000)	.50	.20 ▢▢▢▢▢
CM1918_____		
32¢ **Glen "Pop" Warner,** tagged	.50	.20 ▢▢▢▢▢
CM1919_____		
32¢ **Vince Lombardi,** tagged	.50	.20 ▢▢▢▢▢
CM1920_____		
32¢ **George Halas,** tagged	.50	.20 ▢▢▢▢▢

CM1921_____ 1997. Classic American Dolls Issue

32¢ **"Alabama Baby" and Martha Chase Doll**	.75	.50 ▢▢▢▢▢

CM1897-1916

	MNHVF	UseVF	

CM1922_____

  32¢ **Rutta Sisters "The Columbian Doll"**   .75   .50 ☐☐☐☐☐

CM1923_____

  32¢ **Johnny Gruelle's "Raggedy Ann"**   .75   .50 ☐☐☐☐☐

CM1924_____

  32¢ **Martha Chase Cloth Doll**   .75   .50 ☐☐☐☐☐

CM1925_____

  32¢ **Effanbee Doll Co. "American Child"**   .75   .50 ☐☐☐☐☐

CM1917-1920 ←

CLASSIC
American Dolls

"Alabama Baby" and Martha Chase   "The Columbian Doll"   Johnny Gruelle's "Raggedy Ann"   Martha Chase   "American Child"
"Baby Coos"   Plains Indian   Izannah Walker   "Babyland Rag"   "Scootles"
Ludwig Greiner   "Betsy McCall"   Percy Crosby's "Skippy"   "Maggie Mix-up"   Albert Schoenhut

The above names include doll makers, designers, trade names and common names.

CM1921-1935 →

	MNHVF	UseVF

CM1926_____

    32¢ **Ideal Novelty & Toy Co. "Baby Coos"**   .75   .50 ☐☐☐☐☐

CM1927_____

    32¢ **Plains Indian Doll 1920s**   .75   .50 ☐☐☐☐☐

CM1928_____

    32¢ **Izannah Walker Oil-Painted Cloth Doll**   .75   .50 ☐☐☐☐☐

CM1929_____

    32¢ **All-Cloth "Babyland Rag" Doll**   .75   .50 ☐☐☐☐☐

CM1930_____

    32¢ **Rose O'Neill "Scootles" Doll**   .75   .50 ☐☐☐☐☐

CM1931_____

    32¢ **Ludwig Greiner First U.S. Patent Doll**   .75   .50 ☐☐☐☐☐

CM1932_____

    32¢ **"Betsy McCall" American Character Doll**   .75   .50 ☐☐☐☐☐

CM1933_____

    32¢ **Percy Crosby's "Skippy"**   .75   .50 ☐☐☐☐☐

CM1934_____

    32¢ **Alexander Doll Co. "Maggie Mix-up"**   .75   .50 ☐☐☐☐☐

CM1935_____

    32¢ **Schoenut "All Word Perfection Art Dolls"**   .75   .50 ☐☐☐☐☐

CM1936_____ **1997. Humphrey Bogart Issue**

    32¢ **multicolored** tagged (195,000,000)   .50   .20 ☐☐☐☐☐

Because this issue also was made available to collectors in full six-pane printing sheets, gutter pairs and blocks and cross-gutter multiples also exist.

CM1937_____ **1997. Vince Lombardi Issue**

    32¢ **multicolored** tagged (20,000,000)   .50   .20 ☐☐☐☐☐

CM1938_____ **1997. Paul "Bear" Bryant Issue**

    32¢ **multicolored** tagged (20,000,000)   .50   .20 ☐☐☐☐☐

CM1939_____ **1997. Glen "Pop" Warner Issue**

    32¢ **multicolored** tagged (10,000,000)   .50   .20 ☐☐☐☐☐

CM1940_____ **1997. George Halas Issue**

    32¢ **multicolored** tagged (10,000,000)   .50   .20 ☐☐☐☐☐

CM1941_____ **1997. "The Stars And Stripes Forever" Issue**

    32¢ **multicolored** tagged (323,000,000)   .50   .20 ☐☐☐☐☐

CM1942_____ **1997. Opera Singers Issue**

    32¢ **Lily Pons,** tagged (21,500,000)   .50   .20 ☐☐☐☐☐

CM1943_____

    32¢ **Richard Tucker,** tagged   .50   .20 ☐☐☐☐☐

CM1944_____

    32¢ **Lawrence Tibbett,** tagged   .50   .20 ☐☐☐☐☐

CM1945_____

    32¢ **Rosa Ponselle,** tagged   .50   .20 ☐☐☐☐☐

CM1946_____ **1997. Classical Composers and Conductors Issue**

    32¢ **Leopold Stokowski,** tagged (4,300,000) 20-stamp panes   .50   .20 ☐☐☐☐☐

CM1947_____

    32¢ **Arthur Fiedler,** tagged   .50   .20 ☐☐☐☐☐

CM1948_____

    32¢ **George Szell,** tagged   .50   .20 ☐☐☐☐☐

CM1949_____

    32¢ **Eugene Ormandy,** tagged   .50   .20 ☐☐☐☐☐

CM1950_____

    32¢ **Samuel Barber,** tagged   .50   .20 ☐☐☐☐☐

CM1951_____

    32¢ **Ferde Grofe,** tagged   .50   .20 ☐☐☐☐☐

CM1936

CM1937

CM1938

CM1939

CM1940

CM1942-1945

CM1941

CM1954

CM1946-1953

CM1955

CM1956-1960

CM1961

	MNHVF	UseVF

CM1952_____
    32¢ **Charles Ives,** tagged — .50 — .20 ☐☐☐☐☐
CM1953_____
    32¢ **Louis Moreau Gottschalk, Gottschalk,** tagged — .50 — .20 ☐☐☐☐☐
CM1954_____   **1997. Padre Felix Varela Issue**
    32¢ **purple** tagged (25,250,000) — .50 — .20 ☐☐☐☐☐
CM1955_____   **1997. U.S. Department of the Air Force Issue**
    32¢ **multicolored** tagged (45,250,000) — .50 — .20 ☐☐☐☐☐
CM1956_____   **1997. Classic Movie Monsters Issue**
    32¢ **Lon Chaney, as Phantom of the Opera,** (29,000,000) — .50 — .20 ☐☐☐☐☐
CM1957_____
    32¢ **Bela Lugosi, as Dracula,** tagged — .50 — .20 ☐☐☐☐☐
CM1958_____
    32¢ **Boris Karloff, in Frankenstein,** tagged — .50 — .20 ☐☐☐☐☐
CM1959_____
    32¢ **Boris Karloff, as The Mummy,** tagged — .50 — .20 ☐☐☐☐☐
CM1960_____
    32¢ **Lon Chaney Jr., as The Wolf Man,** tagged — .50 — .20 ☐☐☐☐☐

Because this issue also was made available to collectors in full nine-pane printing sheets, gutter pairs and blocks and cross-gutter multiples also exist.

CM1961_____   **1997. First Supersonic Flight Issue**
    32¢ **multicolored** tagged (173,000,000) — .50 — .20 ☐☐☐☐☐
CM1962_____   **1997. Women in Military Service Issue**
    32¢ **multicolored** tagged (37,000,000) — .50 — .20 ☐☐☐☐☐
CM1963_____   **1997. Kwanzaa Issue**
    32¢ **multicolored** tagged (133,000,000) — .50 — .20 ☐☐☐☐☐

Because this issue also was made available to collectors in full six-pane printing sheets, gutter pairs and blocks and cross-gutter multiples also exist.

CM1964_____   **1998. Year of The Tiger New Year Issue**
    32¢ **multicolored** tagged — .50 — .20 ☐☐☐☐☐
CM1965_____   **1998. Winter Sports Issue**
    32¢ **multicolored** tagged — .50 — .20 ☐☐☐☐☐
CM1966_____   **1998. Madam C.J. Walker Issue**
    32¢ **multicolored** tagged — .50 — .20 ☐☐☐☐☐
CM1967_____   **1998. Celebrate the Century 1900s Issue**
    $4.80 **Pane of 15,** tagged — 12.50 — 9.50 ☐☐☐☐☐
CM1968_____   **1998. Celebrate the Century 1910s Issue**
    $4.80 **Pane of 15,** tagged — 12.50 — 9.50 ☐☐☐☐☐
CM1969_____   **1998. Spanish American War Issue**
    32¢ **red & black** tagged — .50 — .20 ☐☐☐☐☐
CM1970_____   **1998. Flowering Trees Issue**
    32¢ **Southern Magnolia,** tagged — .50 — .20 ☐☐☐☐☐
CM1971_____
    32¢ **Blue Paloverde,** tagged — .50 — .20 ☐☐☐☐☐
CM1972_____
    32¢ **Yellow Poplar,** tagged — .50 — .20 ☐☐☐☐☐
CM1973_____
    32¢ **Prairie Crab Apple,** tagged — .50 — .20 ☐☐☐☐☐
CM1974_____
    32¢ **Pacific Dogwood,** tagged — .50 — .20 ☐☐☐☐☐
CM1975_____   **1998. Alexander Calder Issue**
    32¢ **Black Cascade, 13 verticals,** tagged — .50 — .20 ☐☐☐☐☐
CM1976_____
    32¢ **Untitled,** tagged — .50 — .20 ☐☐☐☐☐

CM1967

CM1962

CM963

CM1964

CM1965

CM1966

CM1968

	MNHVF	UseVF

CM1977 _____
   32¢ **Rearing Stallion,** tagged .50 .20 ☐☐☐☐☐
CM1978 _____
   32¢ **Portrait of a young man,** tagged .50 .20 ☐☐☐☐☐
CM1979 _____
   32¢ **Un Effet du Japonais,** tagged .50 .20 ☐☐☐☐☐
CM1980 _____   **1998. Cinco de Mayo Issue**
   32¢ **multicolored** .50 .20 ☐☐☐☐☐
CM1981 _____   **1998. Sylvester and Tweety Issue**
   $3.20 **Pane of 10,** tagged 5.00 ☐☐☐☐☐
CM1982 _____
   $3.20 **Pane of 10,** tagged 5.00 ☐☐☐☐☐

This issue also was made available in top and bottom half printing sheets of six 10-stamp panes each. Vertical rouletting between the two panes is missing on these half sheets. A plate number, trimmed away or individual panes, appears adjacent to the bottom-left pane in the bottom half of the printing sheet only.

CMSP1 _____   **1998. Breast Cancer Research Semipostal Issue**
   40¢ **multicolored** .80 .30 ☐☐☐☐☐
CM1983 _____
   $4.80 **Sheetlet of 15,** tagged15.00 9.50 ☐☐☐☐☐

CM1969

CM1970-1974

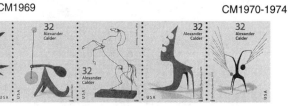

CM1975-1979

CM1980

CM1981-1982

CMSP1

	MNHVF	UseVF

CM1984_____   **1998. Wisconsin Statehood Sesquicentennial Issue**

| 32¢ **multicolored** | .50 | .20 ☐☐☐☐☐ |

CM1985_____   **1998. Trans-Mississippi Color Issue**

| $3.80 **Pane of 9** | 7.50 | 3.50 ☐☐☐☐☐ |

CM1986_____   **1998. Trans-Mississippi Color Issue**

| $9 **Pane,** 9 examples of CM1985h | 15.00 | ☐☐☐☐☐ |

CM1987_____   **1998. Berlin Airlift Issue**

| 32¢ **multicolored** | .50 | .20 ☐☐☐☐☐ |

CM1988_____   **1998. Folk Musicians Issue**

| 32¢ **Woody Guthrie,** tagged | .50 | .20 ☐☐☐☐☐ |

CM1989_____

| 32¢ **Sonny Terry,** tagged | .50 | .20 ☐☐☐☐☐ |

CM1990_____

| 32¢ **Huddie "Leadbelly" Ledbetter** | .50 | .20 ☐☐☐☐☐ |

CM1991_____

| 32¢ **Josh White** | .50 | .20 ☐☐☐☐☐ |

CM1992_____   **1998. Spanish Settlement of the Southwest Issue**

| 32¢ **multicolored** | .50 | .20 ☐☐☐☐☐ |

CM1993_____   **1998. Gospel Singers Issue**

| 32¢ **Mahalia Jackson** | .50 | 2.00 ☐☐☐☐☐ |

CM1994_____

| 32¢ **Roberta Martin** | .50 | .20 ☐☐☐☐☐ |

CM1984

CM1983

	MNHVF	UseVF	

CM1995_____
32¢ **Clara Ward** — .50 — .20 ☐☐☐☐☐
CM1996_____
32¢ **Sister Rosetta Tharpe** — .50 — .20 ☐☐☐☐☐
CM1997_____   **1998. Stephen Vincent Benét Issue**
32¢ **multicolored** — .50 — .20 ☐☐☐☐☐
CM1998_____   **1998. Tropical Birds Issue**
32¢ **Antillean Euphonia** — .50 — .20 ☐☐☐☐☐
CM1999_____
32¢ **Green-throated Carib** — .50 — .20 ☐☐☐☐☐
CM2000_____
32¢ **Crested Honeycreeper** — .50 — .20 ☐☐☐☐☐
CM2001_____
32¢ **Cardinal Honeyeater** — .50 — .20 ☐☐☐☐☐
CM2002_____   **1998. Alfred Hitchcock Issue**
32¢ **black & gray** — .75 — .20 ☐☐☐☐☐
CM2003_____   **1998. Organ & Tissue Donation Issue**
32¢ **multicolored** — .50 — .20 ☐☐☐☐☐
CM2004_____   **1998. Bright Eyes Pet Issue**
32¢ **Dog,** tagged — .50 — .20 ☐☐☐☐☐
CM2005_____
32¢ **Goldfish,** tagged — .50 — .20 ☐☐☐☐☐
CM2006_____
32¢ **Cat,** tagged — .50 — .20 ☐☐☐☐☐
CM2007_____
32¢ **Parakeet,** tagged — .50 — .20 ☐☐☐☐☐
CM2008_____
32¢ **Hamster,** tagged — .50 — .20 ☐☐☐☐☐
CM2009_____   **1998. Klondike Gold Rush Issue**
32¢ **multicolored** tagged — .50 — .20 ☐☐☐☐☐
CM2010_____   **1998. American Art Issue**
32¢ **John Foster** — .50 — .20 ☐☐☐☐☐
CM2011_____
32¢ **The Freake Limner** — .50 — .20 ☐☐☐☐☐
CM2012_____
32¢ **Ammi Phillips** — .50 — .20 ☐☐☐☐☐
CM2013_____
32¢ **Rembrandt Peale** — .50 — .20 ☐☐☐☐☐
CM2014_____
32¢ **John J. Audubon** — .50 — .20 ☐☐☐☐☐
CM2015_____
32¢ **George Caleb Bingham** — .50 — .20 ☐☐☐☐☐
CM2016_____
32¢ **Asher B. Durand** — .50 — .20 ☐☐☐☐☐
CM2017_____
32¢ **Joshua Johnson** — .50 — .20 ☐☐☐☐☐
CM2018_____
32¢ **William M. Harnett** — .50 — .20 ☐☐☐☐☐
CM2019_____
32¢ **Winslow Homer** — .50 — .20 ☐☐☐☐☐
CM2020_____
32¢ **George Catlin** — .50 — .20 ☐☐☐☐☐
CM2021_____
32¢ **Thomas Moran** — .50 — .20 ☐☐☐☐☐

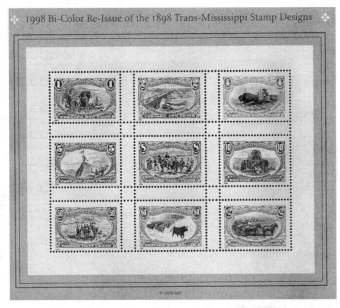

1998 Bi-Color Re-Issue of the 1898 Trans-Mississippi Stamp Designs

© USPS 1997

CM1987

CM1992

CM1985 (CM1986 is a pane of 9 examples of the $1 stamp)

CM1988-1991

CM1997

CM1993-1996

CM1998-2001

CM2002

CM2003

CM2009

CM2004-2008

		MNHVF	UseVF	
CM2022_____				
	32¢ **Albert Bierstadt**	.50	.20	☐☐☐☐☐
CM2023_____				
	32¢ **Frederic Edwin Church**	.50	.20	☐☐☐☐☐
CM2024_____				
	32¢ **Mary Cassatt**	.50	.20	☐☐☐☐☐
CM2025_____				
	32¢ **Edward Hopper**	.50	.20	☐☐☐☐☐
CM2026_____				
	32¢ **Grant Wood**	.50	.20	☐☐☐☐☐
CM2027_____				
	32¢ **Charles Sheeler**	.50	.20	☐☐☐☐☐
CM2028_____				
	32¢ **Franny Kline**	.50	.20	☐☐☐☐☐
CM2029_____				
	32¢ **Mark Rothko**	.50	.20	☐☐☐☐☐
CM2030_____	**1998. Celebrate the Century, 1930s Issue**			
	$4.80 **Sheetlet of 15,** tagged	10.00	7.50	☐☐☐☐☐
CM2031_____	**1998. Ballet Issue**			
	32¢ **multicolored**	.50	.20	☐☐☐☐☐
CM2032_____	**1998. Space Discovery Issue**			
	32¢ **Land craft**	.50	.20	☐☐☐☐☐
CM2033_____				
	32¢ **Space ship**	.50	.20	☐☐☐☐☐

CM2010-2029

		MNHVF	UseVF	
CM2034_____				
32¢ **Figure**		.50	.20	⬜⬜⬜⬜⬜
CM2035_____				
32¢ **Jagged hills**		.50	.20	⬜⬜⬜⬜⬜
CM2036_____				
32¢ **Moon**		.50	.20	⬜⬜⬜⬜⬜
CM2037_____	**1998. Giving & Sharing Issue**			
32¢ **multicolored**		.50	.20	⬜⬜⬜⬜⬜
CM2038_____	**1999. Year of the Hare Issue**			
33¢ **multicolored** tagged		.50	.20	⬜⬜⬜⬜⬜
CM2039_____	**1999. Malcolm X Issue**			
33¢ **multicolored**		.50	.20	⬜⬜⬜⬜⬜
CM2040_____	**1999. Victorian Hearts Issue**			
33¢ **multicolored**		.50	.20	⬜⬜⬜⬜⬜
CM2041_____				
55¢ **multicolored**		.85	.25	⬜⬜⬜⬜⬜
CM2042_____	**1999. Hospice Care Issue**			
33¢ **multicolored** phosphored paper		.50	.20	⬜⬜⬜⬜⬜
CM2043_____	**1999. Celebrate the Century 1940s Issue**			
$4.95 **Commemorative pane of 15,** multicolored tagged		10.00	7.50	⬜⬜⬜⬜⬜
CM2044_____	**1999. Irish Immigration Issue**			
33¢ **multicolored**		.50	.20	⬜⬜⬜⬜⬜
CM2045_____	**1999. Alfred Lunt and Lynn Fontanne Issue**			
33¢ **multicolored**		.50	.20	⬜⬜⬜⬜⬜

CM2030

	MNHVF	UseVF	

CM2046_____   1999. Arctic Animals Issue

33¢ **Arctic Hare, multicolored**   .60   .20

CM2047_____

33¢ **Arctic Fox, multicolored**   .60   .20

CM2048_____

33¢ **Snowy Owl, multicolored**   .60   .20

CM2049_____

33¢ **Polar Bear, multicolored**   .60   .20

CM2050_____

33¢ **Gray Wolf, multicolored**   .60   .20

CM2051_____   1999. Sonoran Desert Issue

$3.30 **multicolored Sheetlet of 10,** blocked tagged   7.50   3.00

CM2052_____   1999. Daffy Duck Issue

$3.30 **Pane of 10,** tagged   7.50

This issue also was made available in top- and bottom-half printing sheets of six 10-stamp panes each. Vertical rou-letting between the two panes is missing on these half sheets. A single plate number, trimmed away on individual panes, appears adjacent to the bottom-left pane in the bottom half of the printing sheet only.

CM2053_____

$3.30 **Pane of 10,** tagged   7.50

CM2054_____   1999. Ayn Rand Issue

33¢ **multicolored**   .50   .20

CM2055_____   1999. Cinco de Mayo Issue

33¢ **multicolored**   .50   .20

CM2056_____   1999. Tropical Flowers Issue

33¢ **Bird of paradise, multicolored**   .50   .20

CM2057_____

33¢ **Royal poinciana, multicolored**   .50   .20

CM2031

CM2032-2036

CM2037

CM2038

CM2039

CM2040

CM2041

Hospice Care

CM2042

CM2043

CM2044

CM2045

CM2046-2050

CM2051

	MNHVF	UseVF
CM2058_____		
33¢ **Gloriosa lily, multicolored**	.50	.20
CM2059_____		
33¢ **Chinese hibiscus, multicolored**	.50	.20
CM2060_____ **1999. John & William Bartram Issue**		
33¢ **multicolored**	.60	.20
CM2061_____ **1999. Celebrate the Century 1950s Issue**		
$4.95 **Commemorative page of 15, multicolored** tagged	10.00	7.50
CM2062_____ **1999. Prostate Cancer Awareness Issue**		
33¢ **multicolored**	.50	.20
CM2063_____ **1999. California Gold Rush Issue**		
33¢ **multicolored**	.50	.20
CM2064_____ **1999. Aquarium Fish Issue**		
33¢ **Black-and-white fish**	.50	.20
CM2065_____		
33¢ **Thermometer**	.50	.20

CM2052

CM2053

	MNHVF	UseVF

CM2066_____
  33¢ **Blue-and-yellow fish** .... .50 ... .20 ☐☐☐☐☐
CM2067_____
  33¢ **red-and-white fish** .... .50 ... .20 ☐☐☐☐☐
This issue was also made available in press sheets.
CM2068_____ **1999. Xtreme Sports Issue**
  33¢ **Skateboarding** .... .50 ... .20 ☐☐☐☐☐
CM2069_____
  33¢ **BMX biking** .... .50 ... .20 ☐☐☐☐☐
CM2070_____
  33¢ **Snowboarding** .... .50 ... .20 ☐☐☐☐☐

CM2054

CM2055

CM2056-2059

CM2060

CM2062

CM2061

	MNHVF	UseVF	

CM2071_____
33¢ **In-line skating** .50 .20

CM2072_____ **1999. American Glass Issue**
33¢ **Freeblown glass** .50 .20

CM2073_____
33¢ **Mold-blown glass** .50 .20

CM2074_____
33¢ **Pressed glass** .50 .20

CM2075_____
33¢ **Art glass** .50 .20

CM2076_____ **1999. James Cagney Issue**
33¢ **multicolored** .50 .20

CM2077_____ **1999. Honoring Those Who Served Issue**
33¢ **multicolored** .50 .20

CM2078_____ **1999. Universal Postal Union Issue**
45¢ **multicolored** .90 .40

CM2079_____ **1999. All Aboard! Issue**
33¢ **multicolored** .50 .20

CM2080_____
33¢ **multicolored** .50 .20

CM2081_____
33¢ **multicolored** .50 .20

CM2063

CM2064-2067

CM2068-2071

CM2072-2075

	MNHVF	UseVF
CM2082_____		
33¢ **multicolored**	.50	.20 ☐☐☐☐☐
CM2083_____		
33¢ **multicolored**	.50	.20 ☐☐☐☐☐
CM2084_____ **1999. Frederic Law Olmsted Issue**		
33¢ **multicolored**	.50	.20 ☐☐☐☐☐
CM2085_____ **1999. Hollywood Composers Issue**		
33¢ **multicolored**	.50	.20 ☐☐☐☐☐
CM2086_____		
33¢ **multicolored**	.50	.20 ☐☐☐☐☐
CM2087_____		
33¢ **multicolored**	.50	.20 ☐☐☐☐☐

CM2076

CM2077

CM2078

CM2084

CM2079-2083

CM2085-2090

		MNHVF	UseVF

CM2088_____

33¢ **multicolored** — .50 — .20 ☐☐☐☐☐

CM2089_____

33¢ **multicolored** — .50 — .20 ☐☐☐☐☐

CM2090_____

33¢ **multicolored** — ☐☐☐☐☐

CM2091_____ **1999. Celebrate the Century 1960s Issue**

$4.95 **Commemorative pane of 15, multicolored,** tagged — 10.00 — 7.50 ☐☐☐☐☐

CM2092_____ **1999. Broadway Songwriters Issue**

33¢ **multicolored** — .50 — .20 ☐☐☐☐☐

CM2093_____

33¢ **multicolored** — .50 — .20 ☐☐☐☐☐

CM2094_____

33¢ **multicolored** — .50 — .20 ☐☐☐☐☐

CM2095_____

33¢ **multicolored** — .50 — .20 ☐☐☐☐☐

CM2096_____

33¢ **multicolored** — .50 — .20 ☐☐☐☐☐

CM2097_____

33¢ **multicolored** — .50 — .20 ☐☐☐☐☐

CM2098_____ **1999. Insects and Spiders Issue**

33¢ **multicolored** — .50 — .20 ☐☐☐☐☐

CM2091

	MNHVF	UseVF

CM2099_____ **1999. Hanukkah Issue**

33¢ **multicolored** — .50 — .20 ☐☐☐☐☐

CM2100_____ **1999. North Atlantic Treaty Organization Issue**

33¢ **multicolored** — .50 — .20 ☐☐☐☐☐

CM2101_____ **1999. Kwanzaa Issue**

33¢ **multicolored** — .50 — .20 ☐☐☐☐☐

CM2102_____ **1999. Celebrate the Century 1970s Issue**

$4.95 **Sheetlet of 15,** tagged — 10.00 — 7.00 ☐☐☐☐☐

CM2103_____ **1999. Year 2000 Issue**

33¢ **multicolored** — .50 — .20 ☐☐☐☐☐

CM2104_____ **2000. Year of the Dragon Issue**

33¢ **multicolored** — .50 — .20 ☐☐☐☐☐

CM2105_____ **2000. Celebrate the Century 1980s Issue**

33¢ **Commemorative pane of 15, multicolored,** tagged — 10.00 — 7.00 ☐☐☐☐☐

CM2106_____ **2000. Patricia Roberts Harris Issue**

33¢ **multicolored** — .50 — .20 ☐☐☐☐☐

CM2107_____ **2000. U.S. Navy Submarines Issue**

33¢ **USS** *Nautilus* — .50 — .20 ☐☐☐☐☐

CM2108_____

33¢ **USS** *Holland* — .50 — .20 ☐☐☐☐☐

CM2109_____

33¢ **S Class submarine** — .50 — .20 ☐☐☐☐☐

CM2099

CM2100

CM2101

CM2092-2097

CM2103

	MNHVF	UseVF	
CM2110_____			
33¢ *Gato* class submarine	.50	.20	☐☐☐☐☐
CM2111_____			
33¢ *Los Angeles* class attack submarine	.50	.20	☐☐☐☐☐
CM2112_____ **2000. Los Angeles Class Submarine Issue**			
33¢ **multicolored**	.50	.20	☐☐☐☐☐
CM2113_____ **2000. Pacific Coast Rain Forest Issue**			
33¢ **multicolored**	.50	.20	☐☐☐☐☐
CM2114_____ **2000. Louise Nevelson Issue**			
33¢ **multicolored**	.50	.20	☐☐☐☐☐
CM2115_____			
33¢ **multicolored**	.50	.20	☐☐☐☐☐
CM2116_____			
33¢ **multicolored**	.50	.20	☐☐☐☐☐
CM2117_____			
33¢ **multicolored**	.50	.20	☐☐☐☐☐
CM2118_____			
33¢ **multicolored**	.50	.20	☐☐☐☐☐

CM2098

CM2102

CM2106

CM2104

CM2107-2111

CM2112

		MNHVF	UseVF

CM2119_____   **2000. Edwin Powell Hubble Issue**

33¢ **Eagle Nebula** .50 .20

CM2120_____

33¢ **Ring Nebula** .50 .20

CM2121_____

33¢ **Lagoon Nebula** .50 .20

CM2122_____

33¢ **Egg Nebula** .50 .20

CM2123_____

33¢ **Galaxy NGC 1316** .50 .20

CM2105 ◄

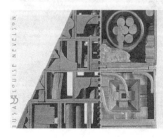

CM2114-2118

		MNHVF	UseVF

CM2124_____ **2000. American Samoa Issue**
33¢ **multicolored** .50 .20 ☐☐☐☐☐

CM2125_____ **2000. Library of Congress Issue**
33¢ **multicolored** .50 .20 ☐☐☐☐☐

CM2126_____ **2000. Celebrate the Century 1990-1999 Issue**
33¢ **Commemorative pane of 15, multicolored,** tagged .50 .20 ☐☐☐☐☐

CM2113

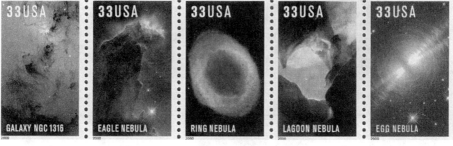

CM2119-2123

CM2124

CM2125

CM2126

	UnFVF	UseFVF

AIRMAIL

A1 _____ **1918. Curtiss Biplane Issue**

6¢ **red orange** (3,395,854) · 75.00 · 30.00 ☐☐☐☐☐

A2 _____

16¢ **green** (3,793,887) · 90.00 · 40.00 ☐☐☐☐☐

A3 _____

24¢ **carmine red & blue** (2,134,888) · 90.00 · 45.00 ☐☐☐☐☐

One sheet of 100 stamps with the blue vignette of the airplane upside down was purchased in a post office at Washington, D.C., by William T. Robey, who sold it to Eugene Klein of Philadelphia, who in turn sold it to Col. Edward H.R. Green. Green retained some of the errors, including the position pieces, and through Klein disposed of the rest. Minkus No. A3v is one of the most famous post office finds in U.S. stamp history.

A4 _____ **1923. The Second Airmail Series Issue**

8¢ **green** (6,414,576) · 25.00 · 15.00 ☐☐☐☐☐

A5 _____

16¢ **indigo** (5,309,275) · 85.00 · 30.00 ☐☐☐☐☐

A6 _____

24¢ **carmine** (5,285,775) · 95.00 · 30.00 ☐☐☐☐☐

A7 _____ **1926-27. Map Issue**

10¢ **blue** (42,092,800) · 3.00 · .45 ☐☐☐☐☐

A8 _____

15¢ **olive brown** (15,597,307) · 3.75 · 2.50 ☐☐☐☐☐

A9 _____

20¢ **yellow green** (17,616,350) · 9.00 · 2.00 ☐☐☐☐☐

A10 _____ **1927. Lindbergh Airmail Issue**

10¢ **indigo** (20,379,179) · 8.00 · 2.00 ☐☐☐☐☐

First-day covers for No. A10 are from Washington, D.C., Little Falls, Minn. (where Lindbergh grew up), St. Louis, Mo., and Detroit, Mich. (his birthplace). FDCs for No. A10n are from Washington, D.C., and Cleveland, Ohio.

A11 _____ **1928. Air Mail Beacon Issue**

5¢ **carmine red & blue** (106,887,675) · 4.50 · .75 ☐☐☐☐☐

A12 _____ **1930. Winged Globe Issue**

5¢ **purple** (97,641,200) · 10.00 · .50 ☐☐☐☐☐

A13 _____ **1930. Graf Zeppelin Issue**

65¢ **green** (93,536) · 325.00 · 240.00 ☐☐☐☐☐

A14 _____

$1.30 **yellow brown** (72,428) · 650.00 · 450.00 ☐☐☐☐☐

A15 _____

$2.60 **blue** (61,296) · 975.00 · 700.00 ☐☐☐☐☐

A16 _____ **1931-34. Winged Globe Issue**

5¢ **reddish violet** (57,340,000) · 5.50 · .60 ☐☐☐☐☐

A17 _____

6¢ **orange** (302,205,100) · 2.50 · .35 ☐☐☐☐☐

A18 _____

8¢ **yellow olive** (76,648,803) · 2.50 · .35 ☐☐☐☐☐

A19 _____ **1933. Century of Progress Zeppelin Issue**

50¢ **green** (324,070) · 90.00 · 75.00 ☐☐☐☐☐

A20 _____ **1935-37. China Clipper Over Pacific Issue**

20¢ **green** (12,794,600) · 10.00 · 1.50 ☐☐☐☐☐

A21 _____

25¢ **blue** (10,205,400) · 1.50 · 1.00 ☐☐☐☐☐

A22 _____

50¢ **carmine** (9,285,300) · 10.00 · 4.50 ☐☐☐☐☐

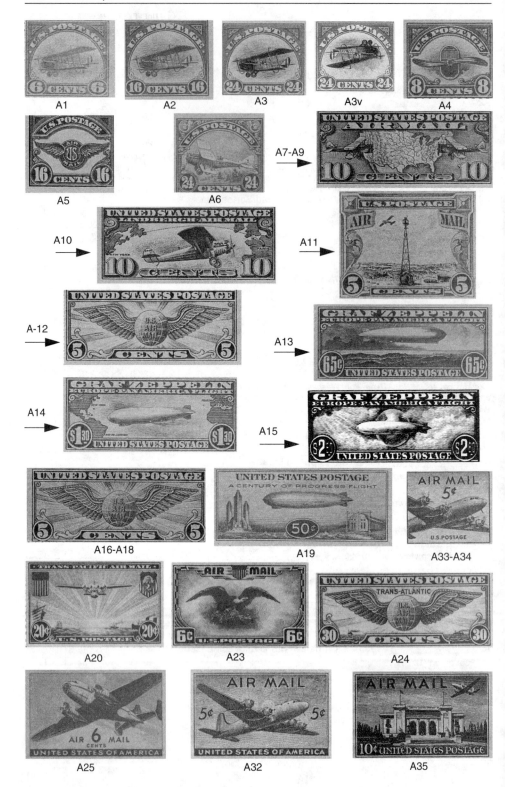

A1

A2

A3

A3v

A4

A5

A6

A7-A9

A10

A11

A-12

A13

A14

A15

A16-A18

A19

A33-A34

A20

A23

A24

A25

A32

A35

	UnFVF	UseFVF

A23 _____ **1938. Eagle and Shield Issue**
6¢ **indigo & carmine** (349,946,500) .50 .20 ☐☐☐☐☐
A24 _____ **1939. Transatlantic Issue**
30¢ **slate blue** (19,768,150) 9.00 1.50 ☐☐☐☐☐
A25 _____ **1941-44. Twin Motored Transport Plane Issue**
6¢ **rose red** (4,746,527,700) .25 .20 ☐☐☐☐☐
A26 _____
8¢ **light olive green** (1,744,878,650) .30 .20 ☐☐☐☐☐
A27 _____
10¢ **violet** (67,117,400) 1.40 .20 ☐☐☐☐☐
A28 _____
15¢ **brown carmine** (78,434,800) 2.75 .40 ☐☐☐☐☐
A29 _____
20¢ **emerald** (42,359,850) 2.75 .40 ☐☐☐☐☐
A30 _____
30¢ **light blue** (59,880,850) 2.75 .50 ☐☐☐☐☐
A31 _____
50¢ **orange** (11,160,600) 14.00 4.00 ☐☐☐☐☐
A32 _____ **1946. Skymaster Issue**
5¢ **carmine** (864,753,100) .25 .20 ☐☐☐☐☐
A33 _____ **1947. Small 5¢ Skymaster Issue**
5¢ **carmine** (971,903,700) .25 .20 ☐☐☐☐☐
A34 _____ **1947. Small 5¢ Skymaster Coil Issue**
5¢ **carmine** (33,244,500) 1.00 1.00 ☐☐☐☐☐
A35 _____ **1947. Pictorial Airmail Issue**
10¢ **black** (207,976,550) .40 .20 ☐☐☐☐☐
A36 _____
15¢ **blue green** (756,186,350) .50 .20 ☐☐☐☐☐
A37 _____
25¢ **blue** (132,956,100) 1.25 .20 ☐☐☐☐☐
A38 _____ **1948. New York City Issue**
5¢ **carmine red** (38,449,100) .25 .20 ☐☐☐☐☐
A39 _____ **1949. Small 6¢ Skymaster Issue**
6¢ **carmine** (5,070,095,200) .25 .20 ☐☐☐☐☐
A40 _____ **1949. Small 6¢ Skymaster Coil Issue**
6¢ **carmine** 3.50 .20 ☐☐☐☐☐
A41 _____ **1949. Alexandria Bicentennial Issue**
6¢ **carmine** (75,085,000) .20 .20 ☐☐☐☐☐
A42 _____ **1949. Universal Postal Union Issue**
10¢ **violet** (21,061,300) .40 .30 ☐☐☐☐☐
A43 _____
15¢ **cobalt** (36,613,100) .50 .40 ☐☐☐☐☐
A44 _____
25¢ **carmine** (16,217,100) .85 .60 ☐☐☐☐☐
A45 _____ **1949. Wright Brothers Issue**
6¢ **carmine purple** (80,405,000) .30 .20 ☐☐☐☐☐
A46 _____ **1952. Hawaii Airmail Issue**
80¢ **bright purple** (18,876,800) 6.00 1.50 ☐☐☐☐☐
A47 _____ **1953. Powered Flight Issue**
6¢ **carmine** (78,415,000) .25 .20 ☐☐☐☐☐
A48 _____ **1954. Eagle Issue**
4¢ **blue** (40,483,600) .25 .20 ☐☐☐☐☐
A49 _____ **1957. Air Force Issue**
6¢ **bright Prussian blue** (63,185,000) .25 .20 ☐☐☐☐☐

A36

A37

A38

A39-A40

A41

A42

A43

A44

A45

A46

A47

A48, 50

A49

A51-A52, A60-61

A53

A54

A55

A56

A57

A58

A59

A62

A63

	UnFVF	UseFVF

A50 _____ **1958. Eagle Issue**
5¢ carmine red (72,480,000)   .25   .20 ☐☐☐☐☐

A51 _____ **1958. Jet Silhouette Issue**
7¢ blue (1,326,960,000)   .25   .20 ☐☐☐☐☐

A52 _____ **1958. Jet Silhouette Coil Issue**
7¢ blue (157,035,000)   2.00   .20 ☐☐☐☐☐

A53 _____ **1959. Alaska Statehood Issue**
7¢ deep blue (90,055,200)   .30   .20 ☐☐☐☐☐

A54 _____ **1959. Balloon Jupiter Issue**
7¢ deep blue & scarlet (79,290,000)   .30   .20 ☐☐☐☐☐

A55 _____ **1959. Pan American Games Issue**
10¢ deep blue & scarlet (38,770,000)   .35   .30 ☐☐☐☐☐

A56 _____ **1959. Hawaii Statehood Issue**
7¢ dull scarlet (84,815,000)   .30   .20 ☐☐☐☐☐

A57 _____ **1960. Liberty Bell Issue**
10¢ black & green (39,960,000)   1.75   .80 ☐☐☐☐☐

A58 _____ **1959. Statue of Liberty Issue**
15¢ black & orange (98,160,000)   .50   .20 ☐☐☐☐☐

A59 _____ **1966. Abraham Lincoln Issue**
25¢ black & brown purple   .75   .20 ☐☐☐☐☐

A60 _____ **1960. Jet Silhouette Issue**
7¢ bright red (1,289,460,000)   .25   .20 ☐☐☐☐☐

A61 _____ **1960. Jet Silhouette Coil Issue**
7¢ bright red (87,140,000)   4.50   .40 ☐☐☐☐☐

A62 _____ **1961. Statue of Liberty Issue**
15¢ black & orange   .50   .20 ☐☐☐☐☐

A63 _____ **1961. Liberty Bell Issue**
13¢ black & scarlet   .50   .20 ☐☐☐☐☐

A64 _____ **1962. Airliner Over Capitol Issue**
8¢ carmine   .30   .20 ☐☐☐☐☐

Type I tagging: mat tagging, using four separate mats that did not cover entire sheet of 400 stamps (untagged areas identify the variety). Stamps from the four corners of a pane have two untagged margins.

Type II tagging: roll tagging, where continuous rolls replaced the tagging mats. Only the plate number selvage margin is partially tagged.

A65 _____ **1962. Airliner Over Capitol Coil Issue**
8¢ carmine   .60   .20 ☐☐☐☐☐

A66 _____ **1963. Montgomery Blair Issue**
15¢ red, maroon & blue (42,245,000)   .75   .60 ☐☐☐☐☐

A67 _____ **1963. Bald Eagle Issue**
6¢ carmine   .25   .20 ☐☐☐☐☐

A68 _____ **1963. Amelia Earhart Issue**
8¢ carmine red & brown purple (63,890,000)   .35   .20 ☐☐☐☐☐

A69 _____ **1964. Robert H. Goddard Issue**
8¢ multicolored (65,170,000)   .45   .20 ☐☐☐☐☐

A70 _____ **1967. Alaska Purchase Issue**
8¢ brown & light brown (64,710,000)   .40   .20 ☐☐☐☐☐

A71 _____ **1967. Columbia Jays Issue**
20¢ blue, brown & yellow, tagged (165,430,000)   1.25   .20 ☐☐☐☐☐

A72 _____ **1968. Star Runway Issue**
10¢ red tagged   .40   .20 ☐☐☐☐☐

A73 _____ **1968. Star Runway Coil Issue**
10¢ red   .40   .20 ☐☐☐☐☐

A74 _____ **1968. Airmail Service Issue**
10¢ black, red & blue (74,180,000)   .40   .20 ☐☐☐☐☐

A64-65

A66

A67

A68

A69

A70

A71

A72-73

A74

A75 (A81 has "21¢")

FIRST MAN ON THE MOON

A76

A77

A78-A79

A82

A83

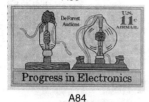

A80

A84

A85, A86

A87

A88

A89

A90

	UnFVF	UseFVF

A75 _____ **1968. USA and Jet Issue**

20¢ **multicolored** — .75 .20 ☐☐☐☐☐

A76 _____ **1969. Moon Landing Issue**

10¢ **multicolored** (152,364,800) — .40 .20 ☐☐☐☐☐

A76v. must have missing red from the entire design, including the dots on top of the yellow area as well as the astronaut's shoulder patch. Stamps with any red present are worth far less than the true red-omitted error.

A77 _____ **1971. Delta Wing Silhouette Issue**

9¢ **red** (25,830,000) — .30 .20 ☐☐☐☐☐

A78 _____ **1971. Jet Silhouette Issue**

11¢ **red** tagged (317,810,000) — .40 .20 ☐☐☐☐☐

A79 _____ **1971. Jet Silhouette Coil Issue**

11¢ **red** — .40 .20 ☐☐☐☐☐

A80 _____ **1971. Head of Liberty Issue**

17¢ **multicolored** tagged — .60 .20 ☐☐☐☐☐

A81 _____ **1971. Jet and "USA" Issue**

21¢ **multicolored** tagged (49,815,000) — .75 .20 ☐☐☐☐☐

A82 _____ **1972. National Park Issue**

11¢ **multicolored** (78,210,000) — .35 .20 ☐☐☐☐☐

A83 _____ **1972. Olympic Issue**

11¢ **multicolored** (92,710,000) — .40 .20 ☐☐☐☐☐

A84 _____ **1973. Progress in Electronics Issue**

11¢ **multicolored** tagged (56,000,000) — .30 .20 ☐☐☐☐☐

A85 _____ **1973. Winged Envelope Issue**

13¢ **red** tagged — .40 .20 ☐☐☐☐☐

A86 _____ **1973. Winged Envelope Coil Issue**

13¢ **red** — .50 .20 ☐☐☐☐☐

A87 _____ **1974. Statue of Liberty Issue**

18¢ **multicolored** tagged — .60 .50 ☐☐☐☐☐

A88 _____ **1974. Mount Rushmore Issue**

26¢ **multicolored** tagged — .75 .20 ☐☐☐☐☐

A89 _____ **1976. Plane and Globes Issue**

25¢ **multicolored** tagged — .75 .20 ☐☐☐☐☐

A90 _____

31¢ **multicolored** tagged — .90 .20 ☐☐☐☐☐

A91 _____ **1978. Orville and Wilbur Wright Issue**

31¢ **multicolored large portraits & biplane** — 1.75 1.50 ☐☐☐☐☐

A92 _____

31¢ **multicolored, small portraits, biplane and hangar** — 1.75 1.50 ☐☐☐☐☐

A93 _____ **1978. Octave Chanute Issue**

21¢ **multicolored, large portrait** — 1.75 1.50 ☐☐☐☐☐

A94 _____

21¢ **multicolored, small portrait** — 1.75 1.50 ☐☐☐☐☐

A95 _____ **1979. High Jumper Issue**

31¢ **multicolored** tagged — 1.00 .35 ☐☐☐☐☐

A96 _____ **1979. Wiley Post Issue**

25¢ **multicolored, large portrait,** tagged — 3.00 2.00 ☐☐☐☐☐

A97 _____

25¢ **multicolored, small portrait,** tagged — 3.00 2.00 ☐☐☐☐☐

A98 _____ **1982. Philip Mazzei Issue**

40¢ **multicolored** tagged — 1.25 .25 ☐☐☐☐☐

A99 _____ **1980. Blanche Stuart Scott Issue**

28¢ **multicolored** tagged — .90 .25 ☐☐☐☐☐

A100 _____ **1980. Glenn Curtiss Issue**

35¢ **multicolored** tagged — 1.00 .25 ☐☐☐☐☐

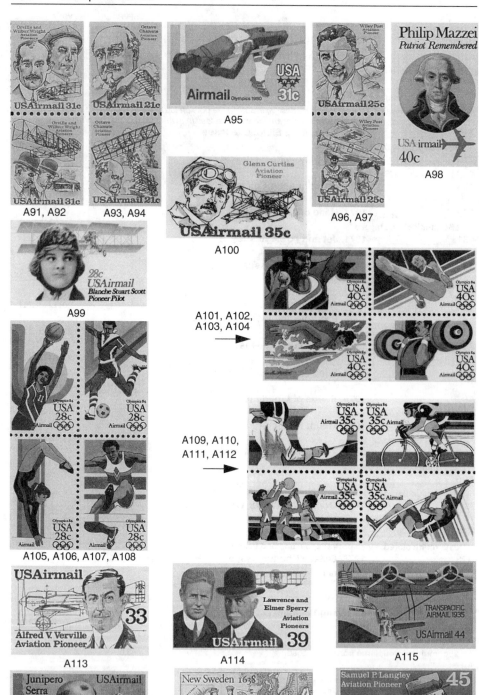

A91, A92   A93, A94

A95

A96, A97

A98

A100

A99

A101, A102,
A103, A104

A109, A110,
A111, A112

A105, A106, A107, A108

A113

A114

A115

A116

A117

A118

	UnFVF	UseFVF	

A101 _____ **1983. Olympic Issues**
40¢ **Men's shot put,** tagged — 1.25 .25 ⬜⬜⬜⬜⬜

A102 _____
40¢ **Men's gymnastics,** tagged — 1.25 .25 ⬜⬜⬜⬜⬜

A103 _____
40¢ **Women's swimming,** tagged — 1.25 .25 ⬜⬜⬜⬜⬜

A104 _____
40¢ **Men's weight lifting,** tagged — 1.25 .25 ⬜⬜⬜⬜⬜

A105 _____ **1983. Olympics Second Issue**
28¢ **Women's gymnastics,** tagged — 1.25 .25 ⬜⬜⬜⬜⬜

A106 _____
28¢ **Men's hurdles,** tagged — 1.25 .25 ⬜⬜⬜⬜⬜

A107 _____
28¢ **Women's basketball,** tagged — 1.25 .25 ⬜⬜⬜⬜⬜

A108 _____
28¢ **Soccer,** tagged — 1.25 .25 ⬜⬜⬜⬜⬜

A109 _____ **1983. Olympics Third Issue**
35¢ **Fencing,** tagged — 1.25 .25 ⬜⬜⬜⬜⬜

A110 _____
35¢ **Cycling,** tagged — 1.25 .25 ⬜⬜⬜⬜⬜

A111 _____
35¢ **Women's volleyball,** tagged — 1.25 .25 ⬜⬜⬜⬜⬜

A112 _____
35¢ **Pole vaulting,** tagged — 1.25 .25 ⬜⬜⬜⬜⬜

A113 _____ **1985. Alfred V. Verville Issue**
33¢ **multicolored** tagged — 1.00 .30 ⬜⬜⬜⬜⬜

A114 _____ **1985. Lawrence and Elmer Sperry Issue**
39¢ **multicolored** tagged — 1.25 .40 ⬜⬜⬜⬜⬜

A115 _____ **1986. Transpacific Airmail Issue**
44¢ **multicolored** tagged — 1.25 .40 ⬜⬜⬜⬜⬜

A116 _____ **1985. Junipero Serra Issue**
44¢ **multicolored** tagged — 1.75 .60 ⬜⬜⬜⬜⬜

A117 _____ **1988. Settlement of New Sweden Issue**
44¢ **multicolored** tagged (22,975,000) — 1.40 .50 ⬜⬜⬜⬜⬜

A118 _____ **1988. Samuel P. Langley Issue**
45¢ **multicolored** tagged — 1.40 .30 ⬜⬜⬜⬜⬜

A119 _____ **1988. Igor Sikorsky Issue**
36¢ **multicolored** tagged — 1.25 .40 ⬜⬜⬜⬜⬜

Traces of red have been detected in all copies of a so-called "red omitted" error of this stamp. Such stamps, on which even minute traces of red are present, are worth far less than a genuine color-omitted error would be.

A120 _____ **1989. French Revolution Bicentennial Issue**
45¢ **multicolored** tagged (38,532,000) — 1.40 .40 ⬜⬜⬜⬜⬜

A121 _____ **1989. America Issue**
45¢ **multicolored** tagged (39,325,000) — 1.50 .30 ⬜⬜⬜⬜⬜

A122 _____ **1989. Future Mail Transportation Souvenir Sheet**
$1.80 **multicolored,** souvenir sheet, tagged (1,944,000) — 7.00 5.00 ⬜⬜⬜⬜⬜

A123 _____ **1989. Future Mail Transportation Issue**
45¢ **Hypersonic airliner,** tagged — 1.25 .25 ⬜⬜⬜⬜⬜

A124 _____
45¢ **Hovercraft,** tagged — 1.25 .25 ⬜⬜⬜⬜⬜

A125 _____
45¢ **Service rover,** tagged — 1.25 .25 ⬜⬜⬜⬜⬜

A126 _____
45¢ **Space Shuttle,** tagged — 1.25 .25 ⬜⬜⬜⬜⬜

		UnFVF	UseFVF

A127 _____ **1990. America Issue**

　45¢ **multicolored** tagged　　　　　　　　　1.50　　.50 ☐☐☐☐☐

A128 _____ **1991. Harriet Quimby Issue**

　50¢ **multicolored** tagged　　　　　　　　　1.50　　.50 ☐☐☐☐☐

A129 _____ **1991. William T. Piper Issue**

　40¢ **multicolored** tagged　　　　　　　　　1.40　　.50 ☐☐☐☐☐

A130 _____ **1991. Antarctic Treaty Issue**

　50¢ **multicolored** tagged　　　　　　　　　1.50　　.60 ☐☐☐☐☐

A131 _____ **1991. America Issue**

　50¢ **multicolored** tagged　　　　　　　　　1.50　　.50 ☐☐☐☐☐

A132 _____ **1993. William T. Piper Issue**

　40¢ **multicolored,** *(July 1993)* tagged　　　1.50　　.50 ☐☐☐☐☐

A119

A120

A121 →

A122 →

A123, A124,
A125, A126
→

A127

A128

A129

A130

A131

A132

	UnFVF	UseFVF

SPECIAL DELIVERY STAMPS

SD1 _____ **1885. Messenger, First Issue**
    10¢ **Prussian blue** — 115.00 — 22.50 ☐☐☐☐☐
SD2 _____ **1888. Messenger, Second Issue**
    10¢ **Prussian blue** — 120.00 — 7.00 ☐☐☐☐☐
SD3 _____ **1893. Messenger, Third Issue**
    10¢ **orange yellow** — 75.00 — 10.00 ☐☐☐☐☐
SD4 _____ **1894. Messenger Issue**
    10¢ **deep blue** — 300.00 — 20.00 ☐☐☐☐☐
SD5 _____ **1895. Messenger Issue**
    10¢ **blue** — 65.00 — 1.75 ☐☐☐☐☐
SD6 _____ **1902. Messenger on Bicycle Issue**
    10¢ **ultramarine** — 75.00 — 3.00 ☐☐☐☐☐
SD7 _____ **1908. Helmet of Mercury Issue**
    10¢ **green** — 50.00 — 30.00 ☐☐☐☐☐
SD8 _____ **1911. Messenger on Bicycle Issue**
    10¢ **ultramarine** — 75.00 — 4.50 ☐☐☐☐☐
SD9 _____ **1914. Messenger on Bicycle Issue**
    10¢ **ultramarine** — 140.00 — 5.00 ☐☐☐☐☐
SD10 _____ **1916. Messenger on Bicycle Issue**
    10¢ **pale ultramarine** — 225.00 — 22.50 ☐☐☐☐☐
SD11 _____ **1917. Messenger on Bicycle Issue**
    10¢ **ultramarine** — 14.50 — .50 ☐☐☐☐☐
SD12 _____ **1922. Messenger and Motorcycle Issue**
    10¢ **gray blue** — 22.50 — .25 ☐☐☐☐☐
SD13 _____
    15¢ **red orange** — 19.00 — 1.00 ☐☐☐☐☐
SD14 _____ **1925. Post Office Delivery Truck Issue**
    20¢ **black** — 2.25 — 1.50 ☐☐☐☐☐
SD15 _____ **1927. Messenger and Motorcycle Issue**
    10¢ **dark lilac** — 1.00 — .20 ☐☐☐☐☐

SD16 _____ **1944. Messenger and Motorcycle Issue**
    13¢ **blue** — 1.00 — .20 ☐☐☐☐☐
SD17 _____ **1931. Messenger and Motorcycle Issue**
    15¢ **yellow orange** — .75 — .20 ☐☐☐☐☐
SD18 _____ **1944. Messenger and Motorcycle Issue**
    17¢ **yellow** — 3.50 — 3.00 ☐☐☐☐☐
SD19 _____ **1951. Post Office Delivery Truck Issue**
    20¢ **black** — 17.50 — .20 ☐☐☐☐☐
SD20 _____ **1954. Letter and Hands Issue**
    20¢ **gray blue** — .75 — .20 ☐☐☐☐☐
SD21 _____ **1957. Letter and Hands Issue**
    30¢ **maroon** — .75 — .20 ☐☐☐☐☐
SD22 _____ **1969. Dual Arrows Issue**
    45¢ **carmine & violet blue** — 1.50 — .50 ☐☐☐☐☐
SD23 _____ **1971. Dual Arrows Issue**
    60¢ **violet blue & carmine** — 1.50 — .25 ☐☐☐☐☐

SD1

SD2, SD3

SD4, SD5

SD6

SD7

SD8-SD11

SD12, SD13, SD15-SD18

SD14, SD19

SD20, SD21

SD22, SD23

	UnFVF	UseFVF

AIRMAIL/SPECIAL DELIVERY

		UnFVF	UseFVF	
ASD1_____	**1934. Blue Airmail Special Delivery Stamp Issue**			
16¢ **Prussian blue** (9,215,750)		.90	.75	☐☐☐☐☐
ASD2_____	**1936. Red and Blue Airmail Special Delivery Stamp Issue**			
16¢ **carmine & blue**		.60	.30	☐☐☐☐☐

ASD1

ASD2

	UnFVF	UseFVF

PARCEL POST STAMPS

		UnFVF	UseFVF	
PP1 _____	**1912. Parcel Post Stamps**			
1¢ **carmine** (209,691,094)		3.00	1.25	☐☐☐☐☐
PP2 _____				
2¢ **carmine** (206,417,253)		3.50	1.00	☐☐☐☐☐
PP3 _____				
3¢ **carmine** (29,027,433)		6.50	4.50	☐☐☐☐☐
PP4 _____				
4¢ **carmine** (76,743,813)		17.50	2.50	☐☐☐☐☐
PP5 _____				
5¢ **carmine** (108,153,993)		17.50	1.75	☐☐☐☐☐
PP6 _____				
10¢ **carmine** (56,896,653)		30.00	2.50	☐☐☐☐☐
PP7 _____				
15¢ **carmine** (21,147,033)		45.00	8.00	☐☐☐☐☐
PP8 _____				
20¢ **carmine** (17,142,393)		85.00	16.00	☐☐☐☐☐
PP9 _____				
25¢ **carmine** (21,940,653)		42.50	5.00	☐☐☐☐☐
PP10 _____				
50¢ **carmine** (2,117,793)		190.00	32.50	☐☐☐☐☐
PP11 _____				
75¢ **carmine** (2,772,615)		55.00	25.00	☐☐☐☐☐
PP12 _____				
$1 **carmine** (1,053,273)		250.00	20.00	☐☐☐☐☐

PARCEL POST/POSTAGE DUE STAMPS

		UnFVF	UseFVF	
PPD1 _____	**1912. Parcel Post Postage Due Stamps**			
1¢ **green** (7,322,400)		6.00	3.50	☐☐☐☐☐
PPD2 _____				
2¢ **green** (3,132,000)		55.00	15.00	☐☐☐☐☐
PPD3 _____				
5¢ **green** (5,840,100)		9.00	3.50	☐☐☐☐☐
PPD4 _____				
10¢ **green** (2,124,540)		125.00	40.00	☐☐☐☐☐
PPD5 _____				
25¢ **green** (2,117,700)		65.00	3.75	☐☐☐☐☐

SPECIAL HANDLING STAMPS

		UnFVF	UseFVF	
SH1 _____	**1925-29. Issue**			
25¢ **green**		22.50	5.50	☐☐☐☐☐
SH2 _____				
10¢ **yellow green**		2.25	1.00	☐☐☐☐☐
SH3 _____				
15¢ **yellow green**		2.25	1.00	☐☐☐☐☐
SH4 _____				
20¢ **yellow green**		3.00	1.75	☐☐☐☐☐
SH5 _____				
25¢ **yellow green** *(1929)*		17.50	7.50	

	UnFVF	UseFVF

REGISTRATION STAMP

REG1_____ **1911. Registration Stamp**

  10¢ **bright blue**   65.00   5.00

	MNHVF	UseVF

CERTIFIED MAIL STAMP

CER1_____ **1955. Certified Mail Stamp**

  15¢ **red**   .50   .35

PP1

PP2

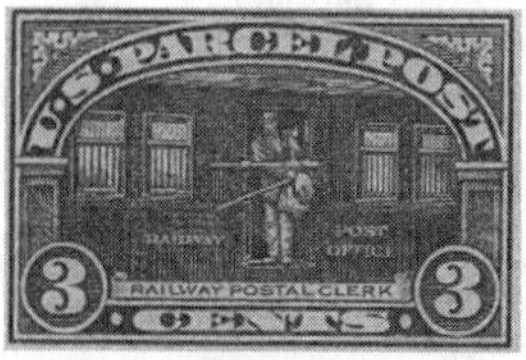

PP3

PP4

PP5

PP6

PP7

PP8

PP9

PP10

PP11

PP12

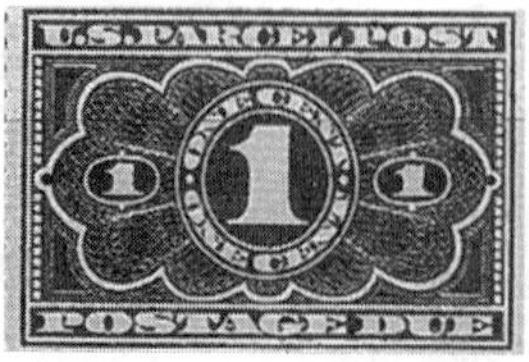

PPD1-PPD5

SH1-SH5

REG1

CER1

	UnFVF	UseFVF

POSTAGE DUE

First Printing

1879. Postage Due Stamps Issue

		UnFVF	UseFVF	
PD1	1¢ **yellow brown**	40.00	8.00	☐☐☐☐☐
PD2	2¢ **yellow brown**	250.00	6.50	☐☐☐☐☐
PD3	3¢ **yellow brown**	35.00	5.00	☐☐☐☐☐
PD4	5¢ **yellow brown**	400.00	38.00	☐☐☐☐☐
PD5	10¢ **yellow brown**	450.00	30.00	☐☐☐☐☐
PD6	30¢ **yellow brown**	200.00	47.50	☐☐☐☐☐
PD7	50¢ **yellow brown**	350.00	55.00	☐☐☐☐☐

Later Printings

		UnFVF	UseFVF	
PD8	1¢ **brown**	40.00	8.00	☐☐☐☐☐
PD9	2¢ **brown**	250.00	5.00	☐☐☐☐☐
PD10	3¢ **brown**	35.00	5.00	☐☐☐☐☐
PD11	5¢ **brown**	400.00	18.00	☐☐☐☐☐
PD12	10¢ **brown**	450.00	30.00	☐☐☐☐☐
PD13	30¢ **brown**	200.00	50.00	☐☐☐☐☐
PD14	50¢ **brown**	350.00	55.00	☐☐☐☐☐

1887. *Previous designs in changed colors.*

		UnFVF	UseFVF	
PD15	1¢ **brown red**	40.00	5.00	☐☐☐☐☐
PD16	2¢ **brown red**	50.00	5.00	☐☐☐☐☐
PD17	3¢ **brown red**	700.00	150.00	☐☐☐☐☐
PD18	5¢ **brown red**	350.00	20.00	☐☐☐☐☐
PD19	10¢ **brown red**	350.00	15.00	☐☐☐☐☐
PD20	20¢ **brown red**	175.00	50.00	☐☐☐☐☐

PD1-28

		UnFVF	UseFVF	

PD21 _____

50¢ **brown red**   1,225.00   175.00 ▢▢▢▢▢

1891. *Previous designs in changed colors. Imperforate varieties of PD22-28 exist, but they were not regularly issued.*

PD22 _____

1¢   **claret**   20.00   1.00 ▢▢▢▢▢

PD23 _____

2¢   **claret**   25.00   1.00 ▢▢▢▢▢

PD24 _____

3¢   **claret**   50.00   8.00 ▢▢▢▢▢

PD25 _____

5¢   **claret**   60.00   8.00 ▢▢▢▢▢

PD26 _____

10¢ **claret**   100.00   17.50 ▢▢▢▢▢

PD27 _____

30¢ **claret**   350.00   150.00 ▢▢▢▢▢

PD28 _____

50¢ **claret**   375.00   150.00 ▢▢▢▢▢

PD29 _____   **1894. New Designs Issue**

1¢   **vermilion** *(1894)*   1,300.00   300.00 ▢▢▢▢▢

SPD1 _____   **1879. Special Printings**

1¢   **brown** (4420)   5,000.00   ▢▢▢▢▢

SPD2 _____

2¢   **brown** (1361)   3,500.00   ▢▢▢▢▢

PD30 _____

1¢   **brown carmine** *(Aug. 14, 1894)*   32.50   5.50 ▢▢▢▢▢

PD31 _____

2¢   **vermilion** *(1894)*   550.00   130.00 ▢▢▢▢▢

PD32 _____

2¢   **brown carmine** *(July 20, 1894)*   35.00   4.00 ▢▢▢▢▢

PD33 _____

3¢   **brown carmine** *(April 27, 1895)*   130.00   26.00 ▢▢▢▢▢

PD34 _____

5¢   **brown carmine** *(April 27, 1895)*   200.00   27.50 ▢▢▢▢▢

PD35 _____

10¢ **brown carmine** *(Sept. 24, 1894)*   200.00   25.00 ▢▢▢▢▢

PD36 _____

30¢ **brown carmine** *(April 27, 1895)*   350.00   90.00 ▢▢▢▢▢

PD37 _____

50¢ **brown carmine** *(April 27, 1895)*   900.00   250.00 ▢▢▢▢▢

1895. *Same as previous designs. Double-line USPS watermark.*

PD38 _____

1¢   **brown carmine** *(Aug. 29, 1895)*   7.50   .75 ▢▢▢▢▢

PD39 _____

2¢   **brown carmine** *(Sept. 14, 1895)*   7.50   .70 ▢▢▢▢▢

PD40 _____

3¢   **brown carmine** *(Oct. 30, 1895)*   47.50   1.50 ▢▢▢▢▢

PD28

PD29-68

	UnFVF	UseFVF
PD41 _____		
5¢ **brown carmine** *(Oct. 15, 1895)*	50.00	1.50 ☐☐☐☐☐
PD42 _____		
10¢ **brown carmine** *(Sept. 14, 1895)*	47.50	3.50 ☐☐☐☐☐
PD43 _____		
30¢ **brown carmine** *(Aug. 21, 1897)*	450.00	50.00 ☐☐☐☐☐
PD44 _____		
50¢ **brown carmine** *(March 17, 1896)*	275.00	35.00 ☐☐☐☐☐

1910. Same as previous designs. Single-line USPS watermark.

	UnFVF	UseFVF
PD45 _____		
1¢ **brown carmine** *(Aug. 30, 1910)*	27.50	2.75 ☐☐☐☐☐
PD46 _____		
2¢ **brown carmine** *(Nov. 25, 1910)*	27.50	1.25 ☐☐☐☐☐
PD47 _____		
3¢ **brown carmine** *(Aug. 31, 1910)*	450.00	30.00 ☐☐☐☐☐
PD48 _____		
5¢ **brown carmine** *(Aug. 31, 1910)*	75.00	6.25 ☐☐☐☐☐
PD49 _____		
10¢ **brown carmine** *(Aug. 31, 1910)*	95.00	12.50 ☐☐☐☐☐
PD50 _____		
50¢ **brown carmine** *(Sept. 23, 1912)*	750.00	120.00 ☐☐☐☐☐

1914. Same as previous designs. Perforated 10.

	UnFVF	UseFVF
PD51 _____		
1¢ **rose red**	50.00	11.00 ☐☐☐☐☐
PD52 _____		
2¢ **vermilion**	45.00	.30 ☐☐☐☐☐
PD53 _____		
2¢ **rose red**	45.00	.30 ☐☐☐☐☐
PD54 _____		
3¢ **rose red**	750.00	38.00 ☐☐☐☐☐
PD55 _____		
5¢ **rose red**	32.00	2.50 ☐☐☐☐☐
PD56 _____		
10¢ **rose red**	50.00	2.00 ☐☐☐☐☐
PD57 _____		
30¢ **rose red**	200.00	16.00 ☐☐☐☐☐
PD58 _____		
50¢ **rose red**	8,200.00	650.00 ☐☐☐☐☐

1916. Same as previous designs. Unwatermarked.

	UnFVF	UseFVF
PD59 _____		
1¢ **rose red**	2,000.00	300.00 ☐☐☐☐☐
PD60 _____		
2¢ **rose red**	125.00	20.00 ☐☐☐☐☐

1917-25. Same as previous designs. Perforated 11.

	UnFVF	UseFVF
PD61 _____		
1/2¢ **carmine** *(April 13, 1925)*	1.00	.25 ☐☐☐☐☐
PD62 _____		
1¢ **carmine**	2.25	.25 ☐☐☐☐☐
PD63 _____		
2¢ **carmine**	2.25	.25 ☐☐☐☐☐
PD64 _____		
3¢ **carmine**	10.00	.25 ☐☐☐☐☐
PD65 _____		
5¢ **carmine**	10.00	.25 ☐☐☐☐☐
PD66 _____		
10¢ **carmine**	15.00	.30 ☐☐☐☐☐

		UnFVF	UseFVF	

PD67 _____
30¢ **carmine** — 80.00 — .75

PD68 _____
50¢ **carmine** — 10.00 — .30 ☐☐☐☐☐

PD69 _____   **1930. New Designs Issue**
1/2¢ **carmine** — 4.00 — 1.25 ☐☐☐☐☐

PD70 _____
1¢ **carmine** — 2.50 — .25 ☐☐☐☐☐

PD71 _____
2¢ **carmine** — 3.50 — .25 ☐☐☐☐☐

PD72 _____
3¢ **carmine** — 20.00 — 1.50 ☐☐☐☐☐

PD73 _____
5¢ **carmine** — 20.00 — 2.50 ☐☐☐☐☐

PD74 _____
10¢ **carmine** — 40.00 — 1.00 ☐☐☐☐☐

PD75 _____
30¢ **carmine** — 110.00 — 2.00 ☐☐☐☐☐

PD76 _____
50¢ **carmine** — 140.00 — .75 ☐☐☐☐☐

PD77 _____
$1 **carmine** — 25.00 — .25 ☐☐☐☐☐

PD78 _____
$5 **carmine** — 40.00 — .25 ☐☐☐☐☐

1931. Same as previous design. Rotary press printing, perforated 11 x 10 1/2.

PD79 _____
1/2¢ **vermilion** — 1.00 — .15 ☐☐☐☐☐

PD80 _____
1¢ **vermilion** — .20 — .15 ☐☐☐☐☐

PD81 _____
2¢ **vermilion** — .20 — .15 ☐☐☐☐☐

PD82 _____
3¢ **vermilion** — .20 — .15 ☐☐☐☐☐

PD83 _____
5¢ **vermilion** — .40 — .15 ☐☐☐☐☐

PD84 _____
10¢ **vermilion** — 1.00 — .15 ☐☐☐☐☐

PD85 _____
30¢ **vermilion** — 8.00 — .25 ☐☐☐☐☐

PD86 _____
30¢ **vermilion** — 10.00 — .25 ☐☐☐☐☐

1956. Perforated 10 1/2 x 11.

PD87 _____
$1 **vermilion** — 35.00 — .25 ☐☐☐☐☐

PD88 _____   **1959-85. New Designs Issue**
1/2¢ **red & black** — 1.25 — .85 ☐☐☐☐☐

PD68

PD69-76, 79-86

PD76

PD77, 87

PD78

	UnFVF	UseFVF	
PD89 _____			
1¢ **red & black**	.15	.15	☐☐☐☐☐
PD90 _____			
2¢ **red & black**	.15	.15	☐☐☐☐☐
PD91 _____			
3¢ **red & black**	.15	.15	☐☐☐☐☐
PD92 _____			
4¢ **red & black**	.15	.15	☐☐☐☐☐
PD93 _____			
5¢ **red & black**	.15	.15	☐☐☐☐☐
PD94 _____			
6¢ **red & black**	.15	.15	☐☐☐☐☐
PD95 _____			
7¢ **red & black**	.15	.15	☐☐☐☐☐
PD96 _____			
8¢ **red & black**	.20	.15	☐☐☐☐☐
PD97 _____			
10¢ **red & black**	.20	.15	☐☐☐☐☐
PD98 _____			
30¢ **red & black**	.50	.15	☐☐☐☐☐
PD99 _____			
50¢ **red & black**	1.00	.15	☐☐☐☐☐
PD100 _____			
$1 **red & black**	1.75	.15	☐☐☐☐☐
PD101 _____			
$5 **red & black**	9.00	.20	☐☐☐☐☐
PD102 _____			
11¢ **red & black** *(Jan. 2, 1978)*	.25	.15	☐☐☐☐☐
PD103 _____			
13¢ **red & black** *(Jan. 2, 1978)*	.25	.15	☐☐☐☐☐
PD104 _____			
17¢ **red & black** *(June 10, 1985)*	.40	.15	☐☐☐☐☐

PD88-100

PD101

		UnFVF	UseFVF

MIGRATORY BIRD HUNTING PERMIT

		UnFVF	UseFVF
RH1 _____	1934. Mallard Issue		
$1 blue		575.00	115.00 □□□□□
RH2 _____	1935. Canvasback Duck Issue		
$1 crimson		525.00	135.00 □□□□□
RH3 _____	1936. Canada Geese Issue		
$1 brown black		300.00	65.00 □□□□□
RH4 _____	1937. Scaup Ducks Issue		
$1 dull green		250.00	45.00 □□□□□
RH5 _____	1938. Pintail Duck Issue		
$1 violet		250.00	45.00 □□□□□
RH6 _____	1939. Green-Winged Teal Issue		
$1 sepia		140.00	40.00 □□□□□
RH7 _____	1940. Black Mallard Issue		
$1 black brown		140.00	40.00 □□□□□
RH8 _____	1941. Ruddy Ducks Issue		
$1 red brown		140.00	35.00 □□□□□
RH9 _____	1942. Baldpates Issue		
$1 sepia		140.00	35.00 □□□□□
RH10 _____	1943. Wood Duck Issue		
$1 carmine red		60.00	35.00 □□□□□
RH11 _____	1944. White-Fronted Geese Issue		
$1 red orange		60.00	25.00 □□□□□
RH12 _____	1945. Shoveller Ducks Issue		
$1 black		45.00	18.00 □□□□□
RH13 _____	1946. Redhead Ducks Issue		
$1 chestnut brown		35.00	13.50 □□□□□
RH14 _____	1947. Snow Geese Issue		
$1 black		35.00	13.50 □□□□□
RH15 _____	1948. Bufflehead Ducks Issue		
$1 light blue		45.00	13.50 □□□□□
RH16 _____	1949. Goldeneye Ducks Issue		
$2 emerald		50.00	13.50 □□□□□
RH17 _____	1950. Trumpeter Swans Issue		
$2 violet		60.00	10.00 □□□□□
RH18 _____	1951. Gadwall Ducks Issue		
$2 gray black		60.00	10.00 □□□□□
RH19 _____	1952. Harlequin Ducks Issue		
$2 deep ultramarine		60.00	10.00 □□□□□
RH20 _____	1953. Blue-Winged Teal Issue		
$2 lavender brown		60.00	12.00 □□□□□
RH21 _____	1954. Ring-Necked Ducks Issue		
$2 black		60.00	8.00 □□□□□
RH22 _____	1955. Blue Geese Issue		
$2 deep blue		60.00	8.00 □□□□□
RH23 _____	1956. American Merganser Issue		
$2 black		60.00	8.00 □□□□□
RH24 _____	1957. American Eider Issue		
$2 yellow emerald		60.00	8.00 □□□□□
RH25 _____	1958. Canada Geese Issue		
$2 black		60.00	8.00 □□□□□
RH26 _____	1959. Retriever Carrying Mallard Issue		
$3 blue, orange brown & black		85.00	8.00 □□□□□

RH1

RH2

RH3

RH4

RH5

RH6

RH7

RH8

RH9

RH10

RH11

RH12

RH13

RH14

RH15

RH16

RH17

RH18

		UnFVF	UseFVF	

RH27 _____ **1960. Redhead Ducks Issue**
$3   multicolored — 65.00 — 8.00 ☐☐☐☐☐

RH28 _____ **1961. Mallards Issue**
$3   blue, brown & yellow brown — 70.00 — 8.00 ☐☐☐☐☐

RH29 _____ **1962. Pintails Issue**
$3   multicolored — 70.00 — 8.00 ☐☐☐☐☐

RH30 _____ **1963. Pacific Brant Issue**
$3   multicolored — 70.00 — 8.00 ☐☐☐☐☐

RH31 _____ **1964. Nene Geese Issue**
$3   multicolored — 70.00 — 8.00 ☐☐☐☐☐

RH32 _____ **1965. Canvasbacks Issue**
$3   multicolored — 70.00 — 8.00 ☐☐☐☐☐

RH33 _____ **1966. Whistling Swans Issue**
$3   deep green, black & blue — 70.00 — 8.00 ☐☐☐☐☐

RH34 _____ **1967. Old Squaw Ducks Issue**
$3   multicolored — 70.00 — 8.00 ☐☐☐☐☐

RH35 _____ **1968. Hooded Mergansers Issue**
$3   multicolored — 55.00 — 8.00 ☐☐☐☐☐

RH36 _____ **1969. White-Winged Scoters Issue**
$3   multicolored — 40.00 — 7.00 ☐☐☐☐☐

RH37 _____ **1970. Ross' Geese Issue**
$3   multicolored — 40.00 — 7.00 ☐☐☐☐☐

RH38 _____ **1971. Cinnamon Teal Issue**
$3   multicolored — 35.00 — 7.00 ☐☐☐☐☐

RH39 _____ **1972. Emperor Geese Issue**
$5   multicolored — 22.50 — 7.00 ☐☐☐☐☐

RH40 _____ **1973. Steller's Eider Issue**
$5   multicolored — 20.00 — 7.00 ☐☐☐☐☐

RH41 _____ **1974. Wood Ducks Issue**
$5   multicolored — 18.00 — 7.00 ☐☐☐☐☐

RH42 _____ **1975. Canvasbacks Issue**
$5   multicolored — 14.00 — 7.00 ☐☐☐☐☐

RH43 _____ **1976. Canada Geese Issue**
$5   green & black — 14.00 — 7.00 ☐☐☐☐☐

RH44 _____ **1977. Ross' Geese Issue**
$5   multicolored — 14.00 — 7.00 ☐☐☐☐☐

RH45 _____ **1978. Hooded Merganser Issue**
$5   multicolored — 14.00 — 7.00 ☐☐☐☐☐

RH46 _____ **1979. Green-Winged Teal Issue**
$7.50 **multicolored** — 17.50 — 7.00 ☐☐☐☐☐

RH47 _____ **1980. Mallards Issue**
$7.50 **multicolored** — 17.50 — 7.00 ☐☐☐☐☐

RH48 _____ **1981. Ruddy Ducks Issue**
$7.50 **multicolored** — 17.50 — 7.00 ☐☐☐☐☐

RH49 _____ **1982. Canvasbacks Issue**
$7.50 **multicolored** — 17.50 — 7.00 ☐☐☐☐☐

RH50 _____ **1983. Pintails Issue**
$7.50 **multicolored** — 17.50 — 7.00 ☐☐☐☐☐

RH51 _____ **1984. Widgeons Issue**
$7.50 **multicolored** — 17.50 — 7.00 ☐☐☐☐☐

NOTE: After No. RH51's period of use had expired, 15 uncut sheets of 120 (four panes of 30 stamps per sheet, separated by gutters) were overprinted "1934-84" and "50th Anniversary" along the margins. These sheets were auctioned off by the U.S. Fish and Wildlife Service, beginning Sept. 1, 1985, with a minimum acceptable bid for each sheet of $2,000. Face value of the sheets, when valid for use, was $900. Fourteen sheets were sold, and one was donated to the Smithsonian Institution. Individual stamps of the sheet cannot be differentiated from normal copies of No. RH51. Various configurations were formed from the sheets and sold to collectors: horizontal and vertical pairs with a gutter between, cross-gutter blocks of four, and margin blocks. Sheets were submitted to The Philatelic Foundation for certification prior to being broken up, and each stamp from each of the sheets has a mark of the expertizer on the reverse. With such marks in place, individual stamps not attached to a margin were sold along with configurations noted above.

RH19

RH20

RH21

RH22

RH23

RH24

RH25

RH26

RH27

RH28

RH29

RH30

RH31

RH32

RH33

RH34

RH35

RH36

	UnFVF	UseFVF

RH51a _____   **1984. Special Commemorative Issue**
  $7.50 **Special Commemorative Issue** (All examples must have P.F. certificates)

RH52 _____   **1985. Cinnamon Teal Issue**
  $7.50 **multicolored**   17.50   7.00 ☐☐☐☐☐

RH53 _____   **1986. Fulvous Whistling Duck Issue**
  $7.50 **multicolored**   17.50   7.00 ☐☐☐☐☐

RH54 _____   **1987. Redhead Issue**
  $10 **multicolored**   20.00   10.00 ☐☐☐☐☐

RH55 _____   **1988. Snow Goose Issue**
  $10 **multicolored**   20.00   7.00 ☐☐☐☐☐

RH56 _____   **1989. Lesser Scaup Issue**
  $12.50 **multicolored**   22.50   7.00 ☐☐☐☐☐

RH57 _____   **1990. Black-Bellied Whistling Duck Issue**
  $12.50 **multicolored**   22.50   7.00 ☐☐☐☐☐

NOTE: printing on back of stamp normally is on top of gum. No. RH57v can only exist unused. Beware of copies with gum removed.

RH58 _____   **1991. King Eiders Issue**
  $15 **multicolored**   27.50   12.50 ☐☐☐☐☐

RH59 _____   **1992. Spectacled Eider Issue**
  $15 **multicolored**   27.50   12.50 ☐☐☐☐☐

RH60 _____   **1993. Canvasback issue**
  $15 **multicolored**   27.50   12.50 ☐☐☐☐☐

RH61 _____   **1994. Red-breasted Mergansers Issue**
  $15 **multicolored**   25.00   10.00 ☐☐☐☐☐

RH62 _____   **1995. Mallard Issue**
  $15 **multicolored**   25.00   10.00 ☐☐☐☐☐

RH63 _____   **1996. Surf Scoter Issue**
  $15 **multicolored**   25.00   10.00 ☐☐☐☐☐

RH64 _____   **1997. Canada Goose Issue**
  $15 **multicolored**   25.00   10.00 ☐☐☐☐☐

RH65 _____   **1998. Barrow's Goldeneye Issue**
  $15 **multicolored**   25.00   10.00 ☐☐☐☐☐

RH66 _____   **1998. Barrow's Goldeneye Self-adhesive Issue**
  $15 **multicolored**   30.00   15.00 ☐☐☐☐☐

RH67 _____   **1999. Greater Scaup Issue**
  $15 **multicolored**   30.00   15.00 ☐☐☐☐☐

RH68 _____   **1999. Greater Scaup Self-adhesive Issue**
  $15 **multicolored**   30.00   15.00 ☐☐☐☐

RH37

RH38

RH39

RH40

RH41

RH42

RH43   RH44   RH45

RH46   RH47   RH48

RH49   RH50   RH51

RH52   RH53   RH54

RH55   RH56   RH57

RH58   RH59   RH60

RH61   RH62   RH63

RH64   RH65

RH66   RH67

RH68

FREE

Minkus-Scott cross-reference

As a purchaser of this new Krause-Minkus Stamps and Prices Mini-Catalog of United States Stamps, you are entitled to receive free a cross-reference booklet. This booklet contains both Minkus to Scott United States catalog number cross-references in an easy-to-use format.

To receive a copy, send the coupon below to Philatelic Division, Krause Publications, 700 E. State St., Iola WI 54990-0001.

Yes, please send my **free**
Minkus-Scott Mini-Catalog of United States Stamps
cross-reference.

Name: _____

Address: _____

City: _____

State: _____ ZIP: _____